AMERICAN
SIGN LANGUAGE
CONCISE
DICTIONARY

AMERICAN SIGN LANGUAGE CONCISE DICTIONARY

Revised Edition

Martin L.A. Sternberg, Ed.D.

ILLUSTRATIONS BY HERBERT ROGOFF AND EDUSELF

Abridged edition of *American Sign Language*

HarperPerennial
A Division of HarperCollins Publishers

To Joseph V. Firsching

AMERICAN SIGN LANGUAGE CONCISE DICTIONARY *(Revised Edition)*.
Copyright © 1994 by Martin L.A. Sternberg. All rights reserved.
Printed in the United States of America. No part of this book may be
used or reproduced in any manner whatsoever without written permission except in the case of brief quotations embodied in critical articles
and reviews. For information address HarperCollins Publishers, Inc.,
10 East 53rd Street, New York, NY 10022.

HarperCollins books may be purchased for educational, business, or
sales promotional use. For information, please write to: Special
Markets Department, HarperCollins Publishers, Inc., 10 East 53rd
Street, New York, NY 10022.

FIRST EDITION

ISBN 0-06-274010-5

05   **39 38 37 36 35 34 33 32 31 30**

Contents

Acknowledgments

The original work from which this revised edition is derived, *American Sign Language: A Comprehensive Dictionary,* is the culmination of a period of endeavor that goes back to 1962. Two abridgments have since appeared: *American Sign Language Dictionary* (1987), and *American Sign Language Concise Dictionary* (1990). The current work is a revised and enlarged edition of the *Concise.*

In order to maintain continuity in the evolution of this project, members of the original General Editorial Committee are listed on pages xi – xiii

My many friends who use sign language have been a constant source of information (and inspiration) in the identification and inclusion of new signs in this book. To them, my sustained appreciation and applause.

Bringing this project into the Computer Age from its index card and hand-illustrated status has been a major challenge, sometimes a source of trepidation and frustration, but ultimately a unique achievement. This could never have been accomplished without the sustained help and guidance of Kenneth S. Rothschild, my teacher, friend, and major supporter, who not only set up the format for the computer but came to my side countless times to help me out when I was in trouble. Lorri Kirzner gave willingly of her knowledge and expertise to resolve transient difficulties I encountered with the database. Her smile and patience make her a very special person.

The illustrations have been produced using the latest current technology, which leaves me breathless when I contemplate the work to produce the original Unabridged

Edition, a project of nineteen years! The new procedure involved making videotapes of the signs using different models and then freeze-framing appropriate poses. These poses in turn produced computer-generated drawings—rapidly and accurately. Randi F. Kleiman coordinated this multi-faceted operation. She is another unique contributor who deserves unfailing appreciation.

Likewise, certain people need special recognition. The two illustrators, Meravi Geffen and Case Ellerbrock, did an outstanding job within the constraints of time and deadline pressures. They were ably assisted by Rachel Ackerman, Eva Cohen, David Fogel, and Jimmy Mizrachi, all under the executive direction of Nissim Halfon. Jack Berberian produced the videotape, which used the talents and modeling skills of Alan R. Barwiolek, Patrice Joyner, and Marie Taccogna.

Herbert Rogoff, the talented artist who did the original freehand drawings appearing in editions past—many of which remain among these pages—is thanked yet again.

Marilee Foglesong, Children's Librarian, New York Public Library, offered valuable suggestions for drawing up an appropriate list of signs for children.

With this project my publisher, HarperCollins, demonstrates a major commitment to the dynamic new world of multimedia publishing. Nancy Dickenson, Director of New Media, has had the vision and drive to design a multifaceted CD-ROM edition of this work. She has been ably assisted by Paul Shostak, a very experienced programmer and software designer.

In spite of her multiple duties as Vice President and Publisher of HarperCollins Interactive for the Adult Trade Group, Carol P. Cohen, who has been involved with this project from its inception, has kept up a lively and close interest in the development of this new edition.

ix   **Acknowledgments**

Robert Wilson, my editor, is the latest and very much the best of a long line of editors under whom I have worked. Thirty-two years is a long time to be affiliated with a single publisher, and Rob's commitment to me and this always-expanding project demonstrates the wisdom of my choice of HarperCollins as my publisher.

Freelance copyeditor Linda H. Hwang improved this edition through her care, diligence, and attention to detail.

Finally, Theodora Zavin, literary adviser, has been a reassuring presence throughout the development of the new edition and the production of the CD-ROM versions.

Martin L. A. Sternberg, ED.D.

General Editorial Committee

(Unabridged Edition)

Editorial Staff

Edna S. Levine, PH.D., LITT.D., *Project Director.* Late Professor Emeritus, New York University, New York, NY.

Martin L.A. Sternberg, ED.D., *Principal Research Scientist and Editor-in-Chief.* Adjunct Professor, Adelphi University, Garden City, NY; Adjunct Associate Professor, Hofstra University, Hempstead, NY.

Herbert Rogoff, *Illustrator.* Former Associate Research Scientist, New York University, New York, NY.

William F. Marquardt, PH.D., *Linguist.* Late Professor of English Education, New York University, New York, NY.

Joseph V. Firsching, *Project Secretary.*

Consulting Committee

Elizabeth E. Benson, LITT.D., *Chief Consultant.* Late Dean of Women and Professor of Speech, Gallaudet University, Washington, DC.

Leon Auerbach, L.H.D., *Senior Consultant.* Late Professor of Mathematics, Gallaudet University, Washington, DC.

Special Consultants

Charles L. Brooks, *Vocational Signs*
Nancy Frishberg, PH.D., *Editorial*
Emil Ladner, *Catholic Signs*
Max Lubin, *Jewish Signs*
The Rev. Steve L. Mathis III, *Protestant Signs*

Mary Ellen Tracy, *Foreign Language Consultant*

Production

Joseph V. Firsching, *Coordinator*
Frank Burkhardt, Ardele Frank, Rosemary Nikolaus,
Bernice Schwartz, Rosalee Truesdale

Editorial Assistants

Jean Calder, *Senior Editorial Assistant*
Lilly Berke, Edna Bock, Nancy Chough, Judith M.
Clifford, Arlene Graham, Pat Rost, Norma Schwartz,
Patrice Smith, Mary Ellen Tracy

Secretarial/Clerical/Typing

Edna Bock, Carole Goldman, Carole Wilkins

Abbreviations

adj.	Adjective
adv.	Adverb, adverbial
adv. phrase	Adverbial phrase
arch.	Archaic
colloq.	Colloquial, colloquialism. Informal or familiar term or expression in sign.
eccles.	Ecclesiastical. Of or pertaining to religious signs. These signs are among the earliest and best developed, inasmuch as the first teachers of deaf people were frequently religious workers, and instruction was often of a religious nature.
e.g.	*Exempli gratia.* L., for example
esp	Especially
i.e.	*Id est.* L., that is
interj.	Interjection
interrog.	Interrogative
L.	Latin
loc.	Localism. A sign peculiar to a local or limited area. This may frequently be the case in a given school for deaf children, a college or postsecondary program catering to their needs, or a geographical area around such school or facility where deaf persons may live or work.
obs.	Obscure, obsolete
pl.	Plural
poss.	Possessive
prep.	Preposition

prep. phrase	Prepositional phrase
pron.	Pronoun
q.v.	*Quod vide.* L., which see
sl.	Slang
v.	Verb
v.i.	Verb intransitive
viz.	*Videlicet.* L., namely
voc.	Vocational. These signs usually pertain to specialized vocabularies used in workshops, trade and vocational classes and schools.
v.t.	Verb transitive
vulg.	Vulgarism. A vulgar term or expression, usually used only in a colloquial sense.

Pronunciation Guide

The primary stress mark (′) is placed after the syllable bearing the heavier stress or accent; the secondary stress mark (′) follows a syllable having a somewhat lighter stress, as in **interrogate** (ĭn tĕr′ ə gāt′).

Symbol	Example	Symbol	Example
ă	add, map	ŏŏ	took, full
ā	ace, rate	p	pit, stop
â(r)	care, air	r	run, poor
ä	plam, father	s	see, pass
b	bat, rub	sh	sure, rush
ch	check, catch	t	talk, sit
d	dog, rod	th	thin, both
ĕ	end, pet	th	this, bathe
ē	even, tree	ŭ	up, done
f	fit, half	ū	unite, vacuum
g	go, log	û(r)	urn, term
h	hope, hate	yōō	use, few
ĭ	it, give	v	vain, eve
ī	ice, write	w	win, away
j	joy, ledge	y	yet, yearn
k	cool, take	z	zest, muse
l	look, rule	zh	vision, pleasure
m	move, seem	ə	the schwa, an un-
n	nice, tin		stressed vowel
ng	ring, song		representing the
ŏ	odd, hot		sound spelled
ō	open, so		*a* in *above*
ô	order, jaw		*e* in *sicken*
oi	oil, boy		*i* in *clarity*
ou	out, now		*o* in *melon*
ōō	pool, food		*u* in *focus*

Explanatory Notes

Sign Rationale

This term, admittedly imprecise semantically, refers to the explanatory material in parentheses which follows the part of speech. This material is an attempt to offer a mnemonic cue to the sign as described verbally. It is a device to aid the user of the dictionary to remember how a sign is formed.

Verbal Description

The sign and its formation are described verbally. Such terms as "S" hand, "D" position, "both 'B' hands," refer to the positions of the hand or hands as they are depicted in the American Manual Alphabet on page xxiii.

Terms such as "counterclockwise," "clockwise," refer to movement from the signer's orientation. Care should be taken not to become confused by illustrations which appear at first glance to contradict a verbal description. In all cases the verbal description should be the one of choice, with the illustration reinforcing it. The reader should place himself or herself mentally in the position of the signer, *i.e.*, the illustration, in order to assume the correct orientation for signing an English gloss word.

Sign Synonyms

Sign synonyms are other glosses for which the same sign is used. They are found at the end of the verbal description, following the italicized *Cf.* and are given in SMALL CAPITAL LETTERS.

It is important to remember that the words listed after

the *Cf.* do not carry an equivalent sense in and of themselves. Because meaning for the signer springs from the sign, apparently unrelated glosses can be expressed by similar movements.

Illustrations

A. Illustrations appearing in sequence should not be regarded as separate depictions of parts of a sign. They are fluid and continuous, and should be used in conjunction with the verbal description of a sign, for they illustrate the main features of the sign as one movement flows into the next.

B. Arrows, broken or solid, indicate direction of movement. Again, they are designed to reinforce the verbal description and, where confusion may arise, the reader is cautioned to review the verbal description, always keeping himself or herself mentally in the position of the illustration (the signer).

C. As a general rule, a hand drawn with dotted or broken lines indicates the sign's initial movement or position of the hand. This is especially true if a similar drawing appears next to it using solid lines. This indicates terminal position in the continuum.

D. Groups of illustrations have been arranged as far as possible in visually logical order. They are read from left to right, or from top to bottom. Where confusion is possible, they have been captioned with letters A, B, C, etc.

E. Small lines outlining parts of the hand, especially when they are repeated, indicate small, repeated, or wavy or jerky motions, as described in the verbal section of an entry.

F. Arrows drawn side by side but pointing in opposite directions indicate repeated movement, as described in the verbal section of an entry.

G. Illustrations giving side or three-quarter views have been so placed to afford maximum visibility and to avoid foreshortening problems. The user of the dictionary should not assume a similar orientation when making the sign. As a general rule, the signer faces the person he or she is signing to.

H. Inclusion of the head in the figures permits proper orientation in the formation of certain signs. The head is omitted where there is no question of ambiguity.

American
Manual
Alphabet

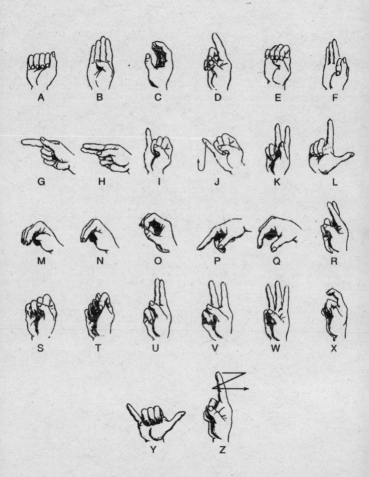

AMERICAN
SIGN LANGUAGE
CONCISE
DICTIONARY

A

ABORTION (ə bôr′ shən), *n*. (The baby is removed from its mother's womb). The right hand grasps the stomach and then is thrown down and open.

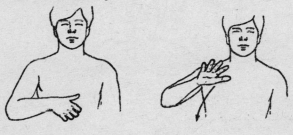

ABOUT 1 (ə bout′), *prep*. (Revolving about.) The left hand is held at chest height, all fingers extended and touching the thumb, and all pointing to the right. The right index finger circles about the left fingers several times.

ABOUT 2, *adj*. Same as ABOUT 1 above, but both hands are held in the "H" position. *Cf.* ALMOST.

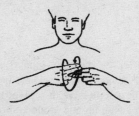

ABOUT 3, *adv*. (In the general area.) The downturned open "5" hand moves in a counterclockwise direction in front of the body. *Cf.* THEREABOUTS.

ACCEPT (ăk sĕpt′), *v*., -CEPTED, -CEPTING. (A taking of something unto oneself.) Both open hands, palms down, are held in front of the chest. They move in unison toward the chest, where they come to rest, all fingers closed.

ACHIEVE (ə chēv′), *v*., -CHIEVED, -CHIEVING. (Penetrating the heights.) The "D" hands, palms back, are held at each side of the head, near the temples. With a pivoting motion of the wrists, the hands swing up and around, simultaneously, to a position above the head, with palms facing out. *Cf.* SUCCEED, SUCCESS, SUCCESSFUL, TRIUMPH.

ACROSS (ə krôs', ə krŏs'), *prep., adv* (A crossing over.) The left hand is held before the chest, palm down and fingers together. The right hand, fingers together, glides over the left, with the right little finger touching the top of the left hand. *Cf.* CROSS, OVER

ACT (ăkt), *v.*, ACTED, ACTING, *n.* (Motion or movement, modified by the letter "A" for "act.") Both "A" hands, palms out, are held at shoulder height and rotate alternately toward the head. *Cf.* PERFORM 2, PERFORMANCE 2, PLAY 2, SHOW 2.

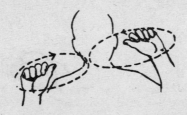

ADD 1 (ăd), *v.*, ADDED, ADDING. (To bring up all together.) The two open hands, palms and fingers facing each other, with the left hand above the right, are brought together, with all fingers closing simultaneously. This sign is used mainly in the sense of adding up figures or items. *Cf.* ADDITION, SUM, SUMMARIZE 2, SUMMARY 2, SUM UP.

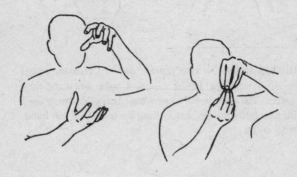

ADD 2, *v.* (Adding on.) The index and middle fingers of the right "H" hand, palm up, are swung up and over until they come to rest on the index and middle fingers of the left "H" hand, held palm down. *Cf.* ADDITION, GAIN, INCREASE, RAISE.

ADDITION (ə dĭsh' ən), *n*. See ADD 1.

ADDRESS (ăd' rĕs), *n*., *v*., -DRESSED, -DRESSING. (Same rationale as for LIFE 1, with the initials "L".) The upturned thumbs of the "A" hands move in unison up the chest. *Cf.* ALIVE, LIFE 1, LIVE 1, LIVING.

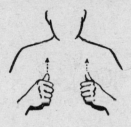

ADMINISTRATION 1 (ad min is trā' shən), *n*. (Handling the reins.) The signer manipulates a pair of imaginary reins back and forth.

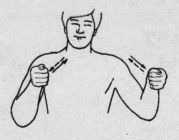

ADMINISTRATION 2, *n.* (A fingerspelled loan sign.) The letters A-D-M are spelled out.

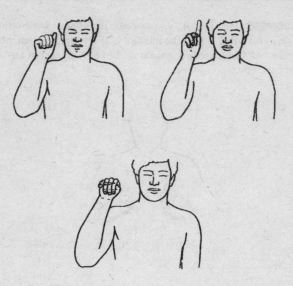

ADOPT (ə dopt′), *v.* (Take and keep.) The right hand grasps onto an imaginary object to the right, and then the two hands assume the "K" position, palms facing each other, with the right resting on the left.

ADULT (ə dult′), *n., adj.* (The letter "A" the FEMALE and MALE root signs.) The thumbtip of the right "A" hand is placed first on the right jawline, and then moves up to touch the right temple.

ADVICE (ăd vīs´), *n.* (Take something, *advice*, and disseminate it.) The left hand, held limp in front of the body, has its fingers pointing down. The fingers of the right hand, held all together, are placed on the top of the left hand, and then move forward, off the left hand, assuming a "5" position, palm down. *Cf.* ADVISE, INFLUENCE.

ADVISE (ăd vīz´), *v.*, -VISED, -VISING. See ADVICE.

AFRAID (ə frād´), *adj.* (The heart is suddenly covered with fear.) Both hands, fingers together, are placed side by side, palms facing the chest. They quickly open and come together over the heart, one on top of the other. *Cf.* FEAR 1, FRIGHT, FRIGHTEN, SCARE (D), TERROR 1.

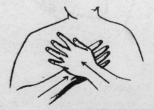

AFRICA (af' ri kə), *n.* (Outlining the continent.) The "C" hand, palm facing out, traces the African continent. As the hand moves down to the narrow part, the fingers come together.

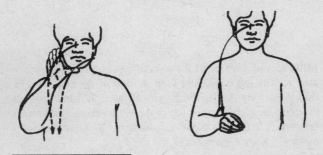

AFTER (ăf tər, äf´-), *prep.* (Something occurring *after* a fixed place in time, represented by the hand nearest the body.) The right hand, held flat, palm facing the body, fingertips pointing left, represents the fixed place in time. The left hand is placed against the back of the right, and moves straight out from the body. The relative positions of the two hands may be reversed, with the left remaining stationary near the body and the right moving out.

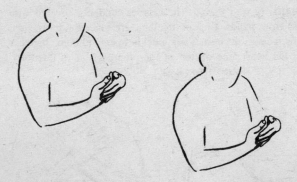

AFTER A WHILE (hwīl), *adv. phrase*. (A moving on of the minute hand of the clock.) The right "L" hand, its thumb thrust into the palm of the left and acting as a pivot, moves forward a short distance. *Cf.* AFTERWARD, LATER 1.

AFTERNOON (ăf′ tər nōōn′, äf′ -), *n., adj*. (The sun is midway between zenith and sunset.) The right arm, fingers together and pointing forward, rests on the back of the left hand, its fingers also together and pointing somewhat to the right. The right arm remains in a position about 45° from the vertical.

AFTERWARD (ăf′ tər wərd, äf′ -), *adv*. See AFTER A WHILE.

AGAIN (ə gĕn'), *adv.* The left hand, open in the "5" position, palm up, is held before the chest. The right hand, in the right-angle position, fingers pointing up, arches over and into the left palm. *Cf.* REPEAT.

AGAINST (ə gĕnst', -gānst'), *prep.* (Opposed to; restraint.) The tips of the right fingers, held together, are thrust purposefully into the open left palm, whose fingers are also together and pointing forward. *Cf.* OPPOSE.

AGGRAVATE 1 (ag' rə vāt), *v.*, -VATED, -VATING. (The stomach turns.) The right claw hand makes a series of counter-clockwise circles on the stomach. A look of distress or annoyance is assumed.

AGGRAVATE 2, *v.* (The emotions well up and explode.) Both downturned hands are placed at the stomach, right fingers pointing left and left fingers pointing right. Both hands move up slowly and then come apart explosively, with palms now facing each other. An expression of distress or annoyance is assumed.

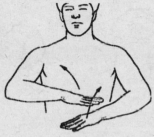

AGREE (ə grē), *v.*, -GREED, -GREEING. (Of the same mind; thinking the same way.) The index finger of the right "D" hand, palm back, touches the forehead (the modified sign for THINK, *q.v.*), and then the two index fingers, both in the "D" position, palms down, are brought together so they are side by side, pointing away from the body (the sign for SAME). *Cf.* AGREEMENT, CONSENT.

AGREEMENT (-mənt), *n.* See AGREE.

AIM (ām), *v.*, AIMED, AIMING, *n.* (A thought directed upward, toward a goal.) The index finger of the right "D" hand touches the forehead, and then moves up to the index finger of the left "D" hand, which is held above eye level. The two index fingers stop just short of touching. *Cf.* GOAL.

AIRPLANE (âr′ plăn′), *n.* (The wings of the airplane.) The "Y" hand, palm down and drawn up near the shoulder, moves forward, up and away from the body. Either hand may be used. *Cf.* FLY 1, PLANE 1.

ALARM (ə lärm′), *n.* (The striker hits the bell.) The right index finger, pointing down or out, strikes the opposite palm repeatedly.

ALASKA (ə las′ kə), *n.* (The letter "A" ; the fur-lined hood.)
The right "A" hand moves from the left side of the face to the
right, describing an arc over the head.

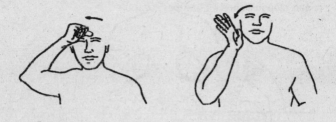

ALCOHOL (al′ kə hôl), *n.* (The size of the jigger.) The right
hand, with index and little fingers extended and remaining fingers held against the palm by the thumb, strikes the back of the
downturned "S" hand.

ALIKE (ə līk′), *adv.* (Matching fingers are brought together.)
The outstretched index fingers are brought together, either
once or several times. *Cf.* LIKE 2, SAME 1, SIMILAR.

ALIVE (ə līv′), *adj.* (The fountain [of *life*] wells up from within the body.) The upturned thumbs of the "A" hands move in unison up the chest. *Cf.* ADDRESS, LIFE 1, LIVE 1, LIVING.

ALL (ôl), *adj., n., pron.* (Encompassing; a gathering together.) Both hands are held in the right angle position, palms facing the body, and the right hand in front of the left. The right hand makes a sweeping outward movement around the left, and comes to rest with the back of the right hand resting in the left palm. *Cf.* ENTIRE.

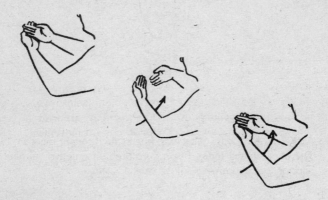

ALL ALONG (ə lông′, əlŏng′), *adv. phrase.* (From a point up and over.) In the "D" position, palms down, both index fingers touch the right shoulder and then are brought up and over, ending in a palm-up position, pointing straight ahead of the body. *Cf.* EVER SINCE, SINCE 1, SO FAR, THUS FAR.

ALLIGATOR (al′ ɔ gā tər), *n.* (The mouth.) Both "5" hands are held against each other, fingertips pointing forward. With the heels of the hands connected, the hands come apart in a wide arc, imitating the opening of a large mouth.

ALLOW (ə lou′), *v.*, -LOWED, -LOWING. (A permissive upswinging of the hands, as if giving in.) Both hands, palms facing and fingers pointing away from the body, are held at chest level, almost a foot apart. With an upward movement, using their wrists as pivots, the hands sweep up until the fingers point almost straight up. *Cf.* GRANT 1, LET, LET US, MAY 3, PERMISSION 1, PERMIT 1.

ALL RIGHT (rīt), *phrase*. (A straightening out.) The right hand, fingers together and palm facing left, is placed in the upturned left palm, whose fingers point away from the body. The right hand slides straight out along the left palm, over the left fingers, and stops with its heel resting on the left fingertips. *Cf.* O.K. 1, RIGHT 1, YOU'RE WELCOME 2.

ALMOST (ôl' mōst, ôl mōst'), *adv*. The left hand is held at chest level in the right angle position, with fingers pointing up and the back of the hand facing right. The right fingers are swept up along the back of the left hand.

ALONE (ə lōn'), *adj*. (One, wandering around in a circle.) The index finger, pointing straight up, palm facing the body (the number *one*), is rotated before the face in a counterclockwise direction. *Cf.* LONE, ONLY.

ALSO (ôl′ sō), *adv* (A likeness; a sameness.) Both index fingers, held together at one side of the body near waist level, point forward. As they travel to the other side of the body they separate an inch or two and come together again.

ALTRUISM (al′ tro͞o iz əm) *n*. (The heart is open.) The right hand is held against the heart. It moves out and forward with a flourish, ending with the palm facing left.

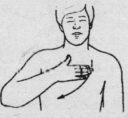

ALWAYS (ôl′ wăz, -wĭz), *adv*. (Around the clock.) The index finger of the right "D" hand points outward, away from the body, with palm facing left. The arm is rotated clockwise.

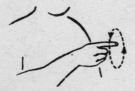

AM 1 (ăm; *unstressed* əm), *v.* (Part of the verb to BE.) The tip of the right index finger, held in the "D" position, palm facing left, is held at the lips, and the hand moves straight out and away from the lips. *Cf.* ARE 1, BE 1.

AM 2, *v.* (The "A" hand.) The tip of the right thumb, in the "A" position, palm facing left, is held at the lips. Then the hand moves straight out and away from the lips.

AMAZE (ə māz´), *v.*, -MAZED, -MAZING. (The eyes pop open in amazement.) Both hands are held in modified "O" positions with thumb and index fingers of each hand near the eyes. These fingers suddenly flick open, and the eyes simultaneously pop open wide. *Cf.* AMAZEMENT, SURPRISE.

AMAZEMENT (-mənt), *n*. See AMAZE.

AMBITIOUS (ăm bĭsh´ əs), *adj*. (Rubbing the hands together in zeal or ambition.) The open hands are rubbed vigorously back and forth against each other. *Cf*. EAGER, EAGERNESS, ENTHUSIASM, ENTHUSIASTIC.

AMBULANCE (am´ byə ləns), *n*. (The flashing light.) The right hand, fingers extended, is positioned above the head. It rotates in imitation of a flashing emergency light.

AMEND (ə mend´), *v*. (Add something on.) The open left hand is held either with palm facing the body or facing right. The right hand, palm down and a space maintained between the thumb and the other fingers, swivels up and grasps the little finger edge of the left hand, as if inserting a clip on a stack of papers.

AMERICA (ə měr′ ə kə) *n.* (The fences built by the early settlers as protection against the Indians.) The extended fingers of both hands are interlocked, and are swept in an arc from left to right as if encompassing an imaginary house or stockade.

AMOUNT *n.* (Throwing up a number of things before the eyes; a display of fingers to indicate a question of how many or how much.) The right hand, palm up, is held before the chest, all fingers touching the thumb. The hand is tossed straight up, while the fingers open to the "5" position. *Cf.* HOW MANY?, HOW MUCH?

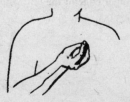

AND (ănd; *unstressed* ǝnd; ǝn), *conj.* The right "5" hand, palm facing the body, fingers facing left, moves from left to right, meanwhile closing until all its fingers touch around its thumb.

ANGER (ăn' gǝr), *n.* (A violent welling-up of the emotions.) The curved fingers of the right hand are placed in the center of the chest, and fly up suddenly and violently. An expression of anger is worn. *Cf.* ANGRY 2, FURY, MAD, RAGE.

ANGLE (ang' gǝl) *n.* (Outlining an angle.) The left hand is held in the "L" position, palm facing forward. The right index finger moves down the left index and along the thumb, tracing a right angle as it does.

ANGRY 1 (ăn′ grĭ), *adj*. (Wrinkling the brow.) The "5" hand is held palm toward the face. The fingers open and close partly, several times, while an angry expression is worn on the face.

ANGRY 2, *adj*. See ANGER.

ANNOUNCE (ə nouns′), *v*., -NOUNCED, -NOUNCING. (An issuance from the mouth.) Both index fingers are placed at the lips, with palms facing the body. They are rotated once and swung out in arcs, until the left index finger points somewhat to the left and the right index somewhat to the right. Sometimes the rotation of the fingers is omitted in favor of a simple swinging out from the lips. *Cf*. ANNOUNCEMENT.

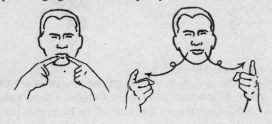

ANNOUNCEMENT (mɔnt), *n*. See ANNOUNCE.

ANNOY (ə noi′), *v*., -NOYED, -NOYING. (Obstruct, block.) The left hand, fingers together and palm flat, is held before the body, facing somewhat down. The little finger side of the right hand, held with palm flat, makes one or several up-down chopping motions against the left hand, between its thumb and index finger. *Cf.* ANNOYANCE, BOTHER, DISTURB, INTERFERE, INTERFERENCE, INTERFERE WITH, INTERRUPT, PREVENT, PREVENTION.

ANNOYANCE (ə noi′ əns) *n*. See ANNOY.

ANOTHER (ə nŭth′ ər), *adj*. (Moving over to *another* position.) The right "A" hand, thumb up, is pivoted from the wrist and swung over to the right, so that the thumb now points to the right. *Cf.* OTHER.

ANSWER (ăn′ sər; än′-), *n., v.,* -SWERED, -SWERING. (Directing a reply from the mouth to someone.) The tip of the right index finger, held in the "D" position, palm facing the body, is placed on the lips, while the left "D" hand, palm also facing the body, is held about a foot in front of the right hand. The right index finger, swinging around, moves toward and stops in a pointing position a few inches from the left index fingertip. *Cf.* REPLY, RESPOND, RESPONSE 1.

ANY (ĕn′ ĭ), *adj., pron.* The "A" hand, palm down and thumb pointing left, pivots around on the wrist, so the thumb now points down.

APART (ə pärt′), *adv.* (The hands are moved *apart*.) Both hands, in the "A" position, thumbs up, are held together, with knuckles touching. With a deliberate movement they come apart. *Cf.* DIVORCE 1, SEPARATE 1.

APOLOGIZE 1 (ə pŏl′ ə jīz′), *v.*, -GIZED, -GIZING. (The heart is circled, to indicate feeling, modified by the letter "S" for SORRY.) The right "S" hand, palm facing the body, is rotated several times over the area of the heart. *Cf.* APOLOGY 1, REGRET, REGRETFUL, SORROW, SORROWFUL 2, SORRY.

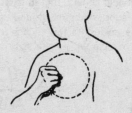

APOLOGIZE 2, *v*. (A wiped-off and cleaned slate.) The right hand wipes off the left palm several times. *Cf*. APOLOGY 2, EXCUSE, FORGIVE, PARDON.

APOLOGY 1 (ə pŏl′ ə jĭ), *n*. See APOLOGIZE 1.

APOLOGY 2, *n*. See APOLOGIZE 2.

APPEAR (ə pĭr′), *v*. -PEARED, -PEARING. (Popping up before the eyes.) The right index finger, pointing up, pops up between the index and middle fingers of the left hand, whose palm faces down. *Cf*. POP UP.

APPLAUD (ə plôd'), v., -PLAUDED, -PLAUDING. (Good words coming from the mouth; clapping hands.) The fingertips of the right hand, palm flat and facing the body, are brought up to the lips, so that they touch (part of the sign for GOOD, q.v.). The hands are then clapped together several times. Cf. APPLAUSE, CONGRATULATE 1, CONGRATULATIONS 1, PRAISE.

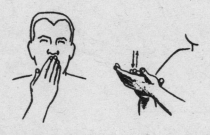

APPLAUSE (ə plôz'), n. See APPLAUD.

APPLE (ăp'əl), n. (A chewing of the letter "A" for *apple*.) The right "A" hand is held at the right cheek, with the thumb tip touching the cheek and palm facing out. In this position the hand is swung over and back from the wrist several times, using the thumb as a pivot.

APPOINTMENT (ə point'mənt), n. (A binding of the hands together; a commitment.) The right "S" hand, palm down, is positioned above the left "S" hand, also palm down. The right hand circles above the left in a clockwise manner and is brought down on the back of the left hand. At the same instant both hands move down in unison a short distance. *Cf.* RESER-VATION 1, RESERVE.

ARE 1 (är), *v.* (Part of the verb to BE.) The tip of the right index finger, held in the "D" position, palm facing left, is held at the lips, and the hand moves straight out and away from the lips. *Cf.* AM 1, BE 1.

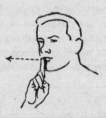

ARE 2, *v.* This is the same sign as for ARE 1, except that the "R" hand is used. It is an initialized version of ARE 1.

ARGUE (är′ gū), *v.*, -GUED, -GUING. (An expounding back and forth.) The index fingers here represent the two sides of the argument. First the left index finger is slapped into the open right palm, and then the right makes the same movement into the left palm. This is repeated back and forth several times. *Cf.* ARGUMENT.

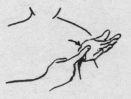

ARGUMENT (-mənt), *n.* See ARGUE.

ARRANGE (ə rănj′), *v.*, -RANGED, -RANGING. (Placing things in order.) The hands, palms facing, fingers together and pointing away from the body, are positioned at the left side and held about a foot apart. With a slight up-down motion, as if describing waves, the hands travel in unison from left to right. *Cf.* ARRANGEMENT, ORDER 2, PLAN, PREPARE 1, PUT IN ORDER, READY 1.

ARRANGEMENT (ə rănj′ mənt), *n.* See ARRANGE.

ARRIVAL (ə rī′ vəl), *n.* (Arrival at a designated place.) The right hand, palm facing the body and fingers pointing up, is brought forward from a position near the right shoulder and placed in the upturned palm of the left hand (the designated place). *Cf.* ARRIVE.

ARRIVE (ə rīv´), *v.*, -RIVED, -RIVING. See ARRIVAL.

ARTICULATE (är tik´ yə lit), *adj.* (Speaking with skill.) The right index finger, pointing left, describes a continuous small circle in front of the mouth. This is a sign for SPEAK. It is followed by the sign for SKILL: the right hand grasps the little finger edge of the left firmly. As it leaves this position, moving down and out, it assumes the position, palm facing left.

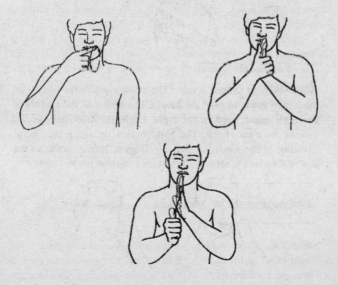

ARTIFICIAL (är tə fish′ əl), *adj* (Words deflected from their path, straight out from the lips.) The index finger of the right "D" hand, pointing to the left, moves in front of the lips, from-right to left.

AS A MATTER OF FACT *phrase*. (Straightforward, from the lips.) The right index finger is placed up against the lips. It moves up and forward, in a small arc.

ASHAMED (ə shāmd′), *adj*. (The color rises in the cheek; an attempt is made to hide the head.) The backs of the fingers of the right hand, held in the right angle position, are placed against the right cheek. The hand moves up along the cheek, pivoting at the wrist, so that the fingers finally point to the rear. *Cf.* BASHFUL, SHAME 1, SHAMEFUL, SHAME ON YOU, SHY 1.

ASK 1 (ăsk, äsk), *v.*, ASKED, ASKING. (Pray tell.) Both hands, held upright about a foot in front of the chest, with palms facing and fingers pointing straight up, are positioned about a foot apart. Moving toward the chest, they come together until they touch, as if in prayer. *Cf.* REQUEST.

ASK 2 (*colloq.*), *v.* (Fire a question.) The right hand, held in a modified "S" position with palm facing out, assumes a position with the thumb resting on the fingernail of the index finger. The index finger is flicked out and forward, usually directed at the person being asked a question. Reversing the direction so that the index finger flicks out toward the speaker indicates the passive voice of the verb *i.e.* to be ASKED. *Cf.* INQUIRE, INTERROGATE, INTERROGATION.

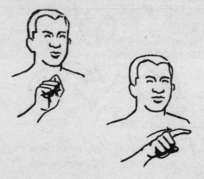

ASLEEP (ə slēp′), *adv.* (The eyes are closed.) The fingers of the right open hand, facing the forehead, are placed on the forehead. The hand moves down and away from the head, with the fingers closing so that they all touch. The eyes meanwhile close, and the head bows slightly, as in sleep. *Cf.* SLEEP 1.

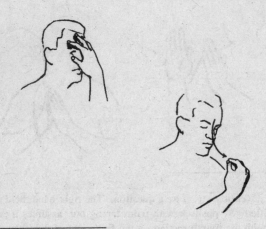

ASSEMBLE (ə sem′ bəl), *v.*, -BLED, -BLING. (Many people coming together in one place.) The downturned "5" hands, fingers wriggling, come toward each other until the fingertips almost touch.

ASSET (as′ et), *n.* (Putting a plus into the pocket.) The index fingers form a plus (+) sign, and then the right "F" hand moves down an inch or two against the right side of the body, as if placing a coin into a pocket.

ASSIST (ə sĭst′), *n.*, *v.*, -SISTED, -SISTING. (Helping up; supporting.) The left "S" hand, thumb side up, rests in the open right palm. In this position the left hand is pushed up a short distance by the right. *Cf.* ASSISTANCE, HELP.

ASSISTANCE (ə sĭs′ təns), *n.* See ASSIST.

ASSUME (ə sōōm′), *v.*, -SUMED, -SUMING. (To take up.) Both hands, held palms down in the " 5" position, are at chest level. With a grasping upward movement, both close into "S" positions before the face. *Cf.* PICK UP 1, TAKE UP.

ATTACH (ə tăch′), v., -TACHED, -TACHING. (Joining together.) Both hands, held in the modified "5" position, palms out, move toward each other. The thumbs and index fingers of both hands then connect. *Cf.* BELONG, CONNECT, JOIN.

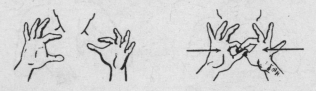

ATTEMPT 1 (ə tĕmpt′), n., v., -TEMPTED, -TEMPTING. (Trying to push through.) The "A" hands, palms facing before the body, are swung around and a bit down, so that the palms now face out. The movement indicates an attempt to push through a barrier. *Cf.* EFFORT 1, TRY 1.

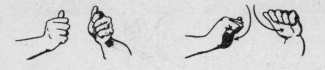

ATTEMPT 2, n., v. (Trying to push through, using the "T" hands, for "try") This is the same sign as ATTEMPT 1, except that the "T" hands are employed. *Cf.* EFFORT 2, TRY 2.

ATTITUDE (ăt´ ə tūd´, -tood´), *n.* (The letter "A" ; the inclina-
tion of the heart.) The right "A" hand describes a counterclockwise circle around the heart, and comes to rest against the
heart.

ATTRACT (ə trăkt´), *v.*, -TRACTED, -TRACTING. (Bringing
everything together, to one point.) The open "5" hands, palms
down and held at chest level, draw together until all the fingertips touch. *Cf.* ATTRACTION, ATTRACTIVE.

ATTRACTION (ə trăk´ shən), *n.* See ATTRACT.

ATTRACTIVE (ə trăk´ tĭv), *adj.* See ATTRACT.

AUNT (ănt, änt), *n.* (A female, defined by the letter "A") The
"A" hand, thumb near the right jawline (see sign for
FEMALE), quivers back and forth several times.

AUTHORITY (ə thôr′ ə tē), *n.* (The letter "A" ; the muscle.)
The right "A" hand describes an arc on the left arm muscle as
it moves from shoulder to the crook of the elbow.

AUTISM (ô′ tiz əm), *n.* (Cut off from the world.) Both "C"
hands, palms facing, are positioned at the temples. They move
around so that they now cover the eyes.

AUTOMATIC (ô tə mat′ ik), *n., adj.* (The shift lever attached
to the car steering column.) The left index finger, slightly
curved, is held up. The right index finger, also slightly curved,
palm up, slides up and down the left index finger.

AUTOMOBILE (ô′ tə mə bēl′, ô′ tə mō′ bēl, -mə bēl′), *n.* (The steering wheel.) The hands grasp an imaginary steering wheel and manipulate it. *Cf.* CAR, DRIVE.

AUTUMN (ô′ təm), *n.* (A chopping down during harvest time.) The right hand, fingers together and palm facing down, makes several chopping motions against the left elbow, to indicate the felling of growing things in autumn.

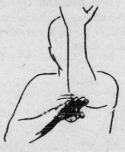

AVOID 1 (ə void′), *v.*, -VOIDED, -VOIDING. (Ducking back and forth, away from something.) Both "A" hands, thumbs pointing straight up, are held some distance before the chest, with the left hand in front of the right. The right hand, swinging back and forth, moves away from the left and toward the chest. *Cf.* EVADE, EVASION.

AVOID 2, *v*. (To push away and recoil from; avoid.) The two open hands, palms facing left, are pushed deliberately to the left, as if pushing something away. An expression of disdain or disgust is worn. *Cf.* HATE.

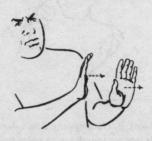

AWAKE (ə wāk´),*v*., *adj*., -WOKE OR -WAKED, -WAKING. (Opening the eyes.) Both hands are closed, with thumb and index finger of each hand held together, extended, and placed at the corners of the closed eyes. Slowly they separate, and the eyes open. *Cf.* AWAKEN, WAKE UP.

AWAKEN (ə wā´ kən), *v*. See AWAKE. -ENED, -ENING

AWFUL (ô´ fəl) *adj*. (Throwing out the hands.) Both hands, their fingertips touching their respective thumbs, are held,

palms facing each other, near the temples. They are thrown out
before the face, assuming "5" positions, palms still facing. *Cf.*
TERRIBLE.

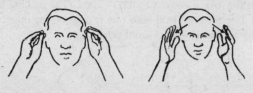

AWKWARD (ôk' wərd), *adj.* (Clumsy in gait; all thumbs.)
The "3" hands, palms down, move alternately up and down
before the body. *Cf.* AWKWARDNESS, CLUMSINESS, CLUMSY.

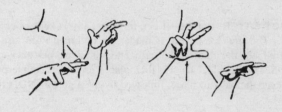

AWKWARDNESS *n.* See AWKWARD.

AXE (aks), *n.* (The chopping.) The left arm is held straight up
from the bent elbow. The little finger edge of the upturned
right hand then makes a series of chopping movements against
the left elbow. *Cf.* HATCHET.

B

BABY (bā' bǐ), *n.*, *adj.*, *v.*,-BIED, -BYING. (The rocking of the baby.) The arms are held with one resting on the other, as if cradling a baby. They rock from side to side.

BABY SITTER (bā' bē sit er), *n.* (The baby is kept or cared for.) The sign for BABY is made: the upturned right arm is placed atop the upturned left arm, and both arms rock back and forth. The right "K" hand is then placed on its left counterpart to keep the baby in place, followed by the sign for INDIVIDUAL.

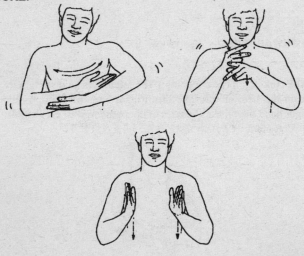

BACON (bā′ kən), *n.* (The curled up slice after frying.) Both hands, in the "H" position, are held with middle and index fingers touching. The hands move apart and the index and middle fingers execute wavy movements as they separate.

BAD (băd), *adj.* (Tasting something, finding it unacceptable, and turning it down.) The tips of the right "B" hand are placed at the lips, and then the hand is thrown down.

BAH (bă), *interj.* The outstretched right hand, palm facing forward, is thrown forward and down in a forceful manner. The signer assumes an expression of annoyance or disapproval. An even more effective nonmanual accompaniment to this sign would be an explosive release of breath. *Cf.* PHOOEY!

BALLET (bal′ā), *n.* (The toes held "en pointe.") Both hands, fingers together, point straight down. They move up and down in successive order.

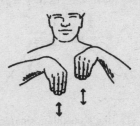

BALLOON (bə lōōn′), *n.* (Blowing up.) The signer mimes blowing up a balloon. The cupped "C" hands expand and the cheeks are puffed out.

BANANA (bə nan′ ə), *n.* (The natural sign.) Go through the motions of peeling a banana, the left index representing the banana and the right fingertips pulling off the skin.

BAR (bär), *n*. (Raising the beer stein or mug.) The thumb of the right "A" or "Y" hand is brought up to the mouth. *Cf.* SALOON.

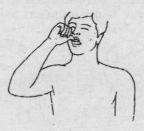

BARBER (bär′ bər), *n*. (The scissors at both sides of the head.) The two "V" hands, palms facing the sides of the head, open and close repeatedly as the hands move alternately back and forth. *Cf.* HAIRCUT.

BASEBALL (bās′ bôl′), *n*. (Swinging a bat.) Both "S" hands, the right behind the left, grip an imaginary bat and move back and forth over the right shoulder, as if preparing to hit a baseball. *Cf.* HIT 2.

BASHFUL (băsh′ fəl), *adj.* (The color rises in the cheek; an attempt is made to hide the head.) The backs of the fingers of the right hand, held in the right angle position, are placed against the right cheek. The hand moves up along the cheek, pivoting at the wrist, so that the fingers finally point to the rear. *Cf.* ASHAMED, SHAME 1, SHAMEFUL, SHAME ON YOU, SHY 1.

BASKETBALL (băs′ kĭt bôl′), *n.* (Shooting a basket.) Both open hands are held with fingers pointing down and somewhat curved, as if grasping a basketball. From this position the hands move around and upward, as if to shoot a basket.

BAT (bat), *n.* (The hooked wings of the creature.) The index fingertips of the "X" hands, palms facing the body, are crossed and hooked on the shoulders, depicting a bat with folded wings.

BATH (băth, bäth), *n.* (The natural sign.) The closed hands move up and down against the chest as if scrubbing it. *Cf.* BATHE.

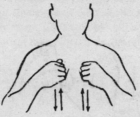

BATHE (băth), *v.*, BATHED, BATHING. See BATH.

BE 1 (bē; unstressed bĭ), *v.*, BEEN, BEING. (Part of the verb to BE.) The tip of the right index finger, held in the "D" position, palm facing left, is held at the lips, and the hand moves straight out and away from the lips. *Cf.* AM 1, ARE 1.

BE 2, *v.* (The "B" hand.) This is the same sign as for BE 1 except that the "B" hand is used.

BEAT *v.* (Forcing the head into a bowed position.) The right "S" hand, placed across the left "S" hand, moves over and down a bit. *Cf.* DEFEAT, OVERCOME.

BEATEN (bē′ tən), *adj.* (The head is forced into a bowed position.) The right "S" hand, palm up, is placed under and across the left "S" hand, whose palm faces down. The right "S" hand moves up and over, toward the body. This sign is used as the passive voice of the verb BEAT.

BEAUTIFUL (bū′ tə fəl), *adj.* (Literally, a good face.) The right hand, fingers closed over the thumb, is placed at or just below the lips (indicating a tasting of something GOOD, *q.v.*). It then describes a counterclockwise circle around the face, opening into the "5" position, to indicate the whole face. At the completion of the circling movement the hand comes to rest in its initial position, at or just below the lips. *Cf.* BEAUTY, PRETTY.

BEAUTY (bū′ tǐ). See BEAUTIFUL.

BE CAREFUL (kâr′ fəl), *v. phrase.* (The "K" for keep in the sense of *keeping carefully*). Both "K" hands are crossed, the right atop the left. The right hand moves up and down a very short distance, several times, each time coming to rest on top of the left.

BECAUSE (bǐ kôz′, -kŏz′), *conj.* (A thought or knowledge uppermost in the mind.) The fingers of the right hand or the index finger, are placed on the center of the forehead, and then the hand is brought strongly up above the head, assuming the "A" position, with thumb pointing up. *Cf.* FOR 2.

BED (bĕd), *n*. (A sleeping place with four legs.) The head is tilted to one side, with the cheek resting in the palm, to represent the head on a pillow. Both index fingers, pointing down, move straight down a short distance, in unison (the two front legs of the bed), and then are brought up slightly, and move down again a bit closer to the body (the rear legs).

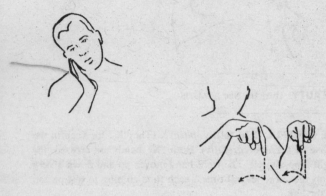

BEER (bĭr), *n*. (Raising a beer stein to the lips.) The right "Y" hand is raised to the lips, as the head tilts back a bit. *Cf.* DRUNK, DRUNKARD, DRUNKENNESS, INTOXICATE, INTOXICATION, LIQUOR.

BEFORE (bĭ fôr'), *adv*. (One hand precedes the other). The left hand is held before the body, fingers together and pointing to the right. The right hand, fingers also together, and pointing to the left, is placed so that its back rests in the left palm. The right hand moves rather quickly toward the body. The sign is used as an indication of time or of precedence: *He arrived before me.*

BEG 1 (bĕg), *v.*, BEGGED, BEGGING. (Holding out the hand and begging). The right open hand, palm up and fingers slightly cupped, is moved up and down by the left hand, positioned under it.

BEG 2, *v.* (An act of supplication.) With the right hand clasped over the left, both hands are shaken gently before the body. The eyes often are directed upward.

BEGIN (bĭ gĭn′), *v.*, -GAN, -GUN, -GINNING. (Turning a key to open up a new venture.) The right index finger, resting between the left index and middle fingers, executes a half turn, once or twice. *Cf.* ORIGIN, START.

BEHIND (bĭ hīnd′), *prep.* (One hand is after or behind the other.) Both hands, in the "A" position, are held knuckles to knuckles. The right hand moves back, describing a small arc, and comes to rest against the left wrist.

BELIEF (bĭ lēf′), *n.* (A thought clasped onto.) The index finger touches the middle of the forehead (where the thought lies), and then both hands are clasped together. *Cf.* BELIEVE.

BELIEVE (bĭ lĕv′), v., -LIEVED, -LIEVING. See BELIEF.

BELONG (bĭ lông′, -lŏng′), v., -LONGED, -LONGING. (Joining together.) Both hands, held in the modified "5" position, palms out, move toward each other. The thumbs and index fingers of both hands then connect. Cf. ATTACH, CONNECT, JOIN.

BELOW 1 (bĭ lo′), adv. (The area below.) Both hands, in the "5" position, palms down, are held before the chest, the right under the left. The right hand moves under the left in a counterclockwise fashion. Cf. FOUNDATION.

BELOW 2, adv. (Underneath something.) The right hand, in the "A" position, thumb pointing straight up, moves down under the left hand, held outstretched, fingers together, palm down. Cf. UNDER 1, UNDERNEATH.

BE QUIET 1 (kwi´ ət), *v. phrase.* (The natural sign.) The index finger is brought up against the pursed lips. *Cf.* QUIET 1, SILENCE 1, SILENT.

BE QUIET 2 (Quiet and peace.) The open hands are crossed before the mouth, the right palm facing left, left facing right. Then both hands, held palms down, move down from the mouth, curving outward to either side of the body. *Cf.* BE STILL, CALM, QUIET 2, SILENCE 2.

BERRY (ber´ ē), *n.* (A small item being picked off a branch.) The right fingertips grasp the tip of the left little finger and twist, as if plucking a berry. This sign is used for any berry, often with classifiers. *Cf.* CHERRY.

BE SEATED *v. phrase.* (The act of sitting.) The extended right index and middle fingers are draped across the back of the same two fingers of the downturned left hand. The hands then move straight downward a short distance. *Cf.* CHAIR, SEAT, SIT.

BEST (bĕst), *adj.* (The most good.) The fingertips of one hand are placed at the lips, as if tasting something (*cf.* GOOD), and then the hand is brought high up above the head into the "A" position, thumb up, indicating the superlative degree.

BE STILL *v. phrase.* See BE QUIET 2.

BETTER (bet´ ər), *adj.* (More good.) The fingertips of one hand are placed at the lips, as if tasting something (*cf.* GOOD). Then the hand is moved up to a position just above the head, where it assumes the "A" position, thumb up. This latter position, less high up than the one indicated in BEST, denotes the comparative degree. *Cf.* PREFER.

BETWEEN (bǐ twēn'), *prep.* (Between the fingers.) The left hand, in the "C" position, is placed before the chest, all fingers facing up. The right hand, in the "B" position, is placed between the left fingers and moves back and forth several times. This sign may also be made by pointing the left fingers to the right, with the left thumb pointing up, and the right hand making the same back and forth motion as before, with the right little finger resting on the left index finger.

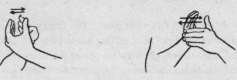

BICYCLE (bī' sə kəl), *n., v.,* -CLED, -CLING. (The motion of the feet on the pedals.) Both hands, in the "S" position, rotate alternately before the chest.

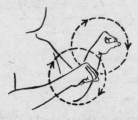

BIG 1 (bǐg), *adj.* (A delineation of something big, modified by the letter "L", which stands for LARGE.) Both "L" hands, palms facing out, are placed before the face, and separate rather widely. *Cf.* LARGE.

BIG 2, *adj*. (The height is indicated.) The right right-angle hand, palm facing the left, is held at the height the signer wishes to indicate. *Cf*. HEIGHT 2, HIGH 2, TALL 2.

BILLIARDS (bil′ yərdz), *n*. (The game of billiards.) The signer, hunched over an imaginary cue stick, mimes striking the ball. *Cf*. POOL.

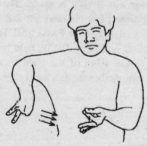

BIRD (bûrd), *n*. (The shape and movement of a beak.) The right thumb and index finger are placed against the mouth, pointing straight out. They open and close.

BIRTH *n.* (The baby is brought forth from the womb.) Both cupped hands, palms facing the body, are placed at the stomach or lower chest, one on top of the other. Both hands are moved out and away from the body in unison, describing a small arc. *Cf.* BORN.

BIRTH CONTROL *n. phrase.* (Preventing a baby from being conceived.) The sign for BABY is made: The upturned right arm rests on its upturned left counterpart, and both arms rock back and forth. Next the sign for PREVENT is made: the left hand, fingers together and palm flat, is held facing somewhat down. The little finger edge of the right hand, striking the thumb side of the left, pushes the left hand slightly forward.

BIRTHDAY (bûrth′ dā′), *n.* The sign for BIRTH is made, followed by the sign for DAY: The left arm, held horizontally, palm down, represents the horizon. The right elbow rests on the back of the left hand, with the right arm in a perpendicular

position. The right "D" hand, palm facing left, moves in an arc
to the left until it is just above the left elbow.

BITTER (bǐt′ ər), *adj.* (Something sour or bitter.) The right
index finger is brought sharply up against the lips, while the
mouth is puckered up as if tasting something sour. *Cf.* DISAP-
POINTED, DISAPPOINTMENT.

BLACK (blăk), *adj.* (The darkest part of the face, *i.e.,* the
brow, is indicated.) The tip of the index finger moves along
the eyebrow.

BLACK EYE *n.* (Swollen eye.) The right claw hand, palm facing the body, is placed over the right eye.

BLANKET (blang′ kit), *n.* (Pulling up the cover.) The downturned hands grasp an imaginary blanket edge and pull it up over the chest.

BLANK MIND *n. phrase.* (Wiping off the mind.) The right middle finger moves across the forehead from left to right, indicating an emptiness within. This sign is derived from BARE or EMPTY.

BLEED (blēd), *v.*, BLED, BLEEDING, *adj.* (Blood trickles down from the hand.) The left "5" hand is held palm facing the body and fingertips pointing right. The right "5" hand touches the back of the left and moves down, with the right fingers wiggling. *Cf.* BLOOD.

BLIND (blīnd), *adj.* (The eyes are blocked.) The tips of the "V" fingers are thrust toward the closed eyes.

BLOOD (blŭd), *n.* See BLEED.

BLOW YOUR STACK *sl. phrase.* (The lid blows off the pot.) The downturned right hand rests on the left hand, in the "C" or "O" position. The right hand suddenly goes up, its wrist swiveling back and forth as it does.

BLUE (bloͦo), *n., adj.* (The letter "B.") The right "B" hand shakes slightly, pivoted at the wrist.

BLUNT (blunt), *adj.* (The letter "B"; straight forward.) The right "B" hand is placed on the forehead, palm facing left. It moves straight out forcefully.

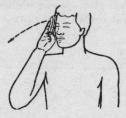

BLUSH (blŭsh), *v.,* BLUSHED, BLUSHING. (The red rises in the cheeks.) The sign for RED is made: The tip of the right index finger of the "D" hand moves down over the lips, which are red. Both hands are then placed palms facing the cheeks, and move up along the face, to indicate the rise of color. *Cf.* EMBARRASS, EMBARRASSED.

BOARD OF DIRECTORS *n.* (The letters "B-D"; the Roman toga.) The right "B" hand, starting at either shoulder, sweeps across the chest, ending in a "D" at the opposite shoulder.

BOARD OF TRUSTEES *n.* (The letters "B-T"; the Roman toga.) The right "B" hand, starting at either shoulder, sweeps across the chest, ending in a "T" at the opposite shoulder.

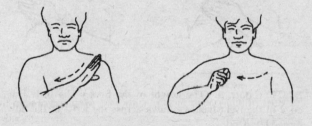

BOAT (bōt), *n.* (The shape; the bobbing on the waves.) Both hands are cupped together to form the hull of a boat. They move forward in a bobbing motion.

BODY (bŏd' ĭ), *n*. (The body is indicated.) One or both hands are placed against the chest and then are removed and replaced at a point a bit below the first.

BOOK (bŏŏk), *n*. (Opening a book.) The open hands are held together, fingers pointing away from the body. They open with little fingers remaining in contact, as in the opening of a book.

BOOT (bŏŏt), *n*. (The height of the boot.) The little finger edge of the right hand is drawn across the wrist of the downturned left hand.

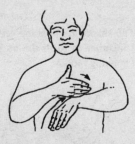

BORDER/BORDERLINE (bôr ' dər), *n., v.* (The line.) The fingertips of the downturned right hand are drawn along the index finger edge of the left hand, held palm facing the body. The tip of the right little finger alone may be substituted for the right fingertips.

BORE (bôr), *v.*, BORED, BORING, *n.* (A dryness, indicated by a wiping of the lips.) The "X" finger is drawn across the lips, from left to right, as if wiping them. *Cf.* DRY.

BORING 1 (bôr′ ing), *adj.* (The nose is pressed, as if to a grindstone wheel.) The right index finger touches the tip of the nose, as a bored expression is assumed. The right hand is sometimes pivoted back and forth slightly, as the fingertip remains against the nose.

BORING 2, *adj.* (The movement of the grindstone.) The left hand is held with palm facing right. The thumb edge of the right "S" hand is placed on the left palm and does a series of clockwise circles. This sign may be preceded by the index finger briefly touching the nose.

BORN (bôrn), *adj.* (The baby is brought forth from the womb.) Both cupped hands, palms facing the body, are placed at the stomach or lower chest, one on top of the other. Both hands are moved out and away from the body in unison, describing a small arc. *Cf.* BIRTH.

BORROW (bŏr′ ō, bôr′ ō), *v.*, -ROWED, -ROWING. (Bring to oneself.) The "K" hands are crossed and moved in toward the body.

 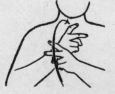

BOTH (bōth), *adj., pron.* (Two fingers are drawn together.)
The right "2" hand, palm facing the body, is drawn down
through the left "C" hand. As it does, the right index and middle fingers come together.

BOTHER (bŏth′ər), *v.,* -ERED, -ERING. (Obstruct, block.) The
left hand, fingers together and palm flat, is held before the
body, facing somewhat down. The little finger side of the right
hand, held with palm flat, makes one or several up-down chopping motions against the left hand, between its thumb and
index finger. *Cf.* ANNOY, ANNOYANCE, DISTURB, INTERFERE,
INTERFERENCE, INTERFERE WITH, INTERRUPT, PREVENT, PREVEN-
TION.

Box 66

BOX (bŏks), *n*. (The dimensions are indicated.) The open hands, palms facing and fingers pointing out, are dropped an inch or two simultaneously. They then shift their relative positions so that both palms face the body, with one hand in front of the other. In this new position they again drop an inch or two simultaneously. *Cf.* PACKAGE, ROOM 1.

BOY 1 (boi), *n*. (A young male.) The MALE root sign is made: The thumb and extended fingers of the right hand are brought up to grasp an imaginary cap brim, representing the tipping of caps by men in olden days. The downturned right hand then indicates the short height of a small boy.

BOY 2, *n*. (A modification of the MALE root sign; the familiar sign for BOY 1.) The right hand, palm down, is held at the forehead. The fingers open and close once or twice.

BRACELET (brăs' lit), *n.* (The natural sign.) The curved thumb and index finger of the open right hand are wrapped around the left wrist.

BRAG (brăg), *v.*, DRAGGED, BRAGGING. (Indicating the self, repeatedly.) The thumbs of both "A" hands are alternately thrust into the chest a number of times.

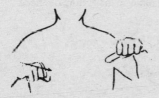

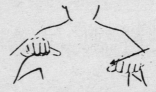

BRAVE (brăv), *adj.*, *n.*, *v.*, BRAVED, BRAVING. (Strength emanating from the body.) Both "5" hands are placed palms against the chest. They move out and away, forcefully, closing and assuming the "S" position. *Cf.* BRAVERY, HEALTH, HEALTHY, MIGHTY 2, STRENGTH, WELL.

BRAVERY (brā' və rĭ), *n.* See BRAVE.

BREAD (brĕd), *n.* (Act of cutting a loaf of bread.) The left arm is held against the chest, representing a loaf of bread. The little finger edge of the right hand is drawn down over the back of the left hand several times, to indicate the cutting of slices.

BREAK (brāk), *n.*, *v.*, BROKE, BROKEN, BREAKING. (The natural sign.) The hands grasp an imaginary object and break it in two.

BREATH (brĕth), *n.* (The rise and fall of the chest in respiration.) The hands, folded over the chest, move forward and back to the chest, to indicate the breathing. *Cf.* BREATHE.

BREATHE (brĕth), *v.*, BREATHED, BREATHING. See BREATH.

BRICK (brik), *n.* (The color red and the shape.) The sign for RED is made: the index finger moves down across the lips. The thumbs and index fingers then outline the shape of a brick, moving apart to indicate the length, and then closing to show the height.

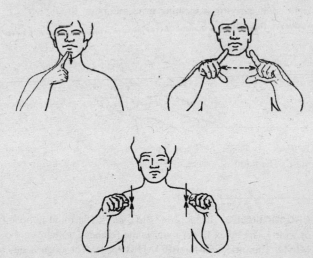

BRIEF (brēf) *adj*. (To make short; to measure off a short space). The index and middle fingers of the right "H" hand are placed across the top of the index and middle fingers of the left "H" hand, and move a short distance back and forth, along the length of the left index finger. *Cf.* SHORT 1, SHORTEN.

BRING (brĭng), *v.*, BROUGHT, BRINGING. (Carrying something over.) Both open hands, palms up, move in an arc from left to right, as if carrying something from one point to another. *Cf.* CARRY 2, DELIVER.

BROAD-MINDED (brôd´ mĭn´ dĭd), *adj*. (The mind is open, or wide.) The index finger touches the forehead to indicate the MIND. Then the sign for BROAD is made: The open hands, fingers pointing out and palms facing each other, separate from their initial position an inch or two apart.

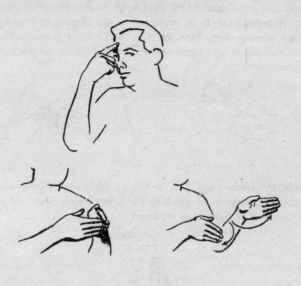

BROKE (brŏk), *(sl.)*, *adj.* (The head is chopped off.) The tips of the right fingers are thrust forcefully into the right side of the neck.

BROTHER (brŭ*th*′ ər), *n*. (A male who is the same, *i.e.,* from the same family.) The root sign for MALE is made: The thumb and extended fingers of the right hand are brought up to grasp an imaginary cap brim, representing the tipping of caps by men in olden days. Then the sign for SAME 1 is made: The outstretched index fingers are brought together, either once or several times.

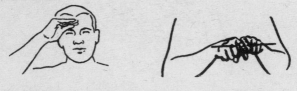

BROWN (broun), *adj*. The "B" hand is placed against the face, with the index finger touching the upper cheek. The hand is then drawn straight down the cheek.

BUCKLE (buk′ əl), *n., v.* (Locking the buckle's catch). Both hands are held palms facing the waist, with curved thumbs, index and middle fingers. These fingers slide together, knuckles interlocking, as if fastening the catch of a buckle.

BUILD (bĭld), v., BUILT, BUILDING. (Piling bricks one on top of another.) The downturned hands are placed repeatedly atop each other. Each time this is done the arms rise a bit, to indicate the raising of a building. *Cf.* CONSTRUCT, CONSTRUCTION.

BURN (bûrn), n., v., BURNED or BURNT, BURNING. (The leaping of flames.) The "5" hands are held with palms facing the body. They move up and down alternately, while the fingers wiggle. *Cf.* FIRE 1, FLAME.

BUSYBODY (biz′ ĕ bod ĕ), n. (One whose nose is into others' business.) The nose is touched with the index finger, which is then curved and thrust into a hole formed by the other hand.

BUT (bŭt; *unstressed* bət), *conj.* (A divergence or a difference; the opposite of SAME, *q.v.*) The index fingers of both "D" hands, palms facing down, are crossed near their tips. The hands are drawn apart.

BUTTER (bŭt´ ər), *n., v.,* -TERED, -TERING. (The spreading of butter.) The tips of the fingers of the downturned right "U" hand are brushed repeatedly over the upturned left palm.

BUY (bī), *n., v.,* BOUGHT, BUYING. (Giving out money.) The sign for MONEY is made: The upturned right hand, grasping some imaginary bills, is brought down into the upturned left palm, and then the right hand moves forward and up in a small arc, opening up as it does.

C

CAFETERIA 1 (kaf ə tir′ ē ə), *n.* (The letter "C"; a restaurant.) The right "C" hand is placed at the left corner of the mouth and moves over to the right corner.

CAFETERIA 2 *n.* (Eating and pushing the tray.) The signer lifts food to the mouth twice and guides a tray from left to right.

CAGE (kāj), *n., v.* (The bars.) Both "4" hands are held up, right facing left and left facing right. They switch positions and may move down slightly.

CAKE (kāk), *n.* (The rising of the cake.) The fingertips of the right "5" hand are placed in the upturned left palm. The right rises slowly an inch or two above the left.

CALCULATOR (kal' kyə lā tər), *n.* (The function and shape.) The left open hand, palm up, represents the keyboard. The index or middle finger of the right hand taps in numbers at random. The right thumb and index are then drawn down the left palm, outlining the shape of the calculator.

CALENDAR (kal' ən dər), *n.* (Turning the pages.) The right "C" hand, palm facing left, moves up the left palm, over the fingertips, and down the back of the hand.

CALL 1 (kôl), *v.*, CALLED, CALLING. (To tap someone for attention.) The right hand is placed upon the back of the left, held palm down. The right hand then moves up and in toward the body, assuming the "A" position. As an optional addition, the right hand may then assume a beckoning movement.

CALL 2, *n., v.* (The natural sign.) The cupped right hand is held against the right cheek. The mouth is slightly open.

CALLED *adj.* (NAME, indicating who is named.) The sign for NAME is made: The right "H" hand, palm facing left, is brought down on the left "H" hand, palm facing right. The hands, in this position, move forward a few inches. *Cf.* NAMED.

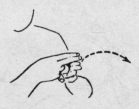

CALM (käm), *adj., v.,* CALMED, CALMING. (Quiet and peace.) The open hands are crossed before the mouth, the right palm facing left, left facing right. Then both hands, held palms down, move down from the mouth, curving outward to either side of the body. *Cf.* BE QUIET 2, BE STILL, QUIET 2, SILENCE 2.

CAN (kăn, kən),*v.* (An affirmative movement of the hands, likened to a nodding of the head, to indicate ability or power to accomplish something.) Both "A" hands, held palms down, move down in unison a short distance before the chest. *Cf.* CAPABLE, MAY 2, POSSIBLE.

CANCEL (kăn´ səl), *n., v.,*-CELED, -CELING. (A canceling out.) The right index finger makes a cross on the open left palm. *Cf.* CORRECT 2.

CANDY *n.* (Wiping the lips; licking the finger.) The right index finger, pointing left, is drawn across the lips from left to right.

CANNOT (kăn´ ŏt), *v.* (One finger encounters an unyielding quality in striking another.) The right index finger strikes the left and continues moving down. The left index finger remains in place. *Cf.* CAN'T, UNABLE.

CAN'T (kănt, känt), *v.* See CANNOT.

CAPABLE (kā´ pə bəl), *adj.* (An affirmative movement of the hands, likened to a nodding of the head, to indicate ability or power to accomplish something.) Both "A" hands, held palm down, move down in unison a short distance before the chest. *Cf.* CAN, MAY 2, POSSIBLE.

CAPITAL LETTER *n.* (The size.) The right index and thumb, forming a "C", are held far apart. This sign is usually made only in context; here we are discussing printing.

CAR (kär), *n.* (The steering wheel.) The hands grasp an imaginary steering wheel and manipulate it. *Cf.* AUTOMOBILE, DRIVE.

CARE 1 (kâr), *n., v.,* CARED, CARING. (Slow, careful movement.) The "K" hands are crossed, the right above the left, little finger edges down. In this position they describe a small clockwise circle in front of the chest. *Cf.* CARE FOR, CAREFUL 1.

CARE 2, *n., v.* (A variant of CARE 1) With the hands in the same position as in CARE 1, they are moved up and down a short distance. *Cf.* CAREFUL 2, KEEP, MAINTAIN, PRESERVE, TAKE CARE OF.

_____

CARE FOR (fôr), *v. phrase.* See CARE 1.

_____

CAREFUL 1 (kâr´ fəl), *adj.* See CARE 1.

_____

CAREFUL 2, *adj.* See CARE 2.

_____

CARELESS (kâr´ lĭs), *adj.* (The vision is sidetracked, causing one to lose sight of the object in view.) The right "V" hand, representing the vision, is held in front of the face, palm facing left. The hand, pivoted at the wrist, moves back and forth a number of times.

CARROT (kar′ ət), *n.* (Shredding.) The right thumb vigorously "shaves" the outstretched index of the left "D" hand.

CARRY 1 (kăr′ ĭ), *v.*, -RIED, -RYING. (Act of conveying an object from one point to another.) The open hands are held palms up before the chest on the right side of the body. Describing an arc, they move up and forward in unison.

CARRY 2, *v.* (Carrying something over.) Both open hands, palms up, move in an arch from left to right, as if carrying something from one point to another. *Cf.* BRING, DELIVER.

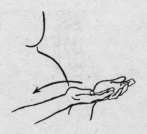

CARTOON(S) (kär tōōn'), *n.* (Funny drawings.) The sign for FUNNY is made: The index and middle fingertips brush repeatedly over the tip of the nose. The sign for DRAW then follows: The tip of the right little finger is repeatedly drawn down over the upturned left palm.

CAT (kăt), *n.* (The whiskers.) The thumbs and index fingers of both hands stroke an imaginary pair of whiskers at either side of the face. The right hand then strokes the back of the left, as if stroking the fur. This latter sign is seldom used today, however. Also one hand may be used in place of two for the stroking of the whiskers.

CATCH 1 (kăch), *v.* (Grasping something and holding it down.) Both hands, palms down, quickly close into the "S" position, the right on top of the left. *Cf.* GRAB, GRASP.

CATCH 2, *v.* (Catching a ball.) Both hands go through the motions of catching a ball.

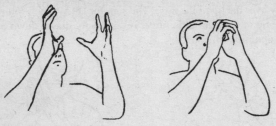

CAUTION (kô´ shən), *n.* (Tapping one to draw attention to danger.) The right hand taps the back of the left several times. *Cf.* WARN.

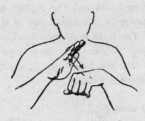

CEILING (sē´ ling), *n.* (An overhead covering.) Both hands are held palms down above the head, index fingers side by side. The arms are separated while the signer looks up.

CELEBRATE (sĕl´ ə brāt´), *v.*, -BRATED, -BRATING. (Waving of flags.) Both upright hands, grasping imaginary flags, wave them in small circles. *Cf.* CELEBRATION, CHEER, REJOICE, VICTORY 1, WIN 1.

CELEBRATION (sĕl´ ə brā´ shən), *n.* See CELEBRATE.

CELERY (sel´ ər ē), *n.* (The "C"; the stalk.) The thumbtip of the right "C" hand is placed on the tip of the left upturned index finger.

CELSIUS (sel´ sē əs), *n.* (The letter "C"; temperature.) The thumb of the right "C" hand moves up and down the upturned left index finger.

CENSUS (sen′ səs), *n.* (Counting people.) The fingertips of the right "F" hand move straight up the palm of the left, from heel to tips of fingers, as if adding up a column of figures. The sign for PEOPLE is then made: both "P" hands, palms down, swing in toward the body in alternate and repeated counterclockwise circles.

CENT (sĕnt), *n.* (The Lincoln head.) The right index finger touches the right temple and moves up and away quickly. This is "one cent." For two cents, the "2" hand is used, etc. *Cf.* CENTS.

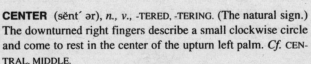

CENTER (sĕnt′ ər), *n., v.,* -TERED, -TERING. (The natural sign.) The downturned right fingers describe a small clockwise circle and come to rest in the center of the upturn left palm. *Cf.* CENTRAL, MIDDLE.

CENTIMETER (sen′ tə mē tər), *n.* (The "C" hands; the distance between.) Both "C" hands, palms out, are held with thumbtips touching. The hands move straight apart.

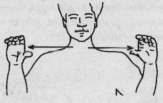

CENTRAL (sĕn′ trəl), *adj.* See CENTER.

CENTS *n. pl.* See CENT.

CHAIR (châr), *n.* (The act of sitting.) The extended right index and middle fingers are draped across the back of the same two fingers of the downturned left hand. The hands then move straight downward a short distance. *Cf.* BE SEATED, SEAT, SIT.

CHAMPAGNE (sham pān′), *n.* (Popping the cork.) The thumb flicks up from its position hidden in the closed hand.

CHANGE 1 (chănj), *n.*, *v.*, CHANGED, CHANGING. (The position of the hands is altered.) Both "A" hands, thumbs up, are held before the chest, several inches apart. The left hand is pivoted over so that its thumb points to the right. Simultaneously, the right hand is moved up and over the left, describing a small arc, with its thumb pointing to the left.

CHANGE 2, *n.*, *v.* (Dividing up or sharing.) The little finger edge of the open right "5" hand, held perpendicular to the index finger edge of the left, sweeps back and forth. This sign is used to mean changing money. Some signers use the right index finger over the left index finger, with the same orientation and motion as described before.

CHASE (chăs), *v.*, CHASED, CHASING. (The natural sign.) The "A" hands are held in front of the body, with the thumbs facing forward, the right palm facing left and the left palm facing right. The left hand is held slightly ahead of the right; it then moves forward in a straight line while the right hand follows after, executing a circular motion or swerving back and forth, as if in pursuit.

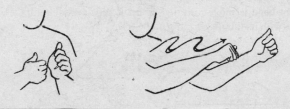

CHAT 1 (chăt), *n.*, *v.*, CHATTED, CHATTING. (Words tossed back and forth.) The open hands are held side by side with palms up, fingers pointing forward and slightly curved. In this position the hands swing back and forth from side to side before the chest. *Cf.* CONVERSATION 2.

CHAT 2, *n.*, *v.* (Moving the hands as in using sign language.) Both "C" hands, palms facing out, move alternately up and down.

CHAT 3, *n., v.* (A modified version of above.) Both hands are held in the "C" position, palms facing out, but only the right hand moves up and down.

CHEAP (chēp), (*colloq.*), *adj.* (Something easily moved, therefore of no consequence.) The right fingertips slap the little finger edge of the upturned left hand.

CHEER (chĭr), *n.* (Waving of flags.) Both upright hands, grasping imaginary flags, wave them in small circles. *Cf.* CELEBRATE, CELEBRATION, REJOICE, VICTORY 1, WIN 1.

CHEERFUL (chĭr′ fəl), *adj.* (A crinkling-up of the face.) Both hands, in the "5" position, palms facing back, are placed on either side of the face. The fingers wiggle back and forth, while a pleasant, happy expression is worn. *Cf.* FRIENDLY, PLEASANT.

CHEESE (chēz), *n.* (The pressing of cheese.) The base of the downturned right hand is pressed against the base of the upturned left hand, and the two rotate back and forth against each other.

CHERRY (cher′ ē), *n.* (Loosening a cherry from a branch.) The fingertips of the right hand grasp the end of the left little finger and twist back and forth as if loosening a cherry from a branch. *Cf.* BERRY.

CHEWING GUM (chŏŏ´ ing gum), *n.* (The chewing motion.)
The thumb of the right "A" hand, held against the right cheek,
swivels forward and back several times. Alternatively, the tips
of the right "V" hand are placed at the right cheek and bend in
and out. *Cf.* GUM.

CHICKEN (chĭk´ ən, -ĭn), *n.* (The bill and the scratching.) The
right index finger and thumb open and close as they are held
pointing out from the mouth. (This is the root sign for any kind
of bird.) The right "X" finger then scratches against the
upturned left palm, as if scratching for food. The scratching is
sometimes omitted.

CHILD (chīld), *n.* (The child's height.) The downturned right
palm is extended before the body, as if resting on a childs
head.

CHILDREN (chĭl´ drən), *n*. (Indicating different heights of children; patting the children on their heads.) The downturned right palm, held before the body, executes a series of movements from left to right, as if patting a number of children on their heads.

CHIMNEY (chim´ nē), *n*. (The shape.) The open hands, palms facing each other, are held a few inches apart. They move up together a short distance, come together an inch or two, and then continue their upward movement.

CHOCOLATE (chŏk´ lit), *n*. (The letter "C"; the icing on the cake.) The right "C" hand makes a counterclockwise circle on the downturned left hand.

CHOICE (chois), *n.* (Making a choice.) The left "V" hand faces the body. The right thumb and index finger close first over the left index fingertip and then over the left middle fingertip. *Cf.* EITHER 2.

CHOOSE (chōōz), *v.*, CHOSE, CHOSEN, CHOOSING. (Taking unto oneself.) The right hand, palm out, is extended before the chest, index finger and thumb in an open position, the other fingers separated and pointing up. The hand is drawn in toward the chest, and the index and thumb close at the same time, indicating something taken to oneself. *Cf.* SELECT 2, TAKE.

CITY (sĭt´ ĭ), *n.* (A collection of rooftops.) The fingertips of both hands are joined, the hands and arms forming a pyramid. The fingertips separate and rejoin a number of times. Both arms may move a bit from left to right each time the fingertips separate and rejoin. *Cf.* COMMUNITY.

CLASS (klăs, kläs), *n.* (A grouping together.) Both "C" hands, palms facing, are held a few inches apart at chest height. They arc swung around in unison, so that the palms now face the body. *Cf.* CLASSED, COMPANY 1, GROUP 1, ORGANIZATION 1.

CLASSED *v.* See CLASS.

CLEAN (klēn), *adj.* (Everything is wiped off the hand, to emphasize an uncluttered or clean condition.) The right hand slowly wipes the upturned left palm, from wrist to fingertips. *Cf.* NICE, PLAIN 2, PURE, PURITY.

CLEAR (klĭr), *adj.* (Rays of light clearing the way.) Both hands are held at chest height, palms out, all fingertips together. They open into the "5" position in unison, the right hand moving toward the right and the left toward the left. The palms of both hands remain facing out. *Cf.* EVIDENT, OBVIOUS, PLAIN 1.

CLOCK (klok), *n.* (A timepiece on the wall.) The signer taps the top of the wrist, indicating a wristwatch. The index fingers and thumbs are then used to form a pair of "C" s, and an imaginary clock is held up, as if hanging it on a wall or placing it on a shelf.

CLOSE 1 (klōs) *adj., adv.* (klōs; *v.* klōz), CLOSED, CLOSING. (The act of closing.) Both "B" hands, held palms out before the body, come together with some force. *Cf.* SHUT.

CLOSE (TO) 2, *adj.* (One hand is near the other.) The left hand, cupped, fingers together, is held before the chest, palm facing the body. The right hand, also cupped, fingers together, moves a very short distance back and forth, as it is held in front of the left. *Cf.* NEAR.

CLOSET (kloz' it), *n.* (The hangers.) The right curved index finger is repeatedly hung over the extended left index finger, starting at the lower knuckle and moving successively to the fingertip. *Cf.* HANGER.

CLOTH (klôth), *n.* (Plucking the fabric.) The right index and middle fingers and thumb pluck the fabric covering the chest.

CLOTHES (klōz, klōthz), *n. pl.* (Draping the clothes on the body.) With fingertips resting on the chest, both hands move down simultaneously. The action is repeated. *Cf.* CLOTHING, DRESS, SHIRT, WEAR.

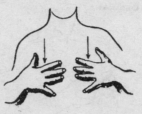

CLOTHING (klō´ thǐng), *n.* See CLOTHES.

CLOWN (klown), *n.* (The big nose.) The fingertips of the right claw hand are placed over the nose.

CLUMSINESS (klŭm´ zǐ nǐs), *n.* (Clumsy in gait; all thumbs.) The "3" hands, palms down, move alternately up and down before the body. *Cf.* AWKWARD, AWKWARDNESS, CLUMSY.

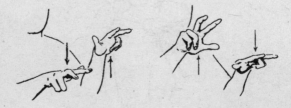

CLUMSY (klŭm´ zĭ), *adj*. See CLUMSINESS.

COAT (kōt), *n*. (The lapels are outlined.) The tips of the "A" thumbs outline the lapels of the coat.

COFFEE (kôf´ ĭ, kŏf´ ĭ), *n*. (Grinding the coffee beans.) The right "S" hand, palm facing left, rotates in a counterclockwise manner, atop the left "S" hand, palm facing right.

COLD 1 (kōld), *adj*. (The trembling from cold.) Both "S" hands, palms facing, are placed at the sides of the body. In this position the arms and hands shiver. *Cf*. SHIVER, WINTER 1.

COLD 2, *n.* (Wiping the nose.) The signer makes the motions of wiping the nose several times with an imaginary handkerchief. This is the common cold.

COLLEGE (kŏl´ ĭj), *n.* (Above ordinary school.) The sign for SCHOOL, *q.v.*, is made, but without the clapping of hands. The upper hand swings up in an arc above the lower. The upper hand may form a "C," instead of assuming a clapping position.

COLLIDE (kə lĭd´), *v.*, -LIDED, -LIDING. The fists come together with force. *Cf.* COLLISION, CRASH.

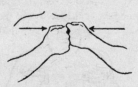

COLLISION (kə lĭzh´ en), *n.* See COLLIDE.

COLOR (kŭl´ ər), *n.* The fingertips of the right "5" hand, palm facing the body, are placed against the chin and wiggle back and forth.

COLUMBUS (kə lum´ bəs), *n.* (The letter "C"; a "name sign.") The thumb of the right "C" hand is placed against the right temple.

COMB (kōm) *n.*, *v.*, COMBED, COMBING. (Act of combing the hair.) The downturned curved fingertips of the right hand, representing the teeth of the comb, are drawn through the hair.

COME 1 (kŭm), *v.*, CAME, COME, COMING. (Movement toward the body.) The index fingers, pointing to each other, are rolled in toward the body.

COME 2, *v.* (The natural sign.) The upright hand beckons.

COMET (kom′ it), *n.* (The comet's tail.) The right "C" hand, palm out, describes a broad sweeping arc in the sky as it moves, ending in the "O" position.

COMFORT (kŭm′ fərt), *n., v.,*-FORTED, -FORTING. (A stroking motion.) Each downturned open hand alternately strokes the

back of the other, moving forward from wrist to fingers. *Cf.*
COMFORTABLE.

COMFORTABLE (kŭmf´ tə bəl, kŭm´ fər tə bəl), *adj.* See
COMFORT.

COMMON (kom´ ən), *adj.* (The same all around.) Both downturned "Y" hands execute counterclockwise circles. *Cf.* STAN-
DARD.

COMMUNITY (kə mū´ nə tǐ), *n.* (A collection of rooftops.)
The fingertips of both hands are joined, the hands and arms
forming a pyramid. The fingertips separate and rejoin a number of times. Both arms may move a bit from left to right each
time the fingertips separate and rejoin. *Cf.* CITY.

COMPANY 1 (kŭm´ pə nē), *n.* (A grouping together.) Both
"C" hands, palms facing, are held a few inches apart at chest
height. They are swung around in unison, so that the palms
now face the body. *Cf.* CLASS, CLASSED, CLUB, GROUP 1, ORGA-
NIZATION 1.

COMPANY 2, *n.* (The abbreviation; a fingerspelled loan sign.)
The letters C-O are fingerspelled. To avoid misunderstanding,
as in "co-worker," the hand may move in a small arc between
the "C" and "O."

COMPARE (kəm pâr´), *v.,* -PARED, -PARING. (Comparing both
palms.) Both open hands are held before the body, with palms
facing each other and fingers pointing upward. The hands then
turn toward the face while the signer looks from one to the
other, as if comparing them.

COMPASSION (kəm păsh´ ən), *n.* (Feelings from the heart, conferred on others.) The middle finger of the open right hand moves up the chest over the heart. The same open hand then moves in a small, clockwise circle in front of the right shoulder, with palm facing forward and fingers pointing up. The signer assumes a kindly expression.

COMPETE 1 (kəm pēt´), *v.,* -PETED, -PETING. (Two opponents come together.) Both hands are closed, with thumbs pointing straight up and palms facing the body. From their initial position about a foot apart, the hands are brought together sharply, so that the knuckles strike. The hands, as they are drawn together, also move down a bit, so that they describe a "V." *Cf.* COMPETITION 1.

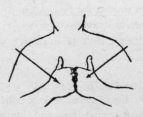

COMPETE 2, *v.* (Opposing objects.) The "A" hands are held side by side before the chest, palms facing each other and thumbs pointing forward. In this position the hands move alternately back and forth, toward and away from the body. *Cf.* COMPETITION 2, RACE.

COMPETITION 1 (kŏm´ pə tĭsh´ ən), *n.* See COMPETE 1.

COMPETITION 2, *n.* See COMPETE 2.

COMPLAIN (kəm plān´), *v.*, -PLAINED, -PLAINING. (The hand is thrust into the chest to force a complaint out.) The curved fingers of the right hand are thrust forcefully into the chest. *Cf.* COMPLAINT, OBJECT, OBJECTION, PROTEST.

COMPLAINT (kəm plānt´), *n.* See COMPLAIN.

COMPLETE (kəm plēt´), *v.*, -PLETED, -PLETING. (Wiping off the top of a container, to indicate its condition of fullness.) The downturned open right hand wipes across the index finger edge of the left "S" hand, whose palm faces right. The movement of the right hand is toward the body. *Cf.* FILL, FULL.

COMPLICATE   (kŏm´ plə kāt´), *v.*, -CATED, -CATING.
(Scrambling or mixing up.) The downturned right hand is positioned above the upturned left. The fingers of both are curved.
Both hands move in opposite horizontal circles. *Cf.* CONFUSE,
CONFUSED, CONFUSION, MIX, MIXED, MIXED UP, MIX-UP.

COMPUTER 1   (kəm pyōō´ tər), *n.* The thumb of the right "C"
hand is placed on the back of the left hand and moves up the
left arm in an arc.

COMPUTER 2, *n.* (Reference to the mind.) The thumb of the right "C" hand touches the forehead or the temple, and the hand twists slightly up and down.

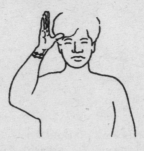

COMPUTER 3, *n.* (The tape in a mainframe drive.) Both index fingers describe clockwise circles.

COMPUTER 4, *n.* Same as COMPUTER 3, using "C" hands.

CONCEITED (kən sē′ tĭd), (*colloq.*), *adj.* (The natural sign.) Both downturned "L" hands are positioned with index fingers at the temples. They move away from the head rather slowly, indicating the size or growth of the head. The head is often moved slightly back and forth as the hands move away. An expression of superiority is assumed.

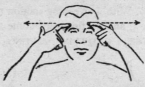

CONCENTRATE (kŏn´ sən trāt´), v., -TRATED, -TRATING, n. (Directing one's attention forward; applying oneself; concentrating.) Both hands, fingers pointing up and together, are held at the sides of the face. They move straight out from the face. *Cf.* CONCENTRATION, FOCUS, MIND 2, PAY ATTENTION (TO).

CONCENTRATION (kŏn´ sən tra´ shən), n. See CONCEN-TRATE.

CONDESCEND (kon di send´), v. (Looking down upon.) Both downturned "V" hands point somewhat down, indicating the gaze is directed down at someone. To indicate the signer is the subject of condescension, the "V" hands are held at eye level, pointing down toward the signer.

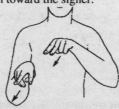

CONFERENCE (kŏn´ fər əns), *n*. (Assemble all together.) Both "5" hands, palms facing, are held with fingers pointing out from the body. With a sweeping motion they are brought in toward the chest, and all fingertips come together. This is repeated. *Cf.* GATHER 2, GATHERING, MEETING.

CONFESS (kən fĕs´), *v*., -FESSED, -FESSING. (Getting something off the chest.) Both hands are held with fingers touching the chest and pointing down. They are then swung up and out, ending with both palms facing up before the body. *Cf.* CONFESSION.

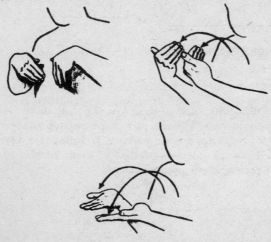

CONFESSION (kən fĕsh ən), *n*. See CONFESS.

CONFIDENCE (kŏn′ fə dəns), *n*. (Planting a flagpole, *i.e.*, planting one's trust.) The "S" hands grasp and plant an imaginary flagpole in the ground. This sign may be preceded by BELIEVE, *q.v.*

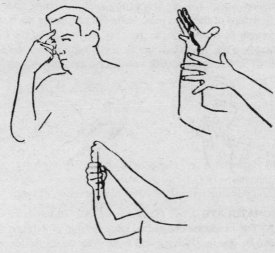

CONFUSE (kən fūz′), *v.*, -FUSED, -FUSING. (Scrambling or mixing up.) The downturned right hand is positioned above the upturned left. The fingers of both are curved. Both hands move in opposite horizontal circles. *Cf.* COMPLICATE, CONFUSED, CONFUSION, MIX, MIXED, MIXED UP, MIX-UP, SCRAMBLE.

CONFUSED (kən fūzd′), *adj*. See CONFUSE.

CONFUSION (kən fū´ zhən), *n.* See CONFUSE.

CONGRATULATE 1 (kən grăch´ ə lāt´), *v.*, -LATED, -LAT-ING.(Good words coming from the mouth; clapping hands.) The fingertips of the right hand, palm flat and facing the body, are brought up to the lips, so that they touch (part of the sign for GOOD, *q.v.*). The hands are then clapped together several times. *Cf.* APPLAUD, APPLAUSE, CONGRATULATIONS 1, PRAISE.

CONGRATULATE 2, *v.* (Shaking the clasped hands in triumph.) The hands are clasped together in front of the face and are shaken vigorously back and forth. The signer smiles. *Cf.* CONGRATULATIONS 2.

CONGRATULATIONS 1 (kən grăch´ ə lā´ shənz), *n. pl.* See CONGRATULATE 1.

CONGRATULATIONS 2, *n. pl.* See CONGRATULATE 2.

CONNECT (kə někt´), *v.*, -NECTED, -NECTING. (Joining together.) Both hands, held in the modified "5" position, palms out,

move toward each other. The thumbs and index fingers of both
hands then connect. *Cf.* ATTACH, BELONG, JOIN.

CONSCIENCE (kŏn´ shəns), *n.* (A guilty heart.) The side of
the right "G" hand strikes against the heart several times.

CONSENSUS (kən sen´ səs), *n.* (Of the same mind all
around.) The sign for AGREE is made: the index finger of the
right hand touches the forehead and then both index fingers
come together side by side, palms down. Both "Y" hands,
palms down, then simultaneously describe a counterclockwise
circle.

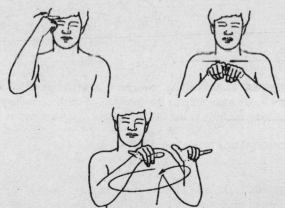

CONSENT (kən sĕnt´), *n.*, *v.*, -SENTED, -SENTING. (Agreement; of the same mind; thinking the same way.) The index finger of the right "D" hand, palm back, touches the forehead (the modified sign for THINK), and then the two index fingers, both in the "D" position, palm down, are brought together so they are side by side, pointing away from the body (the sign for SAME). *Cf.* AGREE.

CONSIDER 1 (kən sĭd´ ər), *v.*, -ERED, -ERING. (A thought is turned over in the mind.) The index finger makes a small circle on the forehead. *Cf.* SPECULATE 1, SPECULATION 1, THINK, THOUGHT, THOUGHTFUL.

CONSIDER 2, *v.* (Turning thoughts over in the mind.) Both index fingers, pointing to the forehead, describe continuous alternating circles. *Cf.* SPECULATE 2, SPECULATION 2, WONDER.

CONSIDER 3, *v.* (The scales move up and down.) The two "F" hands, palms facing each other, move alternately up and down. *Cf.* COURT, EVALUATE 1, IF, JUDGE, JUDGMENT, JUSTICE.

CONSTELLATION (kon stǝ lǎ' shǝn), *n.* (Stars in the sky.) The sign for STARS is made: both index fingers, held together and pointing up, move up alternately. The open right hand, palm facing out, then sweeps up and across the sky.

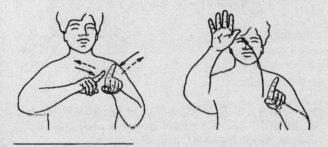

CONSTRUCT (kǝn strŭkt´), *v.*, -STRUCTED, -STRUCTING. (Piling bricks one on top of another.) The downturned hands are placed repeatedly atop each other. Each time this is done the arms rise a bit, to indicate the raising of a building. *Cf.* BUILD, CONSTRUCTION.

CONSTRUCTION (kən strŭk´ shən), *n*. See CONSTRUCT.

CONSUMER 1 (kən soo´ mər), *n*. (One who buys.) The sign for BUY is made: The upturned right hand, grasping imaginary dollar bills, is positioned in the upturned left palm. The hand moves forward in a small arc, opening up as it does. This is followed by the INDIVIDUAL sign.

CONSUMER 2, *n*. (One who uses.) The sign for USE is made: The letter "U" describes a small clockwise circle. This is followed by the INDIVIDUAL sign.

CONTACT 1 (kŏn´ tăkt), *n.*, *v.*, -TACTED, -TACTING. (The natural movement of touching.) The tip of the middle finger of the downturned right "S" hand touches the back of the left hand a number of times. *Cf.* FEEL 1, TOUCH.

CONTACT 2, *v.* (A pinning down.) The left "D" finger represents the one who is caught. The curved index and middle fingers of the right hand, palm facing down, are thrust against the left "D" finger, impaling it.

CONTACT LENSES (kon´ takt lenz´ ez), *n.* (Inserting the lens.) Leaning over the upturned index or middle finger, the signer mimes placing a contact lens in the eye.

CONTENT (kən tĕnt´), *adj.* (The inner feelings settle down.) Both "B" hands (or "5" hands, fingers together) are placed palms down against the chest, the right above the left. Both move down simultaneously a few inches. *Cf.* CONTENTED, SATISFACTION, SATISFIED, SATISFY 1.

CONTENTED (kən tĕn´ tĭd), *adj.* See CONTENT.

CONTINUE (kən tĭn´ ū), *v.,* -TINUED, -TINUING. (Steady, uninterrupted movement.) The "A" hands are held with palms out, thumbs extended and touching, the right behind the left. In this position the hands move forward in a straight, steady line. *Cf.* ENDURE 2, EVER 1, LAST 3, LASTING, PERMANENT, PERSEVERE, PERSIST, REMAIN, STAY 1, STAY STILL.

CONTRAST (*n.* kŏn´ trăst; *v.* kən trăst´), -TRASTED, -TRAST-ING. (Separateness.) The tips of the extended index fingers touch before the chest, the right finger pointing left and the left finger pointing right. The fingers then draw apart sharply to either side. *Cf.* OPPOSITE.

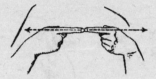

CONTRIBUTE (kən trĭb´ ūt), *v.,* -UTED, -UTING. (A giving of something.) Both "A" hands, with index fingers somewhat draped over the tips of the thumbs, are held palms facing in front of the chest. They are pivoted forward and down, in unison, from the wrists. *Cf.* GIFT, PRESENT 2.

CONTROL 1 (kən trōl´), *v.,* -TROLLED, -TROLLING. (Holding the reins over all.) The "A" hands, palms facing, move alternately back and forth, as if grasping and manipulating reins. The left "A" hand, still in position, swings over so that its palm now faces down. The right hand opens to the "5" position, palm down, and swings over the left which moves slightly to the right. *Cf.* GOVERN, MANAGE, RULE.

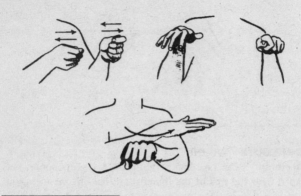

CONTROL 2, *n., v.* (Keeping the feelings down.) The curved fingertips of both hands are placed against the chest. The hands slowly move down as the fingers close into the "S" position. One hand only may also be used.

CONVENTIONAL (kən ven´ shən əl), *adj.* (Bound down by custom or habit.) Both "Y" hands, are held side by side. They move in a continuous counterclockwise direction. *Cf.* CUSTOM, HABIT, LOCKED.

CONVERSATION 1 (kŏn´ vər sā´ shən), *n.* (Movement forward from, and back to, the mouth.) The tips of both index fingers, held pointing up, move alternately forward from, and back to, the lips. *Cf.* CONVERSE, TALK 3.

CONVERSATION 2, *n.* (Words tossed back and forth.) The open hands are held side by side with palms up, fingers pointing forward and slightly curved. In this position the hands swing back and forth from side to side before the chest. *Cf.* CHAT 1.

CONVERSE (kən vûrs´), *v.*, -VERSED, -VERSING. See CONVER-
SATION 1.

COOK (kŏŏk), *n., v.*, COOKED, COOKING. (Turning over a pancake.) The open right hand rests on the upturned left palm. The
right hand flips over and comes to rest with its back on the left
palm. This is the action of turning over a pancake. The sign for
INDIVIDUAL, for a noun, then follows: Both open hands,
palms facing each other, move down the sides of the body,
tracing its outline to the hips.

COOKIE (kŏŏk´ ĭ), *n.* (Act of cutting cookies with a cookie
mold.) The right hand, in the "C" position, palm down, is
placed into the open left palm. It then rises a bit, swings or
twists around a little, and in this new position is placed again
in the open left palm.

COOL (kŏŏl), *adj., v.*, COOLED, COOLING. (Fanning the face.)
Both open hands are held with palms down and fingers spread

and pointing toward the face. The hands move up and down as if fanning the face.

COOPERATE (kō ŏp´ ə rāt´), v., -ATED, -ATING. (Joining in movement.) Both "D" hands, thumbs and index fingers interlocked, rotate in a counterclockwise circle in front of the body.

COP (kŏp), (colloq.), n. (The letter "C" for "cop"; the shape and position of the badge.) The right "C" hand, palm facing left, is placed against the heart. Cf. POLICE.

COPY (kŏp´ ĭ), *n., v.,* COPIED, COPYING. (The natural sign.) The right fingers and thumb close together and move onto the upturned, open left hand, as if taking something from one place to another.

CORRECT 1 (kə rĕkt´), *adj.* The right index finger, held above the left index finger, comes down rather forcefully so that the bottom of the right hand comes to rest on top of the left thumb joint. *Cf.* PROPER, RIGHT 3.

CORRECT 2, *v.,* -RECTED, -RECTING. (A canceling out.) The right index finger makes a cross on the open left palm. *Cf.* CANCEL.

CORRELATION (kôr ə lā′ shən), *n.* (Connection.) The index-
es and thumbs of both hands form a link together. Both hands
move repeatedly left to right and back.

COST (kôst, kŏst), *n., v.,* COST, COSTING. (Nicking into one.)
The knuckle of the right "X" finger is nicked against the palm
of the left hand, held in the "5" position, palm facing right. *Cf.*
EXPENSE, FINE 2, PENALTY, PRICE, TAX, TAXATION.

COSTUME (kos′ tōōm), *n.* (The letter "C"; slipping clothes
on.) Both "C" hands, palms facing, move down the chest
simultaneously. The movement is repeated.

COUGH (kôf), *n.*, *v.* The right claw hand is held with finger-tips on the chest. The fingertips alternately open and bend as the signer mimes coughing.

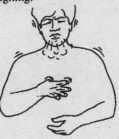

COUNT (kount), *v.*, COUNTED, COUNTING. The thumbtip and index fingertip of the right "F" hand move up along the palm of the open left hand, which is held facing right with fingers pointing up.

COUNTRY 1 (kun´ tri), *n.* (The elbow reinforcement on the jacket of a "country squire" type; also, a place where one commonly "roughs it," *i.e.*, gets rough elbows.) The open right hand describes a continuous counterclockwise circle on the left elbow.

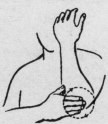

COUNTRY 2, *n.* (An established area.) The right "N" hand, palm down, executes a clockwise circle above the downturned prone left hand. The tips of the "N" fingers then move straight down and come to rest on the back of the left hand. *Cf.* LAND 2, NATION, REPUBLIC.

COURT (kört), *n.* (The scales move up and down.) The two "F" hands, palms facing each other, move alternately up and down. *Cf.* CONSIDER 3, EVALUATE 1, IF, JUDGE, JUDGMENT, JUSTICE.

COW (kou), *n.* (The cow's horns.) The "Y" hands, palms facing away from the body, are placed at the temples, with thumbs touching the head. Both hands are brought out and away simultaneously, in a gentle curve.

COWBOY (kou' boi), *n.* (The pistols.) Using both "L" hands, the signer waves them forward and back repeatedly.

CRASH (krăsh), *n., v.,* CRASHED, CRASHING. The fists come together with force. *Cf.* COLLIDE, COLLISION.

CRAYON (krā' ən), *n.* (Color and writing.) The sign for COLOR is made: The fingertips of the right "5" hand, palm facing the body, are placed on or just in front of the chin and wiggle back and forth. This is followed by the sign for WRITE: the right hand, holding an imaginary writing implement, "writes" on the palm of the upturned left hand.

CRAZY 1 (krā´ zĭ), *adj.* (Turning of wheels in the head.) The open right hand is held palm down before the face, fingers spread, bent, and pointing toward the forehead. The fingers move in circles before the forehead. *Cf.* INSANE, INSANITY.

CRAZY 2, *adj.* (Turning of wheels in the head.) The right index finger revolves in a clockwise circle at the right temple.

CRAZY FOR/ABOUT *phrase.* (Something that makes you dizzy.) The right claw hand, facing the signer, shakes from right to left repeatedly. The mouth is usually held open.

CREATE (krē āt´), *v.*, CREATED, CREATING. (Fashioning something with the hands.) The right "S" hand, palm facing left, is placed on top of its left counterpart, whose palm faces right. The hands are twisted back and forth, striking each other slightly after each twist. *Cf.* MAKE, MEND, PRODUCE.

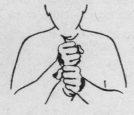 

CREDIT CARD (kred´ it kard), *n.* (The credit card machine is used to make an impression on the sales slip.) The left hand is held palm up. The right hand, closed in a fist, is placed with the edge of the little finger on the left palm. The right hand moves back and forth.

CRIB (krib), *n.* (An interlaced support.) The upturned hands are held with fingers interlocked. They separate and move up, forming a cradle or crib.

CROOK (krŏŏk), *n.* (A mustachioed thief.) The fingertips of
both "H" hands, palms facing the body, are placed above the
lips and are drawn slowly apart, describing a mustache.
Sometimes one hand only is used. This is followed by the sign
for INDIVIDUAL: Both open hands, palms facing each other,
move down the sides of the body, tracing its outline to the
hips. *Cf.* ROB 3, THEFT 2.

CROSS (krôs) *v.*, CROSSED, CROSSING. (A crossing over.) The
left hand is held before the chest, palm down and fingers
together. The right hand, fingers together, glides over the left,
with the right little finger touching the top of the left hand. *Cf.*
ACROSS, OVER.

CROSS-COUNTRY SKIING *n.* (The natural movement.) Using
a swinging rhythm, the signer takes long sliding strides as the
ski poles maneuver back and forth.

CROWD (kroud), *n.* (Many people spread out.) The down-turned claw hands move straight forward. *Cf.* MOB.

CRUEL (krōō´ əl), *adj.* (Striking down against.) Both "A" or "X" hands are held before the chest, the right above the left. The right hand strikes down and out, hitting the left thumb and knuckles with force. *Cf.* MEAN 1.

CRY (krī), *v.,* CRIED, CRYING. (Tears streaming down the cheeks.) Both index fingers, in the "D" position, move down the cheeks, either once or several times. Sometimes one finger only is used.

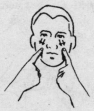

CURIOSITY (kyo͝or′ ĭ ŏs′ ə tĭ), *n.* See CURIOUS 2.

CURIOUS 1 (kyo͝or′ ĭ əs), *adj.* (Something which distorts the vision.) The "C" hand describes a small arc in front of the face. *Cf.* ODD, STRANGE, WEIRD.

CURIOUS 2, *(colloq.), adj.* (The Adam's apple.) The right thumb and index finger pinch the skin over the Adam's apple, while the hand wiggles up and down. *Cf.* CURIOSITY.

CURSE 1 (kûrs), *n., v.,* CURSED, CURSING. (Harsh words and a threatening hand.) The right hand appears to claw words out of the mouth. It ends in the "S" position, above the head, shaking back and forth in a threatening manner. *Cf.* SWEAR 2.

CURSE 2, *n.*, *v.* (Harsh words thrown out.) The right hand, as in CURSE 1, appears to claw words out of the mouth. This time, however, it turns and throws them out, ending in the "5" position. *Cf.* SCREAM, SHOUT.

CUSTOM (kŭs´ təm), *n.* (Bound down to custom or habit.) Both "S" hands, palms down, are crossed and brought down in unison before the chest. *Cf.* CONVENTIONAL, HABIT, LOCKED.

CUTE 1 (kūt), *adj.* (Titillating to the taste.) The fingertips of the right "U" hand, palm facing the body, brush against the chin a number of times, beginning at the lips. *Cf.* SUGAR, SWEET.

CUTE 2, *adj.* (Tickling.) The open right hand is held with fingers spread and pointing up, palm facing the chest. In this position the fingertips wiggle up and down, tickling the chin several times.

D

DAILY (dā' lǐ), *adj.* (Tomorrow after tomorrow.) The sign for TOMORROW, *q.v.*, is made several times: The right "A" hand moves forward several times from its initial resting place on the right cheek. *Cf.* EVERYDAY.

DANCE (dăns, däns), *n., v.,* DANCED, DANCING. (The rhythmic swaying of the feet.) The downturned index and middle fingers of the right "V" hand swing rhythmically back and forth over the upturned left palm. *Cf.* PARTY 2.

DANGER (dăn' jər), *n.* (An encroachment; parrying a knife thrust.) The left "A" hand is held palm toward the body, knuckles facing right. The extended thumb of the right "A" hand is brought sharply over the back of the left. *Cf.* DANGER-OUS.

DANGEROUS *adj.* See DANGER.

DARE (dâr), *n., v.* (The letter "D"; challenge or confront.)
Both hands are held in the "D" position, facing each other. The
right "D" hand is brought up sharply against the left, and both
hands continue away from the body an inch or so.

DAUGHTER (dô′ tər), *n.* (Female baby.) The FEMALE prefix
sign is made: The thumb of the right "A" hand traces a line on
the right jaw from just below the ear to the chin. The sign for
BABY is then made: The right arm is folded on the left arm.
Both palms face up.

DAY (dā), *n., adj.* (The letter "D"; the course of the sun across the sky.) The left arm, held horizontally, palm down, represents the horizon. The right elbow rests on the back of the left hand, with the right arm in a perpendicular position. The right "D" hand, palm facing left, moves in an arc to the left until it is just above the left elbow.

DEAD (dĕd), *adj.* (Turning over on one's side.) The open hands, fingers pointing ahead, are held side by side, with the right palm down and the left palm up. The two hands reverse their relative positions as they move from the left to the right. *Cf.* DEATH, DIE.

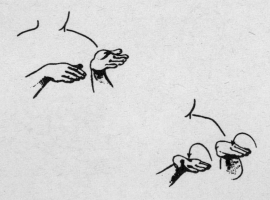

DEAF 1 (dĕf), *adj.* (Deaf and mute.) The tip of the extended right index finger touches first the right ear and then the closed lips.

DEAF 2, *adj.* (The ear is shut.) The right index finger touches the right ear. Both "B" hands, palms out, then draw together until their index finger edges toch.

DEATH (dĕth), *n.* See DEAD.

DECIDE (dĭ sīd′), *v.,* -CIDED, -CIDING. (The mind stops wavering, and the pros and cons are resolved.) The right index finger touches the forehead, the sign for THINK, *q.v.* Both "F" hands, palms facing each other and fingers pointing straight out, then drop down simultaneously. The sign for JUDGE, *q.v.,* explains the rationale behind the movement of the two hands here. *Cf.* DECISION.

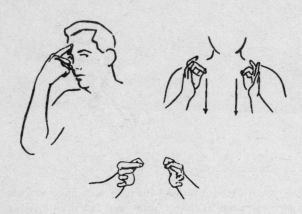

DECISION (dĭ sĭzh′ ən), *n.* See DECIDE.

DECLINE (dĭ klīn′), *v.,* -CLINED, -CLINING. (Going down step by step.) The little finger edge of the open right hand is placed on the upper side of the extended left arm, which is held with the open left hand palm down. The right hand moves down along the left arm in a series of short movements. This is the opposite of IMPROVE, *q.v.*

DECLINE IN HEALTH *phrase*. Both upturned thumbs move down in a series of stages.

DECREASE (*n.* dĕ′ krĕs, *v.* dĭ krĕs′), -CREASED, -CREASING. (The diminishing size or amount.) With palms facing, the right hand is held above the left. The right hand moves slowly down toward the left, but does not touch it. *Cf.* LESS, REDUCE.

DEDUCT (dĭ dŭkt'), *v.*, -DUCTED, -DUCTING. (Removing.) The right "A" hand, resting in the palm of the left "5" hand, moves slightly up and away, describing a small arc. It is then cast downward, opening into the "5" position, palm down, as if removing something from the left hand and casting it down. *Cf.* ELIMINATE, REMOVE, SUBTRACT, SUBTRACTION.

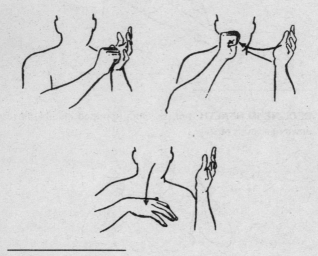

DEFEAT (dĭ fēt'), *v.*, -FEATED, -FEATING. (Forcing the head into a bowed position.) The right "S" hand, placed across the left "S" hand, moves over and down a bit. *Cf.* BEAT, OVERCOME.

DEFEATED *adj.* (Overpowered by great strength.) The right "S" hand (a fist) is held with palm facing the right shoulder. In this position it moves back toward the shoulder, pivoting from the elbow. The left "S" hand, at the same time, is held palm down with knuckles facing right, and is positioned below the right hand and over the right biceps.

DEFEND (dĭ fĕnd′), *v.*, -FENDED, -FENDING. (Hold down firmly; cover and strengthen.) The "S" hands, downturned, are held side by side in front of the body, the arms almost horizontal, and the left hand in front of the right. Both arms move a short distance forward and slightly downward. *Cf.* DEFENSE, GUARD, PROTECT, PROTECTION, SHIELD.

DEFENSE (dĭ fĕns′), *n.* See DEFEND.

DEFINE 1 (dĭ fīn′), *v.*, -FINED, -FINING. (Unraveling something to get at its parts.) The "F" hands, palms facing and fingers pointing straight out, are held about an inch apart. They move alternately back and forth a few inches. *Cf.* DESCRIBE, DESCRIPTION, EXPLAIN.

DEFINE 2, *v.* This is the same sign as for DEFINE 1, except that the "D" hands are used.

DEGREE 1 (di grē′), *n.* (A unit of temperature.) The tip of the right "D" hand travels up and down the upturned left index finger. *Cf.* TEMPERATURE.

DEGREE 2, *n.* (Drawing a percent symbol in the air.) The right

"O" hand traces a percent symbol (%) in the air. *Cf.* PERCENT.

DEGREE 3, *n.* (The rolled up diploma.) With thumbs and index fingers forming circles, both hands, held together initially, separate, describing the shape of a rolled up diploma. *Cf.* DIPLOMA.

DELAY (dĭ lā′), *n., v.,* -LAYED, -LAYING. (Putting off; moving things forward repeatedly.) The "F" hands, palms facing and fingers pointing out from the body, are moved forward simultaneously in a series of short movements. *Cf.* POSTPONE, PROCRASTINATE, PUT OFF.

DELICIOUS (dĭ lĭsh' əs), *adj.* (Smooth to the taste.) The right middle finger is placed on the lips, and then the hand moves down and out a bit. As it does, the thumb rubs over the middle finger. Both hands may be used.

DELIVER (dĭ lĭv' ər), *v,* -ERED, -ERING. (Carrying something over.) Both open hands, palms up, move in an arc from left to right, as if carrying something from one point to another. *Cf.* BRING, CARRY 2.

DEMAND (dĭ mănd', -mänd´), *v.*, -MANDED, -MANDING. (Something specific is moved in toward oneself.) The palm of the left "5" hand faces right. The right index finger is thrust into the left palm, and both hands are drawn sharply in toward the chest. *Cf.* REQUIRE.

DEMONSTRATE (dĕm′ ən strāt′), *v.*, -STRATED, -STRATING. (Directing the attention to something, and bringing it forward.) The right index finger points into the left palm, held facing out before the body. The left palm moves straight out. *Cf.* DISPLAY, EXAMPLE, EXHIBIT, EXHIBITION, REPRESENT, SHOW 1.

DENY 1 (dĭ nī′), *v.*, -NIED, -NYING. (An emphatic NOT 2, *q.v.*) The thumbs of both "A" hands, positioned under the chin, move out simultaneously, each toward their respective sides of the body. The head may be shaken slightly as the hands move out.

DENY 2, *v.* (Turning down.) The right "A" hand swings down sharply, its thumb pointing down. Both hands are sometimes used here.

DEPART (dĭ pärt'), *v.*, -PARTED, -PARTING. (Pulling away.) The downturned open hands are held in a line, with fingers pointing to the left, the right hand behind the left. Both hands move in unison toward the right. As they do so, they assume the "A" position. *Cf.* LEAVE, WITHDRAW 1.

DEPEND (dĭ pĕnd'), *v.*, -PENDED, -PENDING. (Hanging onto.) With the right index finger resting across its left counterpart, both hands drop down a bit. *Cf.* DEPENDABLE, RELY.

DEPENDABLE (dĭ pĕn′ də bəl), *adj*. See DEPEND.

DEPRESSED (dĭ prĕst′), *adj*. (The inner feelings are "down.") Both open hands, palms down, fingers pointing down, slide down the chest to waist level.

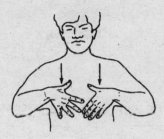

DEPTH (dĕpth), *n*. (The "D" hand, movement downward.) The right "D" hand is held with index finger pointing down. In this position it moves down along the left palm, which is held facing right with fingertips pointing forward.

DESCRIBE (dĭ skrīb′), v., SCRIBED, -SCRIBING. (Unraveling something to get at its parts.) The "F" hands, palms facing and fingers pointing straight out, are held about an inch apart. They move alternately back and forth a few inches. *Cf.* DEFINE 1, DESCRIPTION, EXPLAIN.

DESCRIPTION (dĭ skrĭp′ shən), n. See DESCRIBE.

DESERT (dez′ ərt), n. (A dry area.) The downturned curved right index finger draws across the lips, from left to right. The open hands, palms down, then spread forward and apart, indicating an expanse of land.

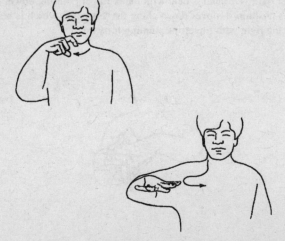

DESIGN (dǐ zīn'), *n.*, *v.* (Drawing and inventing.) The right "I" hand moves across the upturned left palm, from index finger edge to little finger edge, describing a series of curves. Optionally, the signer then places the index finger of the right "4" hand against the forehead and moves straight up.

DESIRE (dǐ zīr'), *n.*, *v.*, -SIRED, -SIRING. (Grasping something and pulling it in.) The upturned "5" hands, held side by side before the chest, close slightly into a grasping position as they move in toward the body. *Cf.* NEED 2, WANT, WISH 1.

DESSERT (dǐ zûrt'), *n.* Both hands, held in the "D" position, palms facing, come together once or twice.

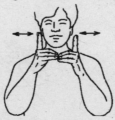

DESTROY (dĭ stroi′), *v.*, -STOYED, -STROYING. (Wiping off.) The left "5" hand, palm up, is held slightly above the right "5" hand, held palm down. The right hand swings up, just brushing over the left palm. Both hands close into the "S" position, and the right is brought back with force to its initial position, striking a glancing blow against the left knuckles as it returns. *Cf.* RUIN.

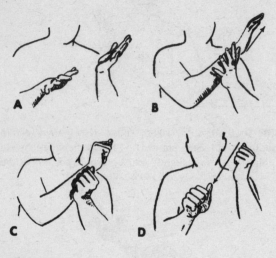

DETACH (dĭ tăch′), *v.*, -TACHED, -TACHING. (An unlocking.) With thumbs and index fingers interlocked initially (the links of a chain), the hands draw apart, showing the break in the chain. *Cf.* DISCONNECT.

DEVELOP (dĭ vĕl′ əp), *v.*, -OPED, -OPING. (The letter "D"; moving upward, as if in growth.) The right "D" hand is placed against the left palm, which is facing right with fingers pointing up. The "D" hand moves straight up to the left fingertips.

DEVIATE 1 (dē′ vĭ āt′), *v.*, -ATED, -ATING. (Going astray.) The open right hand, palm facing left, is placed with its little finger edge resting on the upturned left palm. The right hand curves rather sharply to the left as it moves across the palm. *Cf.* DEVIATION.

DEVIATE 2, *v.* (The natural motion.) The "G" hands are held side by side and touching, palms down, index fingers pointing forward. Then the right hand moves forward, curving toward the right side as it does. *Cf.* DEVIATION.

DEVIATION (dē´ vĭ ā´ shən), *n*. See DEVIATE 1 and 2.

DIAPER (dī´ ə pər), *n., v.* (The natural sign.) The thumbs and index and middle fingers of each hand point down and rest on each hip, as the signer mimes the closing of clips to fasten the diaper.

DIE (dī), *v.*, DIED, DYING. (Turning over on one's side.) The open hands, fingers pointing ahead, are held side by side, with the right palm down and the left palm up. The two hands reverse their relative positions as they move from the left to the right. *Cf.* DEAD, DEATH.

DIFFER (dĭf´ ər), *v.*, -FERED, -FERING. (To think in opposite terms.) The sign for THINK is made: The right index finger touches the forehead. The sign for OPPOSITE is then made:

The "D" hands, palms facing the body and index fingers touching, draw apart sharply. *Cf.* DISAGREE.

DIFFERENCE (dĭf′ ər əns, dĭf′ rəns,), *n.* (Separated many times; different.) The "D" hands, palms down, are crossed at the index fingers or are held side by side. They separate and return to their initial position a number of times. *Cf.* DIFFERENT, DIVERSE 1, DIVERSITY 1, VARIED.

DIFFERENT (dĭf′ ər ənt, dĭf′ rənt), *adj.* See DIFFERENCE.

DIFFICULT 1 (dĭf′ ə kŭlt′), *adj.* (The knuckles are rubbed, to indicate a condition of being worn down.) The knuckles of the curved index and middle fingers of both hands are rubbed up and down against each other. Instead of the up-down rubbing, they may rub against each other in an alternate clockwise-counterclockwise manner. *Cf.* DIFFICULTY, HARD 1, HARDSHIP, POVERTY, PROBLEM 2.

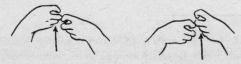

DIFFICULT 2 , *adj.* (Striking a hard object.) The curved index and middle fingers of the right hand, whose palm faces the body or the left, are brought down sharply against the back of the downturned left "S" hand. *Cf.* HARD 2.

DIFFICULTY (dĭf′ ə kŭl′ tĭ, -kəl tĭ), *n.* See DIFFICULT 1.

DINOSAUR (dī′ nə sôr), *n.* (The swinging neck.) The right arm is held upright, with the hand facing forward, all fingers touching the thumb. The hand swivels from right to left in a slow, deliberate movement. The cupped left hand may be used to support the right elbow.

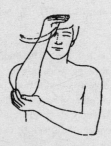

DIPLOMA (di plō′ mə), *n.* (The rolled up diploma.) With thumbs and index fingers forming circles, both hands, held together initially, separate, describing the shape of a rolled up diploma. *Cf.* DEGREE 3.

DIRT (dûrt), *n.* (Fingering the soil.) Both hands, held upright before the body, finger imaginary pinches of soil. *Cf.* GROUND.

DIRTY (dûr′ tĭ), *adj.* (A modification of the pig's snout groveling in a trough.) The downturned right hand is placed under the chin. Its fingers, pointing left, wiggle repeatedly. *Cf.* FILTHY.

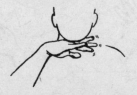

DISAGREE (dĭs´ ə grē´), v., -GREED, -GREEING. (To think in opposite terms.) The sign for THINK is made: The right index finger touches the forehead. The sign for OPPOSITE is then made: The "D" hands, palms facing the body and index fingers touching, draw apart sharply. *Cf.* DIFFER.

DISAPPEAR (dĭs´ ə pir´), v., -PEARED, -PEARING. (A disappearance.) The right open hand, palm facing the body, is held by the left hand and is drawn down and out, ending in a position with fingers drawn together. The left hand, meanwhile, may close into a position with fingers also drawn together. *Cf.* GONE 1.

DISAPPOINT (dĭs′ ə point′), *v.*, -POINTED, -POINTING. (The feelings sink.) The middle fingers of both "5" hands, one above the other, rest on the heart. They both move down a few inches.

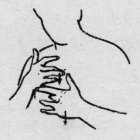

DISAPPOINTED *adj.* (Something sour or bitter.) The right index finger is brought sharply up against the lips, while the mouth is puckered up as if tasting something sour. *Cf.* BITTER, DISAPPOINTMENT.

DISAPPOINTMENT (dĭs′ ə point′ mənt), *n.* See DISAPPOINT-ED.

DISBELIEF (dĭs bĭ lēf′), *n.* (The nose is wrinkled in disbelief.) The right "V" hand faces the nose. The index and middle fingers bend as a cynical expression is assumed. *Cf.* DON'T BELIEVE, DOUBT 1.

DISCO (dis′ kō), *n.* (The natural sign.) The signer mimes dancing to a disco beat.

DISCONNECT (dĭs′ kə nĕkt′), *v.*, -NECTED, -NECTING. (An unlocking.) With thumbs and index fingers interlocked initially (the links of a chain), the hands draw apart, showing the break in the chain. *Cf.* DETACH.

DISCUSS (dĭs kŭs'), *v.*, -CUSSED, -CUSSING. (Expounding one's points.) The right "D" hand is held with the palm facing the body. It moves down repeatedly so that the side of the index finger strikes the upturned left palm. *Cf.* DISCUSSION.

DISCUSSION (dĭs kŭsh' ən), *n* See DISCUSS.

DISHWASHER (dish' wôsh ər), *n.* (The action of the water inside the machine.) Both hands, in the claw position, palms facing and one above the other, move back and forth in opposite clockwise/counterclockwise motions.

DISOBEDIENCE (dĭs' ə bē' dĭ əns), *n.* See DISOBEY.

DISOBEY (dĭs´ ə bā´), *v.*, -BEYED, -BEYING. (Turning the head.) The right "S" hand, held up with its palm facing the body, swings sharply around to the palm-out position. The head meanwhile moves slightly toward the left. *Cf.* DISOBEDIENCE.

DISPLAY (dĭs plā´), *v.*, -PLAYED, -PLAYING. (Directing the attention to something, and bringing it forward.) The right index finger points into the left palm, held facing out before the body. The left palm moves straight out. *Cf.* DEMONSTRATE, EXAMPLE, EXHIBIT, EXHIBITION, REPRESENT, SHOW 1.

DISREGARD (dĭs´ rĭ gärd´), *v.*, -GARDED, -GARDING. (Thumbing the nose.) The index finger of the right "B" hand is placed under the tip of the nose. From this position the right hand moves straight forward, away from the face. *Cf.* IGNORE.

DISSATISFACTION (dĭs´ săt ĭs făk´ shən), *n.* (NOT, SATIS-FIED.) The sign for NOT 1 is made: The crossed downturned open hands draw apart. The sign for SATISFIED then follows: The downturned "B" hands, the right above the left, are positioned on the chest. They move straight down simultaneously. *Cf.* DISSATISFIED.

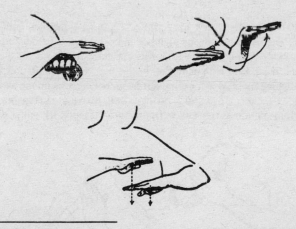

DISSATISFIED (dĭs săt´ ĭs fīd´), *adj.* See DISSATISFACTION.

DISSOLVE (dĭ zŏlv′), *v.*, -SOLVED, -SOLVING. (Fingering the small pieces resulting from the breaking up of something.) The thumbs rub slowly across the fingertips of the upturned hands, from the little fingers to the index fingers, and then continue to the "A" position, palms up. *Cf.* MELT.

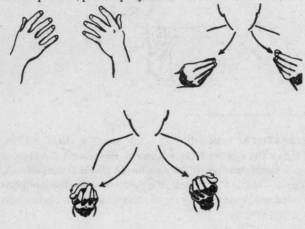

DISTURB (dĭs tûrb′), *v.*, -TURBED, -TURBING. (Obstruct, bother.) The left hand, fingers together and palm flat, is held before the body, facing somewhat down. The little finger side of the right hand, held with palm flat, makes one or several up-down chopping motions against the left hand, between its thumb and index finger. *Cf.* ANNOY, ANNOYANCE, BOTHER, INTERFERE, INTERFERENCE, INTERFERE WITH, INTERRUPT, PREVENT, PREVENTION.

DIVERSE 1 (dĭ vûrs', dī-, dī' vûrs), *adj.* (Separated many times; different.) The "D" hands, palms down, are crossed at the index fingers or are held side by side. They separate and return to their initial position a number of times. *Cf.* DIFFERENCE, DIFFERENT, DIVERSITY 1, VARIED.

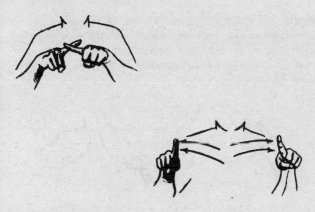

DIVERSE 2, *adj.* (The fingertips indicate many things.) Both hands, in the "D" position, palms out and index fingertips touching, are drawn apart. As they move apart, the index fingers wiggle up and down. *Cf.* DIVERSITY 2, VARIOUS, VARY.

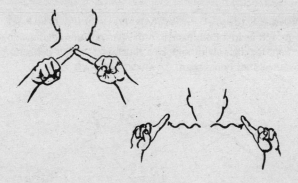

DIVERSITY 1 (dǐ vûr ′ sə tǐ, dī-), *n*. See DIVERSE 1.

DIVERSITY 2, *n*. See DIVERSE 2.

DIVIDE (dǐ vīd′), *v.*, -VIDED, -VIDING. (A splitting apart or dividing.) The two hands are crossed, with the right little finger resting on the left index finger. Both hands are dropped down and separated simultaneously, so that the palms face down. *Cf.* DIVISION.

DIVISION (dǐ vǐzh′ ən), *n*. See DIVIDE.

DIVORCE 1 (dǐ vôrs′), *n., v.*, -VORCED, -VORCING. (The hands are moved apart.) Both hands, in the "A" position, thumbs up, are held together, with knuckles touching. With a deliberate movement they come apart. *Cf.* APART, SEPARATE 1.

DIVORCE 2, *n., v.* (The letter "D"; a separating.) The "D" hands, palms facing and fingertips touching, draw apart.

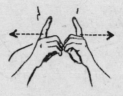

DIZZY (dĭz' e), *adj.* (Images swinging around before the eyes.) The right "5" hand, palm facing the body and fingers somewhat curved, swings around in a continuous counter-clockwise circle before the eyes.

DO (dōō), *v.*, DOES, DID, DONE, DOING. (An activity.) Both open hands, palms down, are swung right and left before the chest. *Cf.* PERFORM 1, PERFORMANCE 1.

DO AS ONE WISHES *phrase.* (Think for yourself.) The sign for THINK is made: The right index finger touches the center of the forehead. The SELF sign follows: The upturned right thumb moves straight forward from the signer toward the person addressed.

DOCTOR (dŏk′ tər), *n.* (The letter "M," from "M.D."; feeling the pulse.) The fingertips of the right "M" hand lightly tap the left pulse a number of times.

DOG (dôg), *n.* (Patting the knee and snapping the fingers to beckon the dog.) The right hand pats the right knee, and then the fingers are snapped.

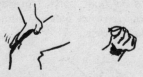

DOLLAR(S) (dŏl′ ər), *n.* (The natural sign; drawing a bill from a billfold.) The right thumb and index finger trace the outlines of a bill on the upturned left palm. Or, the right thumb and fingers may grasp the base of the open left hand, which is held palm facing right and fingers pointing forward; the right hand, in this position, then slides forward along and off the left hand, as if drawing bills from a billfold.

DOLPHIN (dŏl′ fĭn), *n*. (The diving.) The right "B" hand makes a series of undulating dive movements in front of the downturned left arm, which represents the surface of the water.

DONE (dŭn), *v*. (Shaking the hands to rid them of something.) The upright "5" hands, palms facing each other, are suddenly and quickly swung around to a palm-out position. *Cf.* END 3, FINISH.

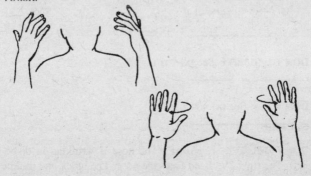

DO NOT 1, *v. phrase.* (The natural sign.) The crossed "5" hands, palms facing out (or down), separate and recross quickly and repeatedly. The head is usually shaken simultaneously. This sign is from NOT 1, *q.v. Cf.* DON'T 1.

DO NOT 2, *v. phrase.* The thumb of the right "A" hand is placed under the chin. From this position it is flicked outward in an arc. This sign is a variant of DO NOT 1. *Cf.* DON'T 2.

DON'T 1 (dōnt) *v.* See DO NOT 1.

DON'T 2 , *v.* See DO NOT 2.

DON'T BELIEVE *v. phrase.* (The nose is wrinkled in disbelief.) The right "V" hand faces the nose. The index and middle fingers bend as a cynical expression is assumed. *Cf.* DISBELIEF 1, DOUBT 1.

DON'T CARE 1, *(colloq.), v. phrase.* (Wiping the nose, *i.e.,* "Keeping the nose clean" or not becoming involved.) The downturned right "D" hand, index finger touching the nose, is suddenly flung down and to the right.

DON'T CARE 2 , *(colloq.), v. phrase.* The thumb of the right "Y" hand touches the right ear. The right "Y" hand is then flung down and to the right. *Cf.* DON'T CARE FOR, DON'T LIKE.

DON'T CARE FOR *(colloq.)*, *v. phrase.* See DON'T CARE 2.

DON'T KNOW *v. phrase.* (Knowledge is lacking.) The sign for KNOW is made: The right fingertips tap the forehead several times. The right hand is then flung over to the right, ending in the "5" position, palm out.

DON'T LIKE *(colloq.)*, *v. phrase.* See DON'T CARE 2.

DON'T WANT *v. phrase.* (The hands are shaken, indicating a wish to rid them of something.) The "5" hands, palms facing the body, suddenly swing around to the palms-down position.

DOOR (dôr), *n.* (The opening and closing of the door.) The "B" hands, palms out and edges touching, are drawn apart and then come together again. *Cf.* DOORWAY, OPEN THE DOOR.

DOORKNOB (dôr′ nob), *n.* (The natural sign.) The signer mimes twisting a doorknob.

DOORWAY (dôr′ wā′), *n.* See DOOR.

DOUBT 1 (dout), *n.*, *v.*, DOUBTED, DOUBTING. (The nose is wrinkled in disbelief.) The right "V" hand faces the nose. The index and middle fingers bend as a cynical expression is assumed. *Cf.* DISBELIEF 1, DON'T BELIEVE.

DOUBT 2, *n.*, *v.* (The wavering.) The downturned "S" hands swing alternately up and down. *Cf.* DOUBTFUL.

DOUBTFUL (dout′ fəl), *adj.* See DOUBT 2.

DOWN (doun), *prep.* (The natural sign.) The right hand, pointing down, moves down an inch or two.

DREAM (drēm), *n., v.,* DREAMED, DREAMT, DREAMING. (A thought wanders off into space.) The right curved index finger opens and closes quickly as it leaves its initial position on the forehead and moves up into the air.

DRESS (drĕs), *n., v.,* DRESSED, DRESSING. (Draping the clothes on the body.) With fingertips resting on the chest, both hands move down simultaneously. The action is repeated. *Cf.* CLOTHES, CLOTHING, SHIRT, WEAR.

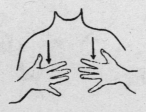

DRINK (drǐngk), *n.*, *v.*, DRANK, DRUNK, DRINKING. (The natural sign.) An imaginary glass is tipped at the open lips.

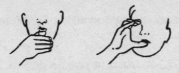

DRIVE (drǐv), *v.*, DROVE, DRIVEN, DRIVING, *n.* (The steering wheel.) The hands grasp an imaginary steering wheel and manipulate it. *Cf.* AUTOMOBILE, CAR.

DRUNK (drŭngk), *adj.* (The act of drinking.) The thumbtip of the right "Y" hand is tilted toward the mouth, as if it were a drinking glass or bottle. The signer tilts his head back slightly, as if drinking. *Cf.* BEER, DRUNKARD, DRUNKENNESS, INTOXICATE, INTOXICATION, LIQUOR.

DRUNKARD (drŭngk′ ərd), *n.* See DRUNK.

DRUNKENNESS (drŭngk′ ən nĭs), *n.* See DRUNK.

DRY (drī), *adj., v.,* DRIED, DRYING. (A dryness, indicated by a wiping of the lips.) The "X" finger is drawn across the lips, from left to right, as if wiping them. *Cf.* BORE.

DUCK (dŭk), *n.* (The broad bill.) The right hand is held with its back resting against the mouth. The thumb, index and middle fingers come together repeatedly, indicating the opening and closing of a broad bill.

DUCKLING (dŭk′ ling) *n.* (A small duck) The sign for DUCK is made: The right hand is held with the back of the hand resting against the mouth. The thumb and index and middle fingers open and close together, depicting the broad bill of the duck. The cupped hands then come together, indicating a small item within.

DUE (dū, dōō), *adj.* (Pointing to the palm, where the money should be placed.) The index finger of one hand is thrust into the upturned palm of the other several times. *Cf.* OWE.

DUMMY (dum' ə), *n.* The thumb of the right "C" hand is placed inside the closed left hand. Pivoting on the thumb, the right hand moves up and over the back of the left.

DURING (dyŏŏr' ĭng , dŏŏr'-), *prep.* (Parallel time.) Both "D" hands, palms down, move forward in unison, away from the body. They may move straight forward or may follow a slight upward arc. *Cf.* MEANTIME, WHILE.

E

EACH (ēch), *adj.* (Peeling off, one by one.) The left "A" hand is held palm facing the right. The knuckles of the right "A" hand are drawn repeatedly down the left thumb, from its tip to its base. *Cf.* EVERY.

EACH OTHER *pron. phrase.* (Mingling with.) Both hands are held in modified "A" positions, thumbs out. The left hand is positioned with its thumb pointing straight up, and the right hand, with its thumb pointing down, revolves above the left thumb in a clockwise direction. *Cf.* MINGLE, ONE ANOTHER.

EAGER (ē′ gər), *adj.* (Rubbing the hands together in zeal or ambition.) The open hands are rubbed vigorously back and forth against each other. *Cf.* AMBITIOUS, EAGERNESS, ENTHUSI-ASM, ENTHUSIASTIC.

EAGERNESS *n.* See EAGER.

EAR (ĭr), *n.* (The natural sign.) The right index finger touches the right ear.

EARLY (ûr′ lē), *adj.* The middle finger of the downturned right hand rests on the back of the downturned left hand. The top hand moves forward, while the middle finger is drawn back against the palm.

EARRING (ĭr′ rĭng′), *n.* (The natural sign.) The signer squeezes the earlobe, which may also be shaken slightly.

EARTH (ûrth), *n.* (The earth and its axes are indicated.) The downturned left "S" hand indicates the earth. The thumb and index finger of the downturned right "5" hand are placed at each edge of the left. In this position the right hand swings back and forth, while maintaining contact with the left.

EASY 1 (ē′ zĭ), *adj.* (The fingertips are easily moved.) The right fingertips brush repeatedly over their upturned left counterparts, causing them to move. *Cf.* SIMPLE 1.

EASY 2, (*loc., colloq.*), *adj.* (Rationale obscure.) The thumb and index finger of the right "F" hand are placed on the chin.

EAT (ēt), *v.*, ATE, EATEN, EATING. (The natural sign.) The closed right hand goes through the natural motion of placing food in the mouth. This movement is repeated. *Cf.* FEED 1, FOOD, MEAL.

EAVESDROP 1 (ēvz' drop), *v.* (Information is pulled into the eye.) The hand is held with thumb below the eye, index and middle fingers pointing forward. The index and middle fingers repeatedly move in and out, as if bringing something into the eye. This is a culturally related sign, taking into account that deaf people gather information with their eyes rather than their ears.

EAVESDROP 2, *v.* (Information is pulled into the ear.) The same hand position as in EAVESDROP 1, above. The thumbtip is placed on the ear, and the index and middle fingers move in and out, as if bringing something into the ear.

ECONOMIC (ek ə nom′ ik), *adj.* (The "E" hand; money.) The back of the upturned right "E" hand is brought down twice on the upturned left open hand.

EDUCATE (ĕj′ ŏŏ kāt′), v., -CATED, -CATING. (Giving forth from the mind.) The fingertips of each hand are placed on the temples. They then swing out and open into the "5" position. *Cf.* INSTRUCT, TEACH.

EFFORT 1 (ĕf′ ərt), n. (Trying to push through.) The "A" hands, palms facing before the body, are swung around and a bit down, so that the palms now face out. The movement indicates an attempt to push through a barrier. *Cf.* ATTEMPT 1, TRY 1.

EFFORT 2, n. (Trying to push through, using the "T" hands, for "try.") This is the same sign as EFFORT 1, except that the "T" hands are employed. *Cf.* ATTEMPT 2, TRY 2.

EFFORT 3, n. (The letter "E"; attempting to break through.) Both "E" hands move forward simultaneously, describing a small, downturned arc.

EGG (ĕg), *n.* (Act of breaking an egg into a bowl.) The right "H" hand is brought down on the left "H" hand, and then both hands are pivoted down and slightly apart. *Cf.* HATCH.

EITHER 1 (ē′ thər *or esp. Brit.,* ī′ thər), *conj.* (Selection between two or among multiple choices.) The left "L" hand is held palm facing the body and thumb pointing straight up. The right index finger touches the left thumbtip and then the left index fingertip.

EITHER 2, *adj.* (Making a choice.) The left "V" hand faces the body. The right thumb and index finger close first over the left index fingertip and then over the left middle fingertip. *Cf.* CHOICE.

EITHER 3, *conj.* (Considering one thing against another.) The "A" hands, palms facing and thumbs pointing straight up, move alternately up and down before the chest. *Cf.* OR, WHETHER, WHICH.

ELECT (ĭ lĕkt′), *n., v.,* -LECTED, -LECTING. (Placing a ballot in a box.) The right hand, holding an imaginary ballot between the thumb and index finger, places it into an imaginary box formed by the left "O" hand, palm facing right. *Cf.* ELECTION, VOTE 1.

ELECTION (ĭ lĕk′ shən), *n.* See ELECT.

ELECTRIC (ĭ lĕk′ trĭk), *adj.* (The points of the electrodes.) The "X" hands are held palms facing the body, thumb edges up. The knuckles of the index fingers touch each other repeatedly. *Cf.* ELECTRICITY.

ELECTRICITY (ĭ lĕk′ trĭs′ ə tĭ), *n.* See ELECTRIC.

ELEGANT (el ′ ə gənt), *adj.* (The feelings are titillated.) With the thumb resting on the upper part of the chest, the fingers are wiggled back and forth. *Cf.* FINE 1, WONDERFUL.

ELEVATOR (ĕl′ ə vā′ tər), *n.* (The letter "E"; the rising.) The right "E" hand, palm facing left and thumb edge up, rises straight up.

ELIMINATE (ĭ lĭm ə nāt′), v., -NATED, -NATING. (Scratching something out and throwing it away.) The fingertips of the open right hand scratch downward across the palm of the upright left hand. In one continuous motion, the right hand then closes as if holding something, and finally opens again forcefully and moticns as if throwing something away. *Cf.* DEDUCT, REMOVE, SUBTRACT, SUBTRACTION.

EMBARRASS (ĕm băr′ əs), v., -RASSED, -RASSING. (The red rises in the cheeks.) The sign for RED is made: The tip of the right index finger of the "D" hand moves down over the lips, which are red. Both hands are then placed palms facing the cheeks, and move up along the face, to indicate the rise of color. *Cf.* BLUSH, EMBARRASSED.

EMBARRASSED *adj*. See EMBARRASS.

EMERGENCY (i mûr′ jən sē), *n., adj.* (The flashing light.)
The right "E" hand is positioned above the head. It rotates in
imitation of a flashing emergency light.

EMOTION 1 (ĭ mō′ shən), *n.* (The welling up of feelings or
emotions in the heart.) The right middle finger, touching the
heart, moves up an inch or two a number of times. *Cf.* FEEL 2,
FEELING.

EMOTION 2, *n.* (The letter "E"; that which moves about in the
chest, *i.e.*, the heart.) The "E" hands, palms facing in, are positioned close to the chest. Both hands describe alternate circles,
the left hand clockwise and the right hand counterclockwise.
The right hand alone may be used.

EMPHASIS (ĕm' fə sĭs), *n.* (Pressing down to emphasize.) The right thumb is pressed down deliberately against the upturned left palm. Both hands move forward a bit. *Cf.* EMPHASIZE, EMPHATIC.

EMPHASIZE (ĕm' fə sīz'), *v.*, -SIZED, -SIZING. See EMPHASIS.

EMPHATIC (ĕm făt' ĭk), adj. See EMPHASIS.

ENCOURAGE (ĕn kûr' ĭj), *v.*, -AGED, -AGING. (Pushing forward.) Both "5" hands are held, palms out, the right fingers facing right and the left fingers left. The hands move straight forward in a series of short movements. *Cf.* MOTIVATE, MOTIVATION, URGE 1.

ENCYCLOPEDIA (en sī klə pē' dē ə), *n.* (The letter "E"; turning the pages.) The upturned left hand indicates the open page. The right "E" hand, palm down, repeatedly brushes against the left palm, from fingertips to heel.

END 1 (ĕnd), *n., v.,* ENDED, ENDING. (The little, *i.e.,* LAST, fingers are indicated.) With the hands in the "I" position, the tip of the right little finger strikes the tip of its left counterpart. *Cf.* FINAL 1, FINALLY 1, LAST 1, LASTLY.

END 2, *n., v.* (A single little, *i.e.,* LAST, finger is indicated.) The tip of the index finger of the right "D" hand strikes the tip of the little finger of the left "I" hand. *Cf.* FINAL 2, FINALLY 2, LAST 2, LASTLY.

END 3, *n.*, *v.* (Shaking the hands to rid them of something.) The upright "5" hands, palms facing each other, are suddenly and quickly swung around to a palm-out position. *Cf.* DONE, FINISH.

ENDORSE 1 (ĕn dôrs′), *v.*, -DORSED, -DORSING. (Holding up.) The right "S" hand pushes up the left "S" hand. *Cf.* SUPPORT, SUSTAIN, SUSTENANCE.

ENDORSE 2, *v.* (One hand upholds the other.) Both hands, in the "S" position, are held palms facing the body, the right under the left. The right hand pushes up the left in a gesture of support.

ENDURE 1 (ĕn dyŏŏr′, -dŏŏr′), *v.*, -DURED, -DURING. (A clenching of the fists; the rise and fall of pain.) Both "S" hands, tightly clenched, revolve about each other, slowly and deliberately, while a pained expression is worn. *Cf.* SUFFER.

ENDURE 2, *v.* (Steady, uninterrupted movement.) The "A" hands are held with palms out, thumbs extended and touching, the right behind the left. In this position the hands move forward in a straight, steady line. *Cf.* CONTINUE, EVER 1, LAST 3, LASTING, PERMANENT, PERSEVERE, PERSIST, REMAIN, STAY 1, STAY STILL.

ENEMY (ĕn′ ə mĭ), *n.* (At sword's point.) The two index fingers, after pointing to each other, are drawn sharply apart. This is followed by the sign for INDIVIDUAL: Both open hands, palms facing each other, move down the sides of the body, tracing its outline to the hips. *Cf.* OPPONENT.

ENERGY (en' ər jē), *n.* (The letter "E"; power or muscle.) The left arm, fist closed, is extended, palm up. The right "E" hand, palm down, describes an arc over the upper muscle area.

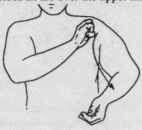

ENGAGED (ĕn gājd'), *adj.* (The letter "E"; the ring finger.) The right "E" hand moves in a clockwise circle over the down-turned left hand, and then comes to rest on the left ring finger.

ENGINE (ĕn' jən), *n.* (The meshing gears.) With the knuckles of both hands interlocked, the hands pivot up and down, imitating the meshing of gear teeth. *Cf.* MACHINE, MOTOR 1.

ENJOY (ĕn joi'), *v.,* -JOYED, -JOYING. (A pleasurable feeling on the heart.) The open right hand is circled on the chest, over the heart. *Cf.* ENJOYMENT, LIKE 3, PLEASE, PLEASURE.

ENJOYMENT (ĕn joi′ mənt), *n.* See ENJOY.

ENOUGH (ĭ nŭf′), *adj.* (A full cup.) The left hand, in the "S" position, is held palm facing right. The right "5" hand, palm down, is brushed outward several times over the top of the left, indicating a wiping off of the top of a cup. *Cf.* PLENTY.

ENTER (ĕn′ tər), *v.*, -TERED, -TERING. (Going in.) The down-turned open right hand sweeps under its downturned left counterpart. *Cf.* ENTRANCE.

ENTHUSIASM (ĕn thoō′ zĭ ăz′ əm), *n.* (Rubbing the hands together in zeal or ambition.) The open hands are rubbed vigorously back and forth against each other. *Cf.* AMBITIOUS, EAGER, EAGERNESS, ENTHUSIASTIC.

ENTHUSIASTIC (ĕn thoō′ zĭ ăs′ tĭk), adj. See ENTHUSIASM.

ENTIRE (ĕn tīr′), *adj.* (Encompassing; a gathering together.) Both hands are held in the right angle position, palms facing the body, and the right hand in front of the left. The right hand makes a sweeping outward movement around the left, and comes to rest with the back of the right hand resting in the left palm. *Cf.* ALL.

ENTRANCE (ĕn trəns′), *n.* See ENTER.

ENVIOUS (ĕn′ vē əs), *adj.* (Biting the finger to suppress the feelings.) The tip of the index finger is bitten. The tip of the little finger is sometimes used. *Cf.* ENVY, JEALOUS, JEALOUSY.

ENVY (en′ vē), *n.* See ENVIOUS.

EPIDEMIC (ep ə dem′ ik), *n.* (Sickness spreads.) The sign for SICK is made: The right middle finger rests on the forehead and its left counterpart on the stomach. Both hands are then held palms down, in the modified "O" position. The hands move out and spread apart, with fingers opening wide.

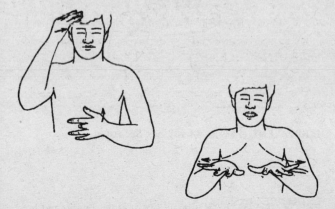

EQUAL (ē′ kwəl), *adj., n., v.,* -QUALED, -QUALING. (Sameness is stressed.) The downturned "B" hands, held at chest height, are brought together repeatedly, so that the index finger edges or fingertips come into contact. *Cf.* EQUIVALENT, EVEN, FAIR, LEVEL.

EQUATOR (i kwā′ tər), *n.* (The letter "E"; circling the globe.) The right "E" hand describes a circle around the left fist, which represents the planet.

EQUIVALENT (ĭ kwĭv′ ə lənt), *adj.* See EQUAL.

ERROR (ĕr′ ər), *n.* (Rationale obscure; the thumb and little finger are said to represent, respectively, right and wrong, with the head poised between the two.) The right "Y" hand, palm facing the body, is brought up to the chin. *Cf.* MISTAKE, WRONG.

ESCALATOR (es′ kə lā tər), *n.* (Standing on moving stairs.) The right index and middle fingers "stand" on the left hand, which is held either up or down. The left hand moves up at an angle, carrying the right hand with it.

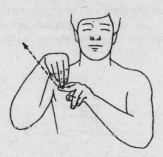

ESCAPE (ĕs kāp′), *v.*, -CAPED, -CAPING. (Emerging from a hiding place.) The downturned right "D" hand is positioned under the downturned open left hand. The right "D" hand suddenly emerges and moves off quickly to the right.

ESKIMO (es′ kə mō), *n.* (The letter "E"; the fur hood.) The "E" hand, palm facing out, describes a circle over the head, from left to right.

ESTABLISH (ĕs tăb′ lĭsh), *v.*, -LISHED, -LISHING. (To set up.) The right "A" hand, thumb up and palm facing left, comes down to rest on the back of the downturned left "S" hand. Before doing so, the right "A" hand may describe a clockwise circle above the left hand, but this is optional. *Cf.* FOUND, FOUNDED.

ETERNITY (ĭ tûr′ nə tĭ), *n.* (Around the clock and ahead into the future.) The right index finger, pointing forward, traces a clockwise circle in the air. The downturned right "Y" hand then moves forward, either in a straight line or in a slight downward curve. *Cf.* EVER 2, EVERLASTING, FOREVER.

EVADE (ĭ vād'), *v.*, -VADED, -VADING. (Ducking back and forth, away from something.) Both "A" hands, thumbs pointing straight up, are held some distance before the chest, with the left hand in front of the right. The right hand, swinging back and forth, moves away from the left and toward the chest. *Cf.* AVOID 1, EVASION.

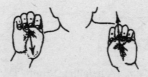

EVALUATE 1 (ĭ văl' yŏŏ āt), *v.*, -ATED, -ATING. (The scales move up and down.) The two "F" hands, palms facing each other, move alternately up and down. *Cf.* CONSIDER 3, COURT, IF, JUDGE, JUDGMENT, JUSTICE.

EVALUATE 2, *v.* (The letter "E"; weighing up and down.) The "E" hands, palms facing out from the body, move alternately up and down.

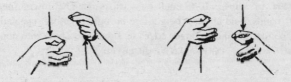

EVALUATE 3, *v.* (Weighing.) Both "E" hands, palms out, move alternately up and down.

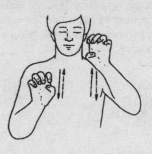

EVASION (ĭ vā zhən), *n.* See EVADE.

EVEN (ē′ vən), *adj.* (Sameness is stressed.) The downturned "B" hands, held at chest height, are brought together repeatedly, so that the index finger edges or fingertips come into contact. *Cf.* EQUAL, EQUIVALENT, FAIR, LEVEL.

EVENT (ĭ vĕnt′), *n.* (A befalling.) Both "D" hands, index fingers pointing away from the body, are simultaneously pivoted over so that the palms face down. *Cf.* HAPPEN 1, INCIDENT.

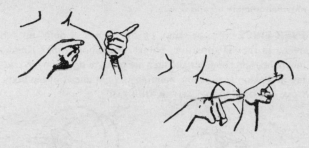

EVER 1 (ĕv′ ər), *adv.* (Steady, uninterrupted movement.) The "A" hands are held with palms out, thumbs extended and touching, the right behind the left. In this position the hands move forward in a straight, steady line. *Cf.* CONTINUE, ENDURE 2, LAST 3, LASTING, PERMANENT, PERSEVERE, PERSIST, REMAIN, STAY 1, STAY STILL.

EVER 2, *adv.* (Around the clock and ahead into the future.) The right index finger, pointing forward, traces a clockwise circle in the air. The downturned right "Y" hand then moves forward, either in a straight line or in a slight downward curve. *Cf.* ETERNITY, EVERLASTING, FOREVER.

EVERLASTING (ĕv′ ər lăs′ tĭng, -läs′-), adj. See EVER 2.

EVER SINCE (ĕv′ ər sĭns), *phrase*. (From a point up and over.) In the "D" position, palms down, both index fingers touch the right shoulder and then are brought up and over, ending in a palm-up position, pointing straight ahead of the body. *Cf.* ALL ALONG, SINCE 1, SO FAR, THUS FAR.

EVERY (ĕv′ rē), *adj*. (Peeling off, one by one.) The left "A" hand is held palm facing the right. The knuckles of the right "A" hand are drawn repeatedly down the left thumb, from its tip to its base. *Cf.* EACH.

EVERYDAY (ĕv′ rē dā′), *adj*. (Tomorrow after tomorrow.) The sign for TOMORROW, *q.v.*, is made several times: The right "A" hand moves forward several times from its initial resting place on the right cheek. *Cf.* DAILY.

EVIDENT (ev′ ə dənt), *adj.* (Rays of light clearing the way.) Both hands are held at chest height, palms out, all fingertips together. They open into the "5" position in unison, the right hand moving toward the right and the left toward the left. The palms of both hands remain facing out. *Cf.* CLEAR, OBVIOUS, PLAIN 1.

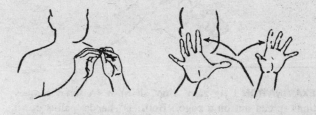

EXACT (ĭg zăkt′), *adj.* (The fingers come together precisely.) The thumb and index finger of each hand, palms facing, the right above the left, form circles. They are brought together with a deliberate movement, so that the fingers and thumbs now touch. Sometimes the right hand, before coming together with the left, executes a slow clockwise circle above the left. *Cf.* EXACTLY, PRECISE, SPECIFIC 1.

EXACTLY (ĭg zăkt′ lē), *adv.* See EXACT.

EXAGGERATE (ĭg zăj´ ə rāt´), (*sl.*)*v.*, -ATED, -ATING. (Stretching out one's words.) The left "S" hand, palm facing right, is held before the mouth. Its right counterpart, palm facing left, is moved forward in a series of short up-and-down arcs.

EXAMINATION 1 (ĭg zăm´ ə nā´ shən), *n.* (A series of questions spread out on a page.) Both "D" hands, palms down, simultaneously execute a single circle, the right hand moving in a clockwise direction and the left in a counterclockwise direction. Upon completion of the circle, both hands open into the "5" position and move straight down a short distance. (The hands actually draw question marks in the air.) *Cf.* TEST.

EXAMINATION 2, *n.* (Firing questions.) The index fingers of both "D" hands repeatedly curve and straighten out as the hands are alternately flung forward and back, as if firing questions. *Cf.* QUERY, QUESTION 1, QUIZ.

EXAMINE (ĭg zăm' ĭn), v., -INED, -INING. (Directing the vision from place to place.) The right "C" hand, palm facing left, moves from right to left across the line of vision, in a series of counterclockwise circles. The signer's gaze remains concentrated and his head turns slowly from right to left. *Cf.* LOOK FOR, SEARCH, SEEK.

EXAMPLE (ĭg zăm' pəl, -zăm'-), n., v., -PLED, -PLING. (Directing the attention to something, and bringing it forward.) The right index finger points into the left palm, held facing out before the body. The left palm moves straight out. *Cf.* DEMONSTRATE, DISPLAY, EXHIBIT, EXHIBITION, REPRESENT, SHOW 1.

EXCELLENT (ĕk' sə lənt), adj. (The hands gesture toward the heavens.) The "5" hands, palms out and arms raised rather high, are positioned somewhat above the line of vision. The arms move abruptly forward and up once or twice. An expression of pleasure or surprise is usually assumed. *Cf.* GREAT 2.

EXCEPT (ĭk sĕpt′), *prep., conj.* (Selecting a particular item from among several.) The index finger and thumb of the right hand grasp and pull up the left index finger. *Cf.* EXCEPTION, SPECIAL.

EXCEPTION (ĭk sĕp′ shən), *n.* See EXCEPT.

EXCHANGE (ĭks chānj′), *v.*, -CHANGED, -CHANGING. (Exchanging places.) The right "A" hand, positioned above the left "A" hand, swings down and under the left, coming up a bit in front of it. *Cf.* REPLACE, SUBSTITUTE, TRADE.

EXCITE (ĭk sīt′), *v.*, CITED, -CITING. (The heart beats violently.) Both middle fingers move up alternately to strike the heart sharply. *Cf.* EXCITEMENT, EXCITING.

EXCITEMENT (ĭk sīt′ mənt), *n.* See EXCITE.

EXCITING (ĭk sī′ tĭng), adj. See EXCITE.

EXCUSE (*n.* ĭk skūs′; *v.* ĭk skūz′), CUSED, -CUSING. (A wiped-off and cleaned slate.) The right hand wipes off the left palm several times. *Cf.* APOLOGIZE 2, APOLOGY 2, FORGIVE, PARDON.

EXHIBIT (ĭg zĭb′ ĭt), *v.*, -ITED, -ITING. (Directing the attention to something, and bringing it forward.) The right index finger points into the left palm, held facing out before the body. The left palm moves straight out. *Cf.* DEMONSTRATE, DISPLAY, EXAMPLE, EXHIBITION, REPRESENT, SHOW 1.

EXHIBITION (ĕk′ sə bĭsh′ ən), *n.* See EXHIBIT.

EXPAND (ĭk spănd′), *v.*, -PANDED, -PANDING. (A large amount.) The "5" hands face each other, fingers curved and touching. They move apart rather quickly. *Cf.* GREAT 1, MUCH.

EXPECT (ĭk spĕkt′), *v.*, -PECTED, -PECTING. (A thought await-ed.) The tip of the right index finger, held in the "D" position, palm facing the body, is placed on the forehead (modified THINK, *q.v.*). Both hands then assume right angle positions, fingers facing, with the left hand held above left shoulder level and the right before the right breast. Both hands, held thus, wave to each other several times. *Cf.* HOPE.

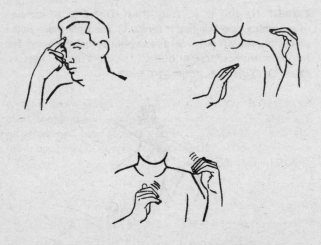

EXPEL (ĭk spĕl′), *v.*, -PELLED, -PELLING. ("Getting the axe";

the head is chopped off.) The upturned open right hand is swung sharply over the index finger edge of the left "S" hand, whose palm faces right. *Cf.* FIRE 2.

EXPENSE (ĭk spĕns'), *n.* (Nicking into one.) The knuckle of the right "X" finger is nicked against the palm of the left hand, held in the "5" position, palm facing right. *Cf.* COST, FINE 2, PENALTY, PRICE, TAX, TAXATION.

EXPENSIVE (ĭk spĕn' sĭv), *adj.* (Throwing away money.) The right "AND" hand lies in the palm of the upturned, open left hand (as if holding money). The right hand then moves up and away from the left, opening abruptly as it does (as if dropping the money it holds).

EXPERIENCE 1 (ĭk spĭr' ĭ əns), *n.* (A sharp-edged hand.) The right hand grasps the little finger-edge of the left firmly. As it leaves this position, moving down and out, it assumes the "A" position, palm facing left. *Cf.* EXPERT, SKILL, SKILLFUL.

EXPERIENCE 2, *n.* (White hair.) The right fingertips gently pull the hair of the right temple. The movement is repeated.

EXPERIENCE SOMETHING *phrase.* (Coming in contact; finish, meaning "to have done so.") The sign for TOUCH is made: The tip of the middle finger of the downturned right "5" hand touches the back of the downturned left hand. This is followed by the sign for FINISH: the upright "5" hands, palms facing each other, are suddenly and quickly swung around to a palm-out position. One hand only may also be used.

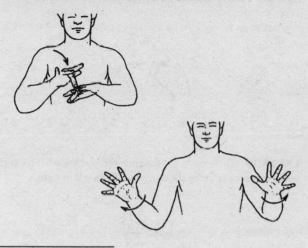

EXPERT (*n.* ĕks' pûrt; *adj.* ĭk spûrt'.). See EXPERIENCE 1.

EXPLAIN (ĭk splān'), *v.*, -PLAINED, -PLAINING. (Unraveling something to get at its parts.) The "F" hands, palms facing and fingers pointing straight out, are held about an inch apart. They move alternately back and forth a few inches. *Cf.* DEFINE 1, DESCRIBE, DESCRIPTION.

EYE (ī) *n., v.,* EYED, EYEING or EYING. (The natural sign.) The right index finger touches the lower lid of the right eye.

EYEBROW (ī′ brou), *n.* (Tracing the eyebrow.) The right index finger runs along the eyebrow, from left to right.

EYEGLASSES (ī′ glăs′ əs), *n. pl.* (The shape.) The thumb and index finger of the right hand, placed flat against the right temple, move back toward the right ear, tracing the line formed by the eyeglass frame. *Cf.* GLASSES.

EYES ROLLING AROUND (*colloq.*), *v. phrase.* (The natural sign.) Both "F" hands, palms facing, are held at eye level. They execute a series of small circular movements before the eyes.

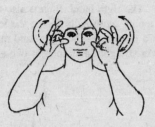

FACE (fās), *v.*, FACED, FACING. (Face to face.) The left hand, fingers together, palm flat and facing the eyes, is held a bit above eye level. The right hand, fingers also together, is held in front of the mouth, with palm facing the left hand. With a sweeping upward movement the right hand moves toward the left, which moves straight up an inch or two at the same time. *Cf.* FACE TO FACE.

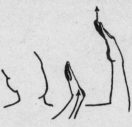

FACE TO FACE *phrase.* See FACE.

FAHRENHEIT (far′ ən hīt), *n.* (The letter "F"; rise and fall of temperature.) The thumb and index finger of the right "F" hand move up and down the upturned left index finger.

FAIL (fāl), *v.*, FAILED, FAILING. (A sliding.) The right "V" hand, palm up, slides along the upturned left palm, from its base to its fingertips.

FAIR (fâr), *adj.* (Sameness is stressed.) The downturned "B" hands, held at chest height, are brought together repeatedly, so that the index finger edges or fingertips come into contact. *Cf.* EQUAL, EQUIVALENT, EVEN, LEVEL.

FALL 1 (fôl), *n.* (The falling of leaves.) The left arm, held upright with palm facing back, represents a tree trunk. The right hand, fingers together and palm down, moves down along the left arm, from the back of the wrist to the elbow, either once or several times. This represents the falling of leaves from the tree branches, indicated by the left fingers.

FALL 2, *n., v.,* FELL, FALLEN, FALLING. (Falling on one's side.) The downturned index and middle fingers of the right "V" hand are placed in a standing position on the upturned left palm. The right "V" hand flips over, coming to rest palm up on the upturned left palm.

FALL FOR *v.* (Swallowing the bait.) The mouth is held wide open. The right hand, fingers pointing to the rear of the signer, moves as if to enter the mouth, but brushes the right cheek as it passes to the rear. This sign is used in the context of someone who has been duped, or has proved gullible.

FALSE (fôls), *adj.* (Words diverted instead of coming straight, or truthfully, out.) The index finger of the right "D" hand, pointing to the left, moves along the lips from right to left. *Cf.* FALSEHOOD, LIAR, LIE 1.

FALSEHOOD (fôls' hŏŏd), *n.* See FALSE.

FAME (fām), *n.* (One's fame radiates far and wide.) The extended index fingers rest on the lips (or on the temples). Moving in small, continuous spirals, they move up and to either side of the head. *Cf.* FAMOUS, PROMINENT.

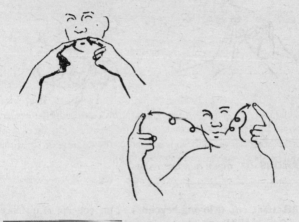

FAMILIAR (fə mil' yər), *adj.* (Patting the head to indicate something of value inside.) The right fingers pat the forehead several times. *Cf.* KNOW.

FAMILY (făm′ ə lǐ), *n.* (The letter "F"; a circle or group.) The thumb and index fingers of both "F" hands are in contact, palms facing. The hands swing open and around, coming together again at their little finger edges, palms now facing the body.

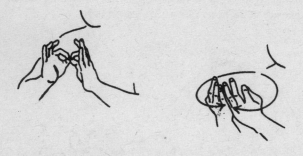

FAMOUS (fā′ məs), *adj.* See FAME.

FAR (fär), *adj.* (Moving beyond, *i.e.,* the concept of distance or "farness.") The "A" hands are held together, thumbs pointing away from the body. The right hand moves straight ahead in a slight arc. The left hand does not move.

FASCINATE (făs' ə nāt´), v., -NATED, -NATING. (Drawing one out.) The index and middle fingers of both hands, one above the other, are placed on the middle part of the chest. Both hands move forward simultaneously. As they do, the index and middle fingers of each hand come together. Cf. INTEREST 1, INTERESTED 1, INTERESTING 1.

FAST (făst), adj. (A quick movement.) The thumbtip of the upright right hand is flicked quickly off the tip of the curved right index finger, as if shooting marbles. Cf. IMMEDIATELY, QUICK, QUICKNESS, SPEED, SPEEDY.

FAT (făt), adj. (The swollen cheeks.) The cheeks are puffed out and the open "C" hands, positioned at either cheek, move away to their respective sides.

FATHER 1 (fä′ ᴛ͟hər), *n.* (Male who holds the baby.) The sign for MALE, *q.v.,* is made: The thumb and extended fingers of the right hand are brought up to grasp an imaginary cap brim, representing the tipping of caps by men in olden days. Both hands are then held open with palms facing up, as if holding a baby. This is the formal sign.

FATHER 2 *(informal)*, *n.* (Derived from the formal sign for FATHER 1, *q.v.*) The thumbtip of the right "5" hand touches the right temple a number of times. The other fingers may also wiggle.

FAVORITE 1 (fä′ vər it), *adj.* (To the taste.) The middle finger is placed against the lips and the signer assumes an expression indicating pleasure.

FAVORITE 2, *adj.* (Hooked on to; a good friend.) Both index fingers interlock and move down forcefully an inch or two. The lips are held together tightly and an expression of pleasure is shown.

FAVORITE 3, *adj.* (Kissing, to indicate a high approval rating.) The back of either fist is kissed, and an expression of pleasure is shown. *Cultural note:* this sign is considered overused by many deaf people. To them it indicates a lack of discrimination (everything is a "favorite").

FAX (faks), *n.*, *v.* (The paper coming out.) The downturned left hand undulates a little as it moves under and out of the downturned right hand.

FEAR 1 (fĭr), *n., v.*, FEARED, FEARING. (The heart is suddenly covered with fear.) Both hands, fingers together, are placed side by side, palms facing the chest. They quickly open and come together over the heart, one on top of the other. *Cf.* AFRAID, FRIGHT, FRIGHTEN, SCARE(D), TERROR 1.

FEAR 2, *n., v.* (The hands attempt to ward off something which causes fear.) The "5" hands, right behind left, move downward before the body, in a wavy motion. *Cf.* TERROR 2.

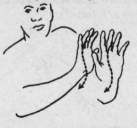

FEED 1 (fēd), *v.*, FED, FEEDING. (The natural sign.) The closed right hand goes through the natural motion of placing food in the mouth. This movement is repeated. *Cf.* EAT, FOOD, MEAL.

FEED 2, *v.* (Placing food before someone; the action of placing food in someone's mouth.) The upturned hands, holding imaginary pieces of food, the right behind the left, move forward simultaneously, in a gesture of placing food in someone's mouth.

FEEDBACK (fēd′ bak), *n.* (The letters "F" and "B"; back and forth.) Both "F" hands are positioned in front of the face, the left facing in and the right facing out. They move in and out alternately, changing from "F" to "B" each time.

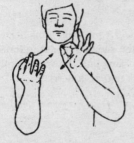 

FEEL 1 (fēl), *v.*, FELT, FEELING. (The natural movement of touching.) The tip of the middle finger of the downturned right "5" hand touches the back of the left hand a number of times. *Cf.* CONTACT 1, TOUCH.

FEEL 2, *v.* (The welling up of feelings or emotions in the heart.) The right middle finger, touching the heart, moves up an inch or two a number of times. *Cf.* EMOTION 1, FEELING.

FEELING (fē′ lǐng), *n.* See FEEL 2.

FEEL TOUCHED (tŭcht), *v. phrase.* (A piercing of the heart.) The tip of the middle finger of the right "5" hand is thrust against the heart. The head, at the same time, moves abruptly back a very slight distance. *Cf.* TOUCHED, TOUCHING.

FEMALE (fē′ māl), *n., adj.* (The bonnet string used by women of old.) The right "A" hand's thumb moves down along the line of the right jaw, from ear almost to chin. This outlines the string used to tie ladies' bonnets in olden days. This is a root sign to modify many others. *Viz:* FEMALE plus BABY:

DAUGHTER; FEMALE plus SAME: SISTER; etc.

FERRIS WHEEL *n.* (The circling seat.) The downturned right index and middle fingers are draped over their downturned left counterparts, which are held rigid. Both hands, thus held, execute a series of large clockwise forward circles, imitating the action of a ferris wheel.

FEW (fu), *adj.* (The fingers are presented in order, to convey the concept of "several.") The right "A" hand is held palm facing up. One by one the fingers open, beginning with the index finger and ending with the little finger. Some use only the index and middle fingers. *Cf.* SEVERAL.

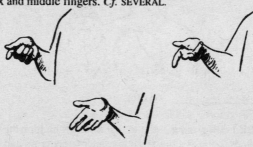

FEW SECONDS AGO, A, *adv. phrase.* (Time moved backward a bit.) The right "D" hand, palm facing the body, is placed in the palm of the left hand, which is facing right. The right hand swings back a bit toward the body, with the index finger describing an arc. *Cf.* JUST A MOMENT AGO, WHILE AGO, A2.

FIGHT 1 (fīt), *n., v.,* FOUGHT, FIGHTING. (The fists in combat.) The "S" hands, palms facing, swing down simultaneously toward each other. They do not touch, however.

FIGHT 2, *n., v.* (The natural sign.) Both clenched fists go through the circular motions of boxing. *Cf.* BOX 2.

FIGURE 1 (fĭg′ yər), *n., v.,* -URED, -URING. (A multiplying.) The "V" hands, palms facing the body, alternately cross and separate, several times. *Cf.* MULTIPLY.

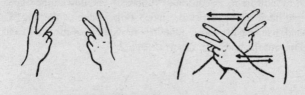

FIGURE 2, *n.*, *v.* (Contours are indicated or outlined.) Both "A" hands, held about a foot apart before the face, with palms facing each other, move down simultaneously in a wavy, undulating motion. *Cf.* FORM 1, SHAPE, STATUE.

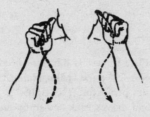

FILE (fil), *n.*, *v.* (Standing up files in proper order.) The left "5" hand, fingers spread, faces right. The open or "B" right hand, palm facing the signer, moves down repeatedly between the different fingers of the left hand.

FILL (fĭl), *v.* FILLED, FILLING. (Wiping off the top of a container, to indicate its condition of fullness.) The downturned open right hand wipes across the index finger edge of the left "S" hand, whose palm faces right. The movement of the right hand is toward the body. *Cf.* COMPLETE, FULL.

FILM (fĭlm), *n.* (The frames of the film speeding through the projector.) The left "5" hand, palm facing right and thumb pointing up, is the projector. The right "5" hand is placed against the left, and moves back and forth quickly. *Cf.* MOVIE (S), MOVING PICTURE.

FILMSTRIP (fĭlm' strĭp), *n.* (A strip of movie film.) The sign for MOVIE is made: The left "5" hand is held palm facing right. The right "5" or "F" hand is placed on the left palm and moves back and forth quickly. The right thumb and index then

move straight down the left palm

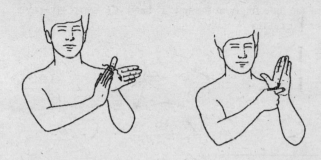

FILTHY (fĭl′ thē), *adj.* (A modification of the pig's snout groveling in a trough.) The downturned right hand is placed under the chin. Its fingers, pointing left, wiggle repeatedly. *Cf.* DIRTY.

FINAL 1 (fī′ nəl), *adj.* (The little, *i.e.*, LAST, fingers are indicated.) With the hands in the "I" position, the tip of the right little finger strikes the tip of its left counterpart. *Cf.* END 1, FINALLY 1, LAST 1, LASTLY.

FINAL 2, *adj.* (A single little, *i.e.*, LAST, finger is indicated.) The tip of the index finger of the right "D" hand strikes the tip of the little finger of the left "I" hand. *Cf.* END 2, FINALLY 2, LAST 2, LASTLY.

FINALLY 1 (fĭ′ nə lē), *adv.* See FINAL 1.

FINALLY 2, *adv.* See FINAL 2.

FINANCE (fi nans′), *v.* (PAY and SUPPORT.) The sign for PAY: The right index finger, resting in the upturned left palm, flicks forward. This is followed by the sign for SUPPORT: The right "S" hand pushes up its left counterpart.

FIND (find), *n.*, *v.*, FOUND, FINDING. (The natural motion of selecting something from the hand.) The thumb and index fingers of the outstretched right hand grasp an imaginary object on the upturned left palm. The right hand then moves straight up. *Cf.* PICK 1, SELECT 1.

FINE 1 (fīn), *adj.*, *interj.* (The feelings are titillated.) With the thumb resting on the upper part of the chest, the fingers are wiggled back and forth. *Cf.* ELEGANT, WONDERFUL.

FINE 2, *n.*, *v.*, FINED, FINING. (Nicking into one.) The knuckle of the right "X" finger is nicked against the palm of the left hand, held in the "5" position, palm facing right. *Cf.* COST, EXPENSE, PENALTY, PRICE, TAX, TAXATION.

FINISH (fĭn' ĭsh), *(colloq.)*, *n.*, *v.*, -ISHED, -ISHING. (Shaking the hands to rid them of something.) The upright "5" hands, palms facing each other, are suddenly and quickly swung around to a palm-out position. *Cf.* DONE, END 3.

FIRE 1 (fīr), *n.*, *v.*, FIRED, FIRING. (The leaping of flames.) The "5" hands are held with palms facing the body. They move up and down alternately, while the fingers wiggle. *Cf.* BURN, FLAME.

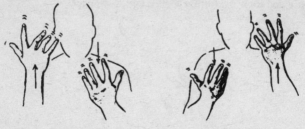

FIRE 2, *v.* ("Getting the axe"; the head is chopped off.) The upturned open right hand is swung sharply over the index finger edge of the left "S" hand, whose palm faces right. *Cf.* EXPEL.

FIREFIGHTER (fĭr′ fī tər), *n.* (The shield on the hat.) The right
"B" hand, palm out, is placed above the forehead

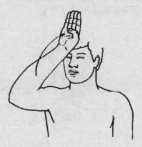

FIRST (fûrst), *adj.* (The first finger is indicated.) The right
index finger touches the upturned left thumb.

FLAME (flām), *n., v.,* FLAMED, FLAMING. (The leaping of
flames.) The "5" hands are held with palms facing the body.
They move up and down alternately, while the fingers wiggle.
Cf. BURN, FIRE 1.

FLATTER (flăt′ ər), *v.*, -TERED, -TERING. (Massaging the ego.) The fingertips of the right hand, pointing forward or left, brush back and forth against the upright left index finger. This sign is used to indicate flattery of someone.

FLAT TIRE *n.* (The natural sign.) The right hand, palm down and fingers pointing forward, is placed with thumb on top of left hand. The right hand closes down suddenly on the right thumb, imitating a flat tire.

FLIRT (flûrt), *v.*, FLIRTED, FLIRTING. (Dazzling one with scintillating looks.) The "5" hands, thumbs touching, swing alter-

nately up and down. The fingers sometimes wiggle, as in
FLATTER 1, *q.v.*

FLOWER (flou′ ər), *n.* (The natural motion of smelling a
flower.) The right hand, grasping an imaginary flower, holds it
first against the right nostril and then against the left.

FLUNK (flŭngk), *v.*, FLUNKED, FLUNKING. The right "F" hand
strikes forcefully against the open left palm, which faces right
with fingers pointing forward.

FLUTE (flōōt), *n.* (Playing the instrument.) The signer mimes playing a flute.

FLY 1 (flī), *v.*, FLEW, FLOWN, FLYING. (The wings of the airplane.) The "Y" hand, palm down and drawn up near the shoulder, moves forward, up and away from the body. Either hand may be used. *Cf.* AIRPLANE, PLANE 1.

FLY 2, *v.*, *n.* (The wings and fuselage of the airplane.) The hand assumes the same position as in FLY 1, but the index finger is also extended, to represent the fuselage of the airplane. Either hand may be used, and the movement is the same as in FLY 1. *Cf.* PLANE 2.

FOCUS (fō′ kəs), *n.*, *v.*, -CUSED, -CUSING. (Directing one's attention forward; applying oneself; concentrating.) Both hands, fingers pointing up and together, are held at the sides of the face. They move straight out from the face. *Cf.* CONCENTRATE, CONCENTRATION, MIND 2, PAY ATTENTION (TO).

FOLLOW (fŏl ´ō), *v.,* -LOWED, -LOWING. (One hand follows the other.) The "A" hands are used, thumbs pointing up. The right is positioned a few inches behind the left. The left hand moves straight forward, while the right follows behind in a series of wavy, movements. *Cf.* FOLLOWING.

FOLLOWING (fŏl´ ō ĭng), *adj.* See FOLLOW.

FOOD (food), *n.* (The natural sign.) The closed right hand goes through the natural motion of placing food in the mouth. This movement is repeated. *Cf.* EAT, FEED 1, MEAL.

FOOLISH (foo'lish), *adj.* (Thoughts flickering back and forth.) The right "Y" hand, thumb almost touching the forehead, is shaken back and forth across the forehead several times. *Cf.* NONSENSE, RIDICULOUS, SILLY.

FOOT (foot), *n.* (The measurement.) The left hand is held palm down. The heel of the right "F" hand is placed on the left wrist, and then moves in an arc to the left fingertips.

FOOTBALL (foot' bôl'), *n.* (The teams lock in combat.) The "5" hands, facing each other, are interlocked suddenly. They are drawn apart and the action is repeated.

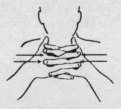

FOR 1 (fôr), *prep.* (The thoughts are directed outward, toward a specific goal or purpose.) The right index finger, resting on the right temple, leaves its position and moves straight out in front of the face.

FOR 2, *prep.* (A thought or knowledge uppermost in the mind.) The fingers of the right hand or the index finger are placed on the center of the forehead, and then the hand is brought strongly up above the head, assuming the "A" position, with thumb pointing up. *Cf.* BECAUSE.

FORBID 1 (fər bĭd′), *v.*, -BADE or -BAD, -BIDDEN or -BID, -BID-DING. (A modification of LAW, *q.v.;* "against the law.") The downturned right "D" or "L" hand is thrust forcefully into the left palm. *Cf.* FORBIDDEN 1, PROHIBIT.

FORBID 2, *v.* (The letter "F"; the same sign as above.) The right "F" hand makes the same sign as in FORBID 1. *Cf.* FORBIDDEN 2.

FORBIDDEN 1 (fər bĭd′ ən), *v.* See FORBID 1.

FORBIDDEN 2, *adj.* See FORBID 2.

FORCE 1 (fōrs), *v.*, FORCED, FORCING. (Forcing the head to bow.) The right "C" hand pushes down on an imaginary neck.

FORCE 2, *v.* (Pushing something forward.) The open right hand is held palm down at chin level, fingers pointing left. From this position the hand turns to point forward, and moves forcefully forward and away from the body, as if pushing something ahead of it.

FOREVER (fôr ĕv′ ər), *adv.* (Around the clock and ahead into the future.) The right index finger, pointing forward, traces a clockwise circle in the air. The downturned right "Y" hand then moves forward, either in a straight line or in a slight downward curve. *Cf.* ETERNITY, EVER 2, EVERLASTING.

FORGET 1 (fər gĕt′), *v.*, -GOT, -GOTTEN, -GETTING. (Wiping knowledge from the mind.) The right hand, fingers pointing left, rests on the forehead. It moves off to the right, assuming the "A" position, thumb up and palm facing the signer's rear.

FORGET 2, *v.* (The thought is gone.) The sign for THINK is made: The index finger makes a small circle on the forehead. This is followed by the sign for GONE 1: The right open hand, palm facing the body, is held by the left hand and is drawn down and out, ending in a position with fingers drawn together. The left hand, meanwhile, has closed into a position with fingers also drawn together.

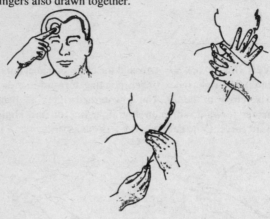

FORGIVE (fər gĭv′), *v.*, -GAVE, -GIVEN, -GIVING. (A wiped-off and cleaned slate.) The right hand wipes off the left palm several times. *Cf.* APOLOGIZE 2, APOLOGY 2, EXCUSE, PARDON.

FORM 1 (fôrm), *n.* (Contours are indicated or outlined.) Both "A" hands, held about a foot apart before the face, with palms facing each other, move down simultaneously in a wavy, undulating motion. *Cf.* FIGURE 2, SHAPE, STATUE.

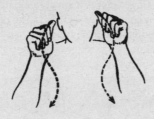

FORM 2 (The letters "F"; outlining the shape.) Both "F" hands, palms facing out, outline the shape of a piece of paper.

FOUND (found), *v.*, FOUNDED, FOUNDING. (To set up.) The right "A" hand, thumb up and palm facing left, comes down to rest on the back of the downturned left "S" hand. Before doing so, the right "A" hand may describe a clockwise circle above the left hand, but this is optional. *Cf.* ESTABLISH, FOUNDED.

FOUNDATION (foun dā′ shən), *n*. (The area below.) Both hands, in the "5" position, palms down, are held before the chest, the right under the left. The right hand moves under the left in a counterclockwise fashion. *Cf*. BELOW 1.

FOUNDED *v*. See FOUND.

FRANKFURTER (The shape in a roll or bun.) The left hand is held with the fingers pointing up. The right index finger is placed between the thumb and the other fingers. *Cf*. HOT DOG.

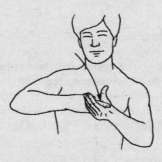

FREE 1 (frē), *adj*., *v*., FREED, FREEING. (Breaking the bonds.) The "S" hands, crossed in front of the body, swing apart and face out. *Cf.* FREEDOM, INDEPENDENCE, INDEPENDENT 1, RESCUE, SAFE, SAVE 1.

FREE 2, *adj., v.* (The letter "F.") The "F" hands make the same sign as in FREE 1.

FREEDOM (frē′ dəm), *n.* See FREE 1.

FREEWAY (frē′ wā), *n.* (Traffic flowing in opposite directions.) The downturned "4" hands pass each other as the right moves repeatedly to the left and the left repeatedly to the right. The downturned "V" hands are often used instead of the "4"s. *Cf.* HIGHWAY.

FREEZE (frēz), *v.*, FROZE, FROZEN, FREEZING. (The stiff fingers.) The fingers of the "5" hands, held palms down, stiffen and contract. *Cf.* FROZEN, ICE.

FREQUENT (*adj.* frē' kwənt; *v.* frĭ kwĕnt '), -QUENTED, -QUENTING. The left hand, open in the "5" position, palm up, is held before the chest. The right hand, in the right-angle position, fingers pointing up, arches over and into the left palm. This is repeated several times. *Cf.* OFTEN.

FRESHMAN (fresh' mən), *n.*, *adj.* (The first year after the preparatory year at Gallaudet University.) The right index finger touches the ring finger of the other hand.

FREUD (froid), *n.* (The letter "F"; PSYCHOLOGY.) The right hand forms the letter "F." The little finger edge is thrust twice into the open left hand, its palm facing out, between thumb and index finger. This is the sign for PSYCHOLOGY, shaping the Greek letter "psi." Strictly speaking, Freud was not a psychologist but a psychoanalytic psychiatrist. This so-called "name sign" applies nevertheless.

FRIEND (frĕnd), *n.* (Locked together in friendship.) The right and left hands are interlocked at the index fingers. The hands separate, change their relative positions, and come together again as before. *Cf.* FRIENDSHIP.

FRIENDLY (frĕnd′ lĕ), *adj.* (A crinkling-up of the face.) Both hands, in the "5" position, palms facing back, are placed on either side of the face. The fingers wiggle back and forth, while a pleasant, happy expression is worn. *Cf.* CHEERFUL, PLEASANT.

FRIENDSHIP (frĕnd' shĭp), *n*. See FRIEND.

FRIGHT (frīt), *n*. (The heart is suddenly covered with fear.) Both hands, fingers together, are placed side by side, palms facing the chest. They quickly open and come together over the heart, one on top of the other. *Cf.* AFRAID, FEAR 1, FRIGHTEN, SCARE(D), TERROR 1.

FRIGHTEN (frī' tən), *v.*, -TENED, -TENING. See FRIGHT.

FROM (frŏm), *prep*. (The "away from" action is indicated.) The knuckle of the right "X" finger is placed against the base of the left "D" or "X" finger, and then moved away in a slight curve toward the body.

FROM TIME TO TIME *adv. phrase*. (Stages forward.) The right hand, held at a right angle, fingers facing left, moves forward from the body in a series of forward movements, describing an arc with each successive movement. *Cf.* NOW AND THEN, ONCE IN A WHILE.

FROZEN (frō′ zən), *adj.* (The stiff fingers.) The fingers of the "5" hands, held palms down, stiffen and contract. *Cf.* FREEZE, ICE.

FRUSTRATED (frŭs′ trāt ĭd), *adj.* (Coming up against a wall; a door is slammed in the face.) The open right hand is brought up sharply, and its back strikes the mouth and nose. The head moves back a bit at the same time.

FULL (fŏŏl), *adj.* (Wiping off the top of a container, to indicate its condition of fullness.) The downturned open right hand wipes across the index finger edge of the left "S" hand, whose palm faces right. The movement of the right hand is toward the body. *Cf.* COMPLETE, FILL.

FUN (fŭn), *n.* (The wrinkled nose--indicative of laughter or fun.) The index and middle fingers of the right "U" hand, whose palm faces the body, are placed on the nose. The right hand swings down in an arc and, palm down, the "U" fingers strike their left counterparts on the downturned left "U" hand, and either stop at that point or continue on.

FUND (fund), *v.* (Support from money.) The sign for MONEY 1 is made: The upturned right hand, grasping some imaginary bills, is brought down into the upturned left palm.

The right "S" hand then pushes up the left "S" hand.

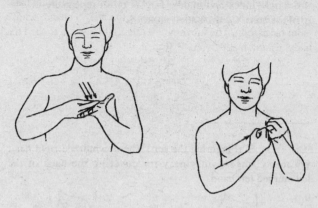

FUND-RAISING *v. phrase.* (Money is raised.) The sign for
MONEY 1 is made: The upturned right hand, grasping some
imaginary bills, is brought down into the upturned left palm a
number of times. Both upturned open hands then move up
together.

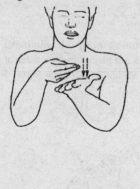

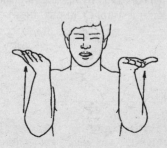

FUNNY (fŭn′ ē), *adj.* (The nose wrinkles in laughter.) The tips of the right index and middle fingers brush repeatedly off the tip of the nose. *Cf.* HUMOR, HUMOROUS.

FUR (fûr), *n.* (Fingering the fur.) The downturned right hand repeatedly fingers imaginary fur covering the back of the downturned left hand.

FURY (fyŏŏr′ ē), *n.* (A violent welling-up of the emotions.) The curved fingers of the right hand are placed in the center of the chest, and fly up suddenly and violently. An expression of anger is worn. *Cf.* ANGER, ANGRY 2, MAD, RAGE.

FUTURE (fū' chər), *n.* (Something ahead or in the future.) The upright, open right hand, palm facing left, moves straight out and slightly up from a position beside the right temple. *Cf.* IN THE FUTURE, LATER 2, LATER ON, WILL, WOULD.

G

GAIN (gān), *v.*, GAINED, GAINING. (Adding on.) The index and middle fingers of the right "H" hand, palm up, are swung up and over until they come to rest on the index and middle fingers of the left "H" hand, held palm down. *Cf.* ADD 2, ADDITION, INCREASE, RAISE.

GALLOP (gal' əp), *v.*, *n.* (The horse's legs.) Both "V" hands, palms down, are held one before the other, fingers curved down. Both hands move forward in unison in a series of circles. Each time they rise, the curved fingers close up, opening again as they fall.

GAMBLE (gam' bəl), *n.*, *v.* (Throwing the dice.) The signer grasps imaginary dice in the closed fist, shakes them up, and throws them out.

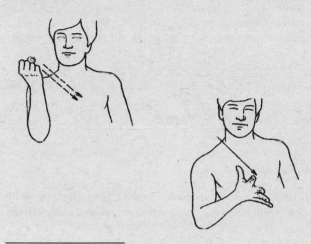

GAME (gām), *n.*, *v.*, GAMED, GAMING. (Two individuals pitted against each other.) The hands are held in the "A" position, thumbs pointing straight up, palms facing the body. They come together forcefully, moving down a bit as they do, and the knuckles of one hand strike those of the other.

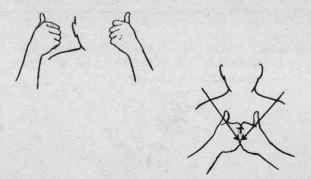

GARDEN (gär′ dən), *n.* (The letter "G"; an area.) The right "G" hand circles counterclockwise around the downturned open left hand.

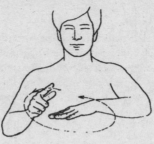

GARLIC (gär′ lik), *n.* (Garlic breath.) The right hand, in the claw position, fingers placed at the open mouth, spins forward.

GAS (găs), *n.* (The act of pouring gasoline into an automobile tank.) The thumb of the right "A" hand is placed into the hole formed by the left "O" hand. *Cf.* GASOLINE.

GASOLINE (găs′ ə lēn′, găs ə lēn′), *n*. See GAS.

GATE (gāt), *n*. (The natural sign.) The fingertips of both open hands touch each other before the body, palms toward the chest, thumbs pointing upward. Then the right fingers swing forward and back to their original position several times, imitating the movement of a gate opening and closing.

GATHER 1 (găłh′ ər), *v*., -ERED, -ERING. (A gathering together.) The right "5" hand, fingers curved and palm facing left, sweeps across and over the upturned left palm, several times, in a circular movement. *Cf.* GATHERING TOGETHER.

GATHER 2, *v.* (Assemble all together.) Both "5" hands, palms facing, are held with fingers pointing out from the body. With a sweeping motion they are brought in toward the chest, and all fingertips come together. This is repeated. *Cf.* CONFERENCE, GATHERING, MEETING.

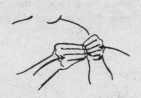

GATHERING (găħ′ ər ĭng), *n.* See GATHER 2.

GATHERING TOGETHER *phrase.* See GATHER 1.

GAY (gā), *n., adj.* (Homosexual.) The tips of the "G" fingers are placed on the chin.

GENEROUS (jĕn′ ər əs), *adj.* (The heart rolls out.) Both right-angle hands roll over each other as they move down and away from their initial position at the heart. *Cf.* KIND 1, MERCY.

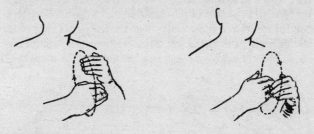

GENTLEMAN (jĕn′ təl mən), *n.* (A fine or polite man.) The MALE prefix sign is made: The right hand grasps the edge of an imaginary cap. The sign for POLITE is then made: The thumb of the right "5" hand is placed slowly and deliberately on the right side of the chest.

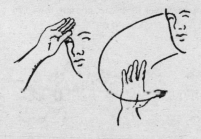

GERBIL (jûr′ bil), *n.* (The letter "G"; MOUSE.) The back of the right "G" hand brushes the nose several times.

GET (gĕt), *v.*, GOT, GOTTEN, GETTING. (A grasping and bringing forward to oneself.) Both hands, in the "5" position, fingers curved, are crossed at the wrists, with the left palm facing right and the right palm facing left. They are brought in toward the chest, while closing into a grasping "S" position. *Cf.* RECEIVE.

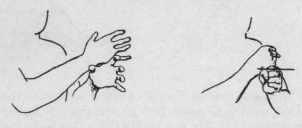

GET UP (ŭp), *v. phrase.* (Getting onto one's feet.) The upturned index and middle fingers of the right hand, representing the legs, are swung up and over in an arc, coming to rest in the upturned left palm. *Cf.* STAND 2, STAND UP.

GIFT (gĭft), *n.* (A giving of something.) Both "A" hands, with index fingers somewhat draped over the tips of the thumbs, are held palms facing in front of the chest. They are pivoted forward and down, in unison, from the wrists. *Cf.* CONTRIBUTE, PRESENT 2.

GIGGLE (gig′ əl), *n., v.* (The mouth contorts repeatedly in laughter.) Both index fingers, at each corner of the mouth, move back quickly and repeatedly, as if forcing the mouth to open in laughter.

GIRL (gûrl), *n.* (A female who is small.) The FEMALE root sign is given: The thumb of the right "A" hand moves down along the line of the right jaw, from ear almost to chin. This outlines the string used to tie ladies' bonnets in olden days. The downturned open right hand is then held at waist level, indicating the short height of the female.

GIVE (gǐv), *v.*, GAVE, GIVEN, GIVING. (Holding something and extending it toward someone.) The right "O" hand is held before the right shoulder and then moved outward in an arc, away from the body.

GIVE ME (mē), *v. phrase.* (Extending the hand toward oneself.) This sign is a reversal of GIVE.

GIVE UP (gǐv ŭp′), *v. phrase.* (Throwing up the hands in a gesture of surrender.) Both "A" hands are held palms down before the chest and then thrown up and back in unison, ending in the "5" position. The head moves back a little as the hands are thrown up. *Cf.* SURRENDER.

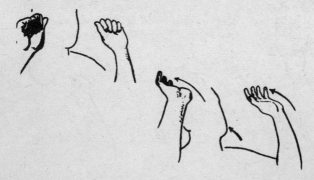

GLAD (glăd), *adj.* (The heart is stirred; the spirits bubble up.) The open right hand, palm facing the body, strikes the heart repeatedly, moving up and off the heart after each strike. *Cf.* HAPPY, JOY, MERRY.

GLASS 1 (glăs, gläs), *n.* (The finger touches a brittle substance.) The index finger is brought up to touch the exposed front teeth.

GLASS 2, *n.* (The shape of a drinking glass.) The little finger edge of the right "C" hand rests in the upturned left palm. The right hand moves straight up a few inches, tracing the shape of a drinking glass.

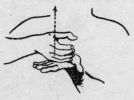

GLASSES (glăs' əs), *n. pl.* (The shape.) The thumb and index finger of the right hand, placed flat against the right temple, move back toward the right ear, tracing the line formed by the eyeglass frame. *Cf.* EYEGLASSES.

GLOOM (glo͞om), *n.* (The facial features drop.) Both "5" hands, palms facing the eyes and fingers slightly curved, drop simultaneously to a level with the mouth. The head drops slightly as the hands move down, and an expression of sadness is assumed. *Cf.* GLOOMY, GRAVE 2, GRIEF, SAD, SORROWFUL 1.

GLOOMY (glo͞o' mĭ), *adj.* See GLOOM.

GO 1 (gō), *v.*, WENT, GONE, GOING. (Continuous motion forward.) With palms facing each other, the index fingers of the "D" hands revolve around each other as both hands move forward.

GO 2, *interj., v.* (The natural sign.) The right index finger is flung out, as a command to go. A stern expression is usually assumed. ·

GO AHEAD (ə hĕd′), *v. phrase.* (Moving forward.) Both right-angle hands, palms facing each other and knuckles facing forward, move forward simultaneously. *Cf.* PROCEED.

GOAL (gōl), *n.* (A thought directed upward, toward a goal.) The index finger of the right "D" hand touches the forehead, and then moves up to the index finger of the left "D" hand, which is held above eye level. The two index fingers stop just short of touching. *Cf.* AIM.

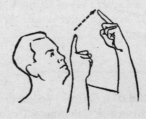

GODFATHER (god' fä ŧħər), *n*. (Second father.) The right "2" hand is twisted around (SECOND), and then the signer makes the sign for FATHER 2: the tip of the thumb of the right "5" hand is placed against the right forehead or temple. The signer may make the two signs in reverse order.

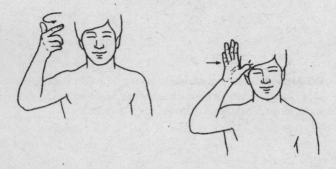

GODMOTHER (god' muŧħ ər), *n*. (Second mother.) The right "2" hand is twisted around (SECOND), and then the signer makes the sign for MOTHER 2: the tip of the thumb of the right "5" hand is placed against the right cheek. The signer may make the two signs in reverse order.

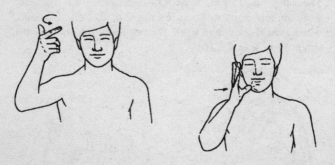

GOLD (gōld), *n*. (Yellow earrings, *i.e.*, gold, which was discovered in California.) The earlobe is pinched, and then the sign for YELLOW is made: The "Y" hand, pivoted at the wrist, is shaken back and forth repeatedly.

 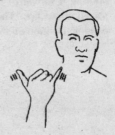

GONE 1 (gôn, gŏn), *adj.* (A disappearance.) The right open hand, palm facing the body, is held by the left hand and is drawn down and out, ending in a position with fingers drawn together. The left hand, meanwhile, may close into a position with fingers also drawn together. *Cf.* DISAPPEAR.

GONE 2, *(sl.), adj.* (A disappearance into the distance. The narrowing perspective is the main feature here.) The right "L" hand, resting on the back of the downturned left hand, moves straight forward suddenly. As it does, the index finger and thumb come together.

GOOD 1 (gŏŏd), *adj.* (Tasting something, approving it, and offering it forward.) The fingertips of the right "5" hand are placed at the lips. The right hand then moves out and into a palm-up position on the upturned left palm.

GOOD 2, *adj.* (Thumbs up.) One or both thumbs are held up.

GOODBYE (gŏŏd´ bī´), *interj.* (A wave of the hand.) The right open hand waves back and forth several times. *Cf.* HELLO.

GOOSE BUMPS *(colloq.), n.* (Fingertips indicate where the bumps appear.) The downturned right claw hand moves up the back of the left arm.

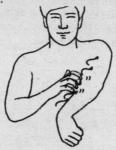

GO TO BED *v. phrase.* (Laying the head on the pillow.) The head is placed on its side, in the open palm, and the eyes are closed.

GOVERN (gŭv′ ərn), *v.,* -ERNED, -ERNING. (Holding the reins over all.) The "A" hands, palms facing, move alternately back and forth, as if grasping and manipulating reins. The left "A" hand, still in position, swings over so that its palm now faces down. The right hand opens to the "5" position, palm down, and swings over the left which moves slightly to the right. *Cf.* CONTROL 1, MANAGE, RULE.

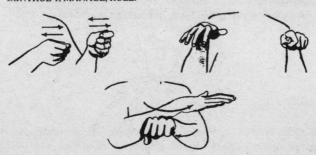

GOVERNMENT (gŭv′ ərn mənt, -ər-), *n*. (The head indicates the head or seat of government.) The right index finger, pointing toward the right temple, describes a small clockwise circle and comes to rest on the right temple.

GRAB (grăb), *v*., GRABBED, GRABBING, *n*. (Grasping something and holding it down.) Both hands, palms down, quickly close into the "S" position, the right on top of the left. *Cf.* CATCH 1, GRASP.

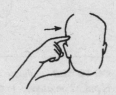

GRADE (grād), *n*. (The letter "G"; the level.) Both "G" hands, palms facing out, move apart, indicating a level or stage.

GRADUATE (*n.* grăj′ ōō ĭt; *v.* grăj′ ōō ăt′), -ATED, -ATING. (The letter "G"; the ribbon around the diploma.) The right "G" hand makes a single clockwise circle, and drops down into the upturned left palm.

GRAM (grăm), *n.* (The letter "G"; weighing.) The right "G" fingers rock back and forth on the extended left index.

GRANDDAUGHTER (gran′ dô tər), *n*. (The letter "G"; DAUGHTER.) The "G" is formed with the right hand. The sign for DAUGHTER is then made: the FEMALE prefix sign is formed, with the thumb of the right hand tracing a line on the right jaw from just below the ear to the chin. The right upturned arm then rests on its left counterpart, as if holding a baby.

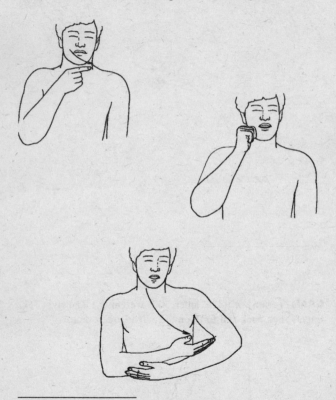

GRANDFATHER 1 (grănd′ fä′ t͟hər), *n*. (A male baby-holder; a predecessor.) The sign for FATHER 2 is made: The thumbtip of the right "5" hand touches the right temple a number of times. Then both open hands, palms up, are extended in front of the chest, as if supporting a baby. From this position they sweep over the left shoulder. The whole sign is smooth and continuous.

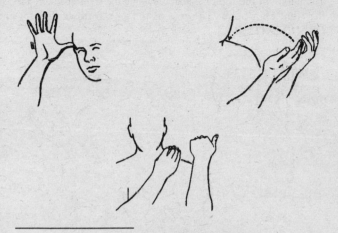

GRANDFATHER 2, *n.* (A variation of GRANDFATHER 1.) The "A" hands are held with the left in front of the right, and the right thumb positioned against the forehead. Both hands open into the "5" position, so that the right little finger touches or almost touches the left thumb. Both hands may, as they open, move forward an inch or two.

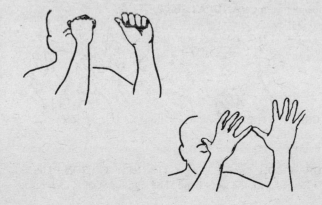

GRANDMOTHER 1 (grănd′ mŭtħ′ ər), *n*. (Same rationale as for GRANDFATHER 1.) The sign for MOTHER 2 is made: The thumb of the right "5" hand rests on the right cheek or on the right chin bone. The rest of the sign follows that for GRANDFATHER 1.

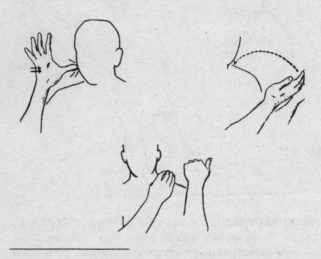

GRANDMOTHER 2, *n*. (A variation of GRANDMOTHER 1.) The "A" hands are positioned as in GRANDFATHER 2 but with the right thumb on the right cheek. They open in the same manner as in GRANDFATHER 2.

GRANDSON (grand′ sun), *n*. (The letter "G"; SON.) The "G" is formed with the right hand. The sign for SON is then made:

the MALE prefix sign is formed, the thumb and extended fingers of the right hand are brought up to grasp an imaginary cap brim. The right upturned arm then rests on its left counterpart, as if holding a baby.

GRANT 1 (gränt, gränt), *v.*, GRANTED, GRANTING. (A permissive upswinging of the hands, as if giving in.) Both hands, palms facing and fingers pointing away from the body, are held at chest level, almost a foot apart. With an upward movement, using their wrists as pivots, the hands sweep up until the fingers point almost straight up. *Cf.* ALLOW, LET, LET'S, LET US, MAY 3, PERMISSION 1, PERMIT 1.

GRANT 2, *v.* The modified "O" hand, little finger edge down, moves forward and down in an arc before the body, as if giving something to someone.

GRAPH (graf), *n.* (Drawing the lines of a graph.) The right "G" hand traces the imaginary up-down lines of a graph in the air.

GRASP (grăsp, gräsp), *v.*, GRASPED, GRASPING. See GRAB.

_____

GRASS (gras), *n.* (The letter "G"; growing.) The index and thumb of the right "G" hand are pushed up through the left hand, which forms a cup.

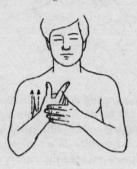

_____

GRAVITY (grav′ ə tĕ), *n.* (The letter "G"; dropping down.) The right "G" hand, positioned under the downturned left palm, drops straight down.

GRAY 1 (grā), *(loc.)*, *adj.* (Rationale unknown.) The right "O" hand traces an S-curve in the air as it moves down before the body. *Cf.* GREY.

GRAY 2, *adj.* (Intermingling of colors, in this case black and white.) The open "5" hands, fingers pointing to one another and palms facing the body, alternately swing in toward and out from the body. Each time they do so, the fingers of one hand pass through the spaces between the fingers of the other. *Cf.* GREY.

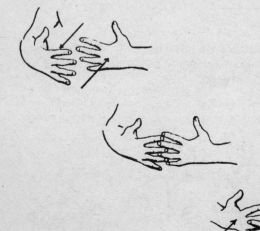

GREAT 1 (grāt), *adj.* (A large amount.) The "5" hands face each other, fingers curved and touching. They move apart rather quickly. *Cf.* EXPAND, MUCH.

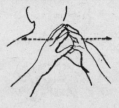

GREAT 2, *adj.* (The hands gesture toward the heavens.) The "5" hands, palms out and arms raised rather high, are positioned somewhat above the line of vision. The arms move abruptly forward and up once or twice. An expression of pleasure or surprise is usually assumed. *Cf.* EXCELLENT.

GREEDY 1 (grē′ dĭ), *adj.* (Pulling things toward oneself.) Both prone open or "V" hands are held in front of the body with fingers bent. The hands are then drawn quickly and forcefully inward, as if raking things toward oneself. *Cf.* SELFISH 1, STINGY 1.

GREEDY 2, *adj.* (Scratching the palm in greed.) The right fingers scratch the upturned left palm several times. A frowning expression is often used. *Cf.* SELFISH 2, STINGY 2.

GREY (grā), *adj.* See GRAY 1, 2.

GRIEF (grēf), *n.* (The facial features drop.) Both "5" hands, palms facing the eyes and fingers slightly curved, drop simultaneously to a level with the mouth. The head drops slightly as the hands move down, and an expression of sadness is assumed. *Cf.* GLOOM, GLOOMY, SAD, SORROWFUL 1.

GROUND (ground), *n.* (Fingering the soil.) Both hands, held upright before the body, finger imaginary pinches of soil. *Cf.* DIRT.

GROUP 1 (groop), *n.* (A grouping together.) Both "C" hands, palms facing, are held a few inches apart at chest height. They are swung around in unison, so that the palms now face the body. *Cf.* CLASS, CLASSED, COMPANY, ORGANIZATION 1.

GROUP 2, *n.* (The letter "G.") The sign for GROUP 1 is made, using the "G" hands.

 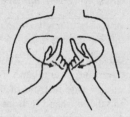

GROVEL (gruv′ əl), *v.* (Walk on knees.) The knuckles of the right index and middle fingers "walk" on the upturned left palm.

GROW (grō), *v.*, GREW, GROWN, GROWING. (Flowers or plants emerge from the ground.) The right fingers, pointing up, emerge from the closed left hand, and they spread open as they do. *Cf.* GROWN, SPRING.

GROWN (grōn), *adj.* See GROW.

GUARD (gärd), *v.*, GUARDED, GUARDING. (Hold down firmly; cover and strengthen.) The "S" hands, downturned, are held side by side in front of the body, the arms almost horizontal, and the left hand in front of the right. Both arms move a short distance forward and slightly downward. *Cf.* DEFEND, DEFENSE, PROTECT, PROTECTION, SHIELD.

GUESS (gĕs), *n., v.*, GUESSED, GUESSING. (A thought is grasped.) The right fingertip touches the forehead; then the

right hand makes a quick grasping movement in front of the
head, ending in the "S" position.

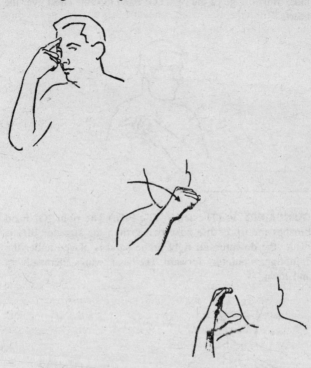

GUIDE (gīd), *n., v.,* GUIDED, GUIDING. (One hand leads the
other). The right hand grasps the tips of the left fingers and
pulls the left hand forward. *Cf.* LEAD.

GUILTY (gĭl′ tĭ), *adj.* (The "G" hand; a guilty heart.) The index finger edge of the right "G" hand taps the chest over the heart.

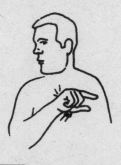

GUINEA PIG *n.* (The letter "G"; PIG.) The right "G" hand brushes the tip of the nose twice, then the sign for PIG is made: the downturned right prone hand is placed under the chin, fingers pointing forward. The hand swings alternately up and down.

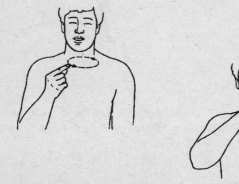

GUM (gum), *n.* (The chewing motion.) The thumb of the right "A" hand, held against the right cheek, swivels forward and back several times. Alternatively, the tips of the right "V" hand

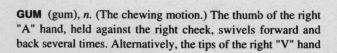

are placed at the right cheek and move in and out. *Cf.* CHEWING GUM.

GYMNASTICS (jim nas′ tiks), *n.* (The body movement.) The right index and middle fingers rest in the upturned left palm. The right hand leaves the left, assuming a palm-up position. The index and middle fingers swing in the air in a clockwise circle, and then the two fingers "land" again in the left palm.

H

HABIT (hăb′ ĭt), *n.* (Bound down to custom or habit.) Both "S" hands, palms down, are crossed and brought down in unison before the chest. *Cf.* CONVENTIONAL, CUSTOM, LOCKED.

HAIR (hâr), *n.* (The natural sign.) A lock of hair is grasped by the right index finger and thumb.

HAIRCUT (hâr′ kut), *n.* (The scissors at both sides of the head.) The two "V" hands, palms facing the sides of the head, open and close repeatedly as the hands move alternately back and forth. *Cf.* BARBER.

HAIR DRYER (hâr′ drī ər), *n.* (Holding the machine above the head.) The right "L" hand, thumb pointing up, aims the index finger at the hair as the hand moves at random over the head.

HAMSTER (ham′ stər), *n.* (The letter "H"; a rodent or rat.) The right "H" fingers brush repeatedly across the tip of the nose.

HAND (hănd), *n.* (The natural sign.) The prone right hand is drawn over the back of the prone left hand. For the plural, the action is repeated with the hands switched. The little finger edge of the right hand may instead be drawn across the back of the left wrist, as if cutting off the left hand; and for the plural the action is repeated with the hands switched.

HANDCUFF (hand′ kuf), *v.*, *n.* (Placing handcuffs on the wrists.) The right index and thumb, forming a "C", close over the left wrist. The left hand then does the same to the right.

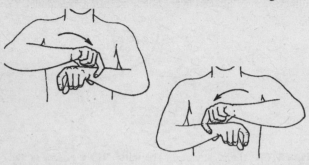

HANG (hăng), *v.*, HUNG, HANGED, HANGING. (Hanging by the throat.) The thumb of the "Y" hand is placed at the right side of the neck, and the head hangs toward the left, as if it were caught in a noose.

HANGER (hang′ ər), *n.* (The hangers.) The right curved index finger is repeatedly hung over the extended left index finger, starting at the lower knuckle and moving successively to the fingertip. *Cf.* CLOSET.

HAPPEN 1 (hăp′ ən), *v.*, -ENED, -ENING. (A befalling.) Both "D" hands, index fingers pointing away from the body, are simultaneously pivoted over so that the palms face down. *Cf.* EVENT, INCIDENT.

HAPPEN 2, *v.* The same sign as for HAPPEN 1, except that the "H" hands are used.

HAPPY (hăp′ ĭ), *adj.* (The heart is stirred; the spirits bubble up.) The open right hand, palm facing the body, strikes the heart repeatedly, moving up and off the heart after each strike. *Cf.* GLAD, JOY, MERRY.

HARD 1 (härd), *adj.* (The knuckles are rubbed, to indicate a condition of being worn down.) The knuckles of the curved index and middle fingers of both hands are rubbed up and down against each other. Instead of the up-down rubbing, they may rub against each other in an alternate clockwise-counterclockwise manner. *Cf.* DIFFICULT 1, DIFFICULTY, HARDSHIP, POVERTY, PROBLEM 2.

HARD 2, *adj.* (Striking a hard object.) The curved index and middle fingers of the right hand, whose palm faces the body or the left, are brought down sharply against the back of the downturned left "S" hand. *Cf.* DIFFICULT 2.

HARD OF HEARING *adj. phrase.* (The "H" is indicated twice.) The right "H" hand drops down an inch or so, rises, moves in a short arc to the right, and drops down an inch or so again.

HARDSHIP (härd′ shĭp), *n.* See HARD 1.

HARM (härm), *n.* (A stabbing pain.) The "D" hands, index fingers pointing to each other, are rotated in elliptical fashion before the chest--simultaneously but in opposite directions. *Cf.* HURT, INJURE, INJURY, PAIN.

HATCH (hăch), *v.* (Cracking the shell.) The right "H" hand is brought down on the left "H" hand, and then both hands are pivoted down and slightly apart. *Cf.* EGG.

HATCHET (hach' it), *n.* (The chopping.) The left arm is held straight up from the bent elbow. The little finger edge of the upturned right hand (or "H" hand) then makes a series of chopping movements against the left elbow. *Cf.* AXE.

HATE (hăt), *n., v.,* HATED, HATING. (To push away and recoil from; avoid.) The two open hands, palms facing left, are pushed deliberately to the left, as if pushing something away. An expression of disdain or disgust is worn. *Cf.* AVOID 2.

HAVE (hăv), *v.,* HAS, HAD, HAVING. (The act of bringing something over to oneself.) The right-angle hands, palms facing and thumbs pointing up, are swept toward the body until the fingertips come to rest against the middle of the chest.

HAVE TO *v. phrase.* (Being pinned down.) The right hand, in the "X" position, palm down, moves forcefully up and down once or twice. An expression of determination is frequently assumed. *Cf.* MUST, NECESSARY, NECESSITY, NEED 1, OUGHT TO, SHOULD.

HAWAII *n.* ("H"; beautiful.) The right "H" hand makes a counterclockwise circle around the face. This movement is from the sign for BEAUTIFUL.

HAY (hā), *n.* (Blades of grass obscuring the view, or the smell of newly mown hay.) The open right hand, palm facing the signer, moves up in front of the lips and nose. The movement is usually repeated. *Cf.* GRASS.

HAYSTACK (hā' stak), *n.* (A pile of hay or grass.) The sign for HAY, above, is made. The downturned cupped hands, held together, then move down and apart, describing a mound or pile.

HE (hē), *pron.* (Pointing at a male.) The MALE prefix sign is made: The right hand grasps an imaginary cap brim. The right index finger then points at an imaginary male. If in context the gender is clear, the prefix sign is usually omitted. *Cf.* HIM.

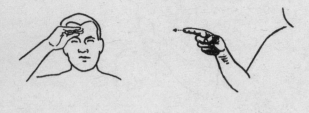

HEAD (hĕd), *n.* (The head is indicated.) The tips of the fingers of the right right-angle hand are placed at the right temple, and then move down in an arc to the right jaw.

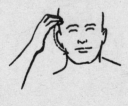

HEADACHE (hĕd′ āk′), *n.* (A stabbing pain in the head.) The index fingers, pointing to each other, move back and forth on the forehead.

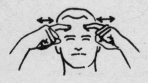

HEADLINE (hed' līn), *n.* (A banner across a newspaper.) The right curved index and thumb sweep across an imaginary newspaper page, from left to right.

HEALTH (hĕlth), *n.* (Strength emanating from the body.) Both "5" hands are placed palms against the chest. They move out and away, forcefully, closing and assuming the "S" position. *Cf.* BRAVE, BRAVERY, HEALTHY, MIGHTY 2, STRENGTH, WELL.

HEALTHY (hĕl' thĭ), *adj.* See HEALTH.

HEARING (hĭr′ ĭng), *n., adj.* (Words tumbling from the mouth, indicating the old association of being able to hear with being able to speak.) The right index finger, pointing left, describes a continuous small circle in front of the mouth. *Cf.* MENTION, SAID, SAY, SPEAK, SPEECH 1, TALK 1, TELL.

HEARING AID 1, *n.* (Behind the ear.) The right curved index finger is hooked onto the right ear, fingertip facing either forward or backward.

HEARING AID 2, *n.* (The wire leading down from the hearing aid.) The thumb and index finger trace an imaginary wire leading down from the ear to the chest.

HEAVY (hĕv′ ĭ), *adj.* (The hands drop under a weight.) The upturned "5" hands, held before the chest, suddenly drop a short distance.

HEIGHT 1 (hīt), *n.* (The height is indicated.) The index finger of the right "D" hand moves straight up against the palm of the left "5" hand. *Cf.* TALL 1.

HEIGHT 2, *n.* (The height is indicated.) The right right-angle hand, palm facing the left, is held at the height the signer wishes to indicate. *Cf.* BIG 2, HIGH 2, TALL 2.

HELICOPTER (hĕl′ ə kop tər), *n*. (The rotor.) The down-turned left "5" hand is placed on the upturned right index and trembles or quivers as the right index pushes it up.

HELL (hĕl), *n*. (The letter "H.") The right "H" hand, palm facing the body, moves sharply in an arc to the right.

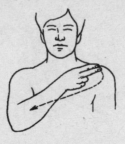

HELLO (hĕ lō′), *interj*. (A wave of the hand.) The right open hand waves back and forth several times. *Cf*. GOODBYE.

HELP (hĕlp), *n., v*., HELPED, HELPING. (Helping up; supporting.) The left "S" hand, thumb side up, rests in the open right palm. In this position the left hand is pushed up a short distance by the right. *Cf.* ASSIST, ASSISTANCE.

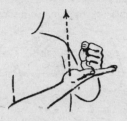

HER (hŭr), *pron.* (Pointing at a female.) The FEMALE prefix sign is made: The right "A" hand's thumb moves down along the line of the right jaw, from ear almost to chin. The right index finger then points at an imaginary female. If in context the gender is clear, the prefix sign is usually omitted. *Cf.* SHE. For the possessive sense of this pronoun, see HERS.

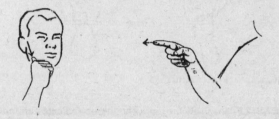

HERE (hǐr), *adv.* The open "5" hands, palms up and fingers slightly curved, move back and forth in front of the body, the right hand to the right and the left hand to the left. *Cf.* WHERE 2.

HERMIT CRAB *n.* (The shape and function.) The downturned bent left "V" fingers creep forward as they pull the right hand, the shell, along.

HERS (hûrz), *pron.* (Belonging to a female.) The FEMALE prefix sign is made. The open right hand, palm facing out, then moves straight forward a few inches. If in context the gender is clear, the prefix sign is usually omitted.

HERSELF (hər sĕlf´), *pron.* (The thumb indicates an individual who is stressed above others.) The FEMALE prefix sign is made. The right "A" hand, thumb upturned, then moves forward an inch or two, either once or twice. If in context the gender is clear, the prefix sign is usually omitted.

HEY! (hā), *interj.* (Waving for attention.) The open hand waves vigorously, with fingers pointing either up or at the person being addressed. This of course takes into account that deaf people communicate visually.

HIDE (hīd), *v.*, HID, HIDDEN, HIDING. (One hand is hidden under the other.) The thumb of the right "A" hand, whose palm faces left, is placed against the lips. The hand then swings down and under the downturned left hand. The initial contact with the lips is sometimes omitted.

HIGH 1 (hī), *adj.* (Something high up.) Both hands, in the right angle position, are held before the face, about a foot apart, palms facing. They are raised abruptly about a foot, in a slight outward curving movement. *Cf.* PROMOTE, PROMOTION.

HIGH 2, *adj.* (The height is indicated.) The right right-angle hand, palm facing the left, is held at the height the signer wishes to indicate. *Cf.* BIG 2, HEIGHT 2, TALL 2.

HIGHWAY (hī′ wā), *n.* (Traffic flowing in opposite directions.) The downturned "4" hands pass each other as the right moves repeatedly to the left and the left repeatedly to the right.

The downturned "V" hands are often used instead of the "4"s. *Cf.* FREEWAY.

HIM (hĭm), *pron.* (Pointing at a male.) The MALE prefix sign is made: The right hand grasps an imaginary cap brim. The right index finger then points at an imaginary male. If in context the gender is clear, the prefix sign is usually omitted. *Cf.* HE.

HIMSELF (hĭm sĕlf'), *pron.* (The thumb indicates an individual who is stressed above others.) The MALE prefix sign is made. The right "A" hand, thumb upturned, then moves forward an inch or two, either once or twice. If in context the gender is clear, the prefix sign is usually omitted.

HIPPOPOTAMUS (hip ə pot′ ə məs), *n.* (The large mouth opens.) Both "C" hands are placed on top of each other, fingertips pointing forward. The hands pivot wide open and close again. Another way to make this sign is with the extended index and little fingers of each hand, with the same open-and-close movement as before. The fingers here represent the teeth.

HIS (hĭz), *poss. pron.* (Belonging to a male.) The MALE prefix sign is made. The open right hand, palm facing out, then moves straight forward a few inches. If in context the gender is clear, the prefix sign is usually omitted.

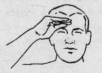 

HIT 1 (hĭt), *n., v.,* HIT, HITTING. (The natural sign.) The right "S" hand strikes its knuckles forcefully against the open left palm, which is held facing right. *Cf.* PUNCH 1, STRIKE 1.

HIT 2, *n., v.* (Hit with a baseball bat.) The signer mimes hitting a ball with a baseball bat. *Cf.* BASEBALL.

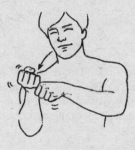

HOCKEY (hok′ē), *n.* (The hockey stick.) The knuckle of the curved right index finger strikes against the upturned left palm, from fingertips to base, as if hitting a hockey puck.

HOME (hōm), *n.* (A place where one eats and sleeps.) The closed fingers of the right hand are placed against the lips (the sign for EAT), and then, opening into a flat palm, against the right cheek (resting the head on a pillow, as in SLEEP). The head leans slightly to the right, as if going to sleep in the right palm, during this latter movement.

HONEST (ŏn′ ĭst), *adj.* (The letter "H" for HONEST; a straight and true path.) The index and middle fingers of the right "H" hand, whose palm faces left, move straight forward along the upturned left palm. *Cf.* HONESTY, SINCERE.

HONESTY (ŏn′ ĭs tĭ), *n.* See HONEST.

HONOR (ŏn′ ər), *n., v.,* -ORED, -ORING. (The letter "H"; a gesture of respect.) The right "H" hand, palm facing left, swings down in an arc from its initial position in front of the forehead.

The head bows slightly during this movement of the hand. *Cf.*
HONORARY.

HONORARY (ŏn' ə rĕr´ ĭ), *adj.* See HONOR.

HOPE (hōp), *n.*, *v.*, HOPED, HOPING. (A thought awaited.) The
tip of the right index finger, held in the "D" position, palm facing the body, is placed on the forehead (modified THINK,
q.v.). Both hands then assume right angle positions, fingers
facing, with the left hand held above left shoulder level and the
right before the right breast. Both hands, held thus, wave to
each other several times. *Cf.* EXPECT.

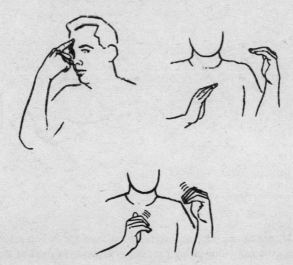

HORSE (hôrs), *n*. (The ears.) The "U" hands are placed palms out at either side of the head. The index and middle fingers move forward and back repeatedly, imitating the movement of a horse's ears.

HOSPITAL (hŏs′ pĭ təl), *n*. (The letter "H"; the red cross on the sleeve.) The index and middle fingers of the right "H" hand trace a cross on the upper part of the left arm.

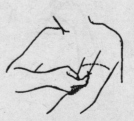

HOT (hŏt), *adj*. (Removing hot food from the mouth.) The cupped hand, palm facing the body, moves up in front of the slightly open mouth. It is then flung down to the palm-down position.

HOT DOG (hot′ dôg), *n.* (The shape in a roll or bun.) The left hand is held with fingers pointing up. The right index finger is placed between the thumb and the other fingers. *Cf.* FRANK-FURTER.

HOT ROD (hot′ rod), *n.* (The stick shift.) The signer mimes shifting automobile gears violently, while holding the top of the steering wheel in the other hand. The body may show bouncing as the car takes off.

HOUSE (hous), *n.* (The shape of the house.) The open hands are held with fingertips touching, so that they form a pyramid a bit above eye level. From this position, the hands separate and move diagonally downward for a short distance; then they continue straight down a few inches. This movement traces the outline of a roof and walls.

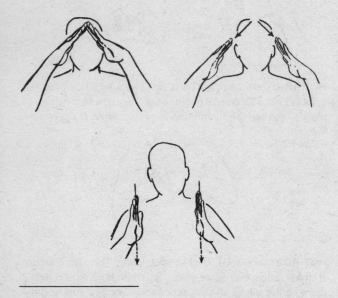

HOW (hou), *adv.* (The hands come into view, to reveal something.) The right-angle hands, palms down and knuckles touching, swing up and open to the palms-up position.

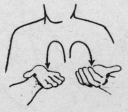

HOW ARE YOU? *phrase.* (What are your feelings?) Both middle fingers quickly sweep up and out from the chest. The eyebrows are raised in inquiry. *Cf.* WHAT'S NEW?, WHAT'S UP?

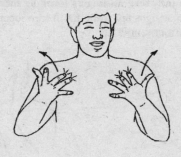

HOWEVER (hou ĕv' ər), *conj.* Both hands, in the "5" position, are held before the chest, fingertips facing each other. With an alternate back-forth movement, the fingertips are made to strike each other. *Cf.* NEVERTHELESS.

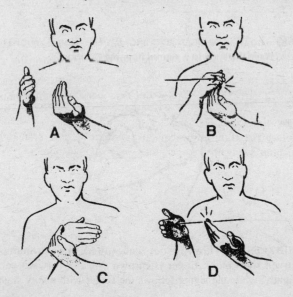

HOW MANY? *interrogative phrase.* (Throwing up a number of things before the eyes; a display of fingers to indicate a question of how many or how much.) The right hand, palm up, is held before the chest, all fingers touching the thumb. The hand is tossed straight up, while the fingers open to the "5" position. *Cf.* AMOUNT, HOW MUCH?

HOW MUCH? *interrogative phrase.* See HOW MANY?

HUG (hŭg), *v.*, HUGGED, HUGGING, *n.* (The natural sign.) The arms clasp the body in a natural hugging position.

HUH? *interj.* (Throwing out a question.) The downturned curved right index finger is thrown out and forward very slightly, while the signer follows the finger with a very slight

forward movement of the body. An expression of inquiry or
perplexity is assumed.

HUMOR (hū′ mər, ū′-), *n.* (The nose wrinkles in laughter.)
The tips of the right index and middle fingers brush repeatedly
off the tip of the nose. *Cf.* FUNNY, HUMOROUS.

HUMOROUS (hū′ mər əs, ū′-), *adj.* See HUMOR.

HUNDRED (hŭn′ drəd), *n., adj.* (The Roman "C," *centum*, for
"hundred.") The letter "C" is formed. This is preceded by a "1"
for a simple hundred, or by whatever number of hundreds one
wishes to indicate.

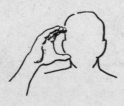

HURRY (hûr´ ĭ), *v.*, -RIED, -RYING. (Letter "H"; quick movements.) The "H" hands, palms facing each other and held about six inches apart, shåke alternately up and down. One hand alone may be used.

HURT (hûrt), *v.*, HURT, HURTING, *n.* (A stabbing pain.) The "D" hands, index fingers pointing to each other, are rotated in elliptical fashion before the chest—simultaneously but in opposite directions. *Cf.* HARM, INJURE, INJURY, PAIN.

HUSBAND (hŭz´ bənd), *n.* (A male joined in marriage.) The MALE prefix sign is formed: The right hand grasps the brim of an imaginary cap. The hands are then clasped together.

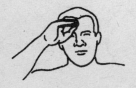

I

I 1 (ī), *pron*. (The letter "I," held to the chest.) The right "I" hand is held with its thumb edge to the chest and little finger pointing up.

I 2, *pron*. (The natural sign.) The signer points to himself. *Cf*. ME.

ICE (īs), *n.*, *v.*, ICED, ICING. (The stiff fingers.) The fingers of the "5" hands, held palms down, stiffen and contract. *Cf*. FREEZE, FROZEN.

ICE CREAM (crēm), *n*. (The eating action.) The upturned left palm represents a dish or plate. The curved index and middle fingers of the right hand represent the spoon. They are drawn up repeatedly from the left palm to the lips.

IF (ĭf), *conj*. (The scales move up and down.) The two "F" hands, palms facing each other, move alternately up and down. *Cf.* CONSIDER 3, COURT, EVALUATE 1, JUDGE, JUDGMENT, JUSTICE.

IGNORANT (ĭg′ nə rənt), *adj*. (The head is struck to emphasize its emptiness or lack of knowledge.) The back of the right "V" hand strikes the forehead once or twice. Two fingers represent prison bars across the mind--the mind is imprisoned.

IGNORE (ĭg nôr'), *v.*, -NORED, -NORING. (Thumbing the nose.) The index finger of the right "B" hand is placed under the tip of the nose. From this position the right hand moves straight forward, away from the face. *Cf.* DISREGARD.

ILL (ĭl), *adj., n., adv.* (The sick parts of the anatomy are indicated.) The right middle finger rests on the forehead, and its left counterpart is placed against the stomach. The signer assumes an expression of sadness or physical distress. *Cf.* SICK.

IMAGINATION (ĭ măj´ ə nā´ shən), *n.* (A thought coming forward from the mind, modified by the letter "I" for "idea.") With the "I" position on the right hand, palm facing the body, touch the little finger to the forehead, and then move the hand up and away in a circular, clockwise motion. The hand may also be moved up and away without this circular motion. *Cf.* IMAGINE.

IMAGINE (ĭ măj´ ĭn), *v.,* -INED, -INING. See IMAGINATION.

IMMEDIATELY (ĭ mē´ dĭ ĭt lĭ), *adv.* (A quick movement.) The thumbtip of the upright right hand is flicked quickly off the tip of the curved right index finger, as if shooting marbles. *Cf.* FAST, QUICK, QUICKNESS, SPEED, SPEEDY.

IMPORTANT (ĭm pôr´ tənt), *adj.* Both "F" hands, palms facing each other, move apart, up, and together in a smooth elliptical fashion, coming together at the tips of the thumbs and index fingers of both hands. *Cf.* SIGNIFICANCE 1, SIGNIFICANT,

VALUABLE, VALUE, WORTH, WORTHWHILE, WORTHY.

IMPOSSIBLE (ĭm pŏs′ ə bəl), *(loc.)*, *adj.* The downturned right "Y" hand is placed in the upturned left palm a number of times. The up-down movement is very slight.

IMPROVE (ĭm proov′), *v.*, -PROVED, -PROVING. (Moving up.) The little finger edge of the right hand rests on the back of the downturned left hand. It moves up the left arm in successive stages, indicating improvement or upward movement.

IN (ĭn), *prep.*, *adv.*, *adj.* (The natural sign.) The fingers of the right hand are thrust into the left. *Cf.* INSIDE, INTO, WITHIN.

IN A FEW DAYS *adv. phrase.* (Several TOMORROWS ahead.) The thumb of the right "A" hand is positioned on the right cheek. One by one, the remaining fingers appear, starting with the index finger. Usually, when all five fingers have been presented, the hand moves forward a few inches, to signify the concept of the future.

IN A WEEK *adv. phrase.* (A week around the corner.) The upright, right "D" hand is placed palm-to-palm against the left "5" hand, whose palm faces right. The right "D" hand moves along the left palm from base to fingertips and then curves to the left, around the left fingertips.

INCIDENT (ĭn′ sə dənt), *n.* (A befalling.) Both "D" hands, index fingers pointing away from the body, are simultaneously pivoted over so that the palms face down. *Cf.* EVENT, HAPPEN 1.

INCLUDE (ĭn klo͞od'), *v.*, -CLUDED, -CLUDING. (All; the whole.)
The left hand is held in the "C" position, fingers pointing right.
The right hand, in the "5" position, fingers facing out from the
body, palm down, is held above the left. With a horizontal
swing to the right, the right hand describes an arc, as the fingers close and are thrust into the left "C" hand, which closes
over it. *Cf.* INCLUSIVE.

INCLUSIVE (ĭn klo͞o ' sĭv), *adj.* See INCLUDE.

INCOME (ĭn' kŭm), *n.* (A regular taking in.) The outstretched
open left hand, held palm facing right, moves in toward the
body, assuming the "A" position, palm still facing right. This
is repeated several times.

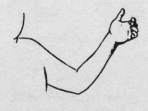

INCREASE (*n.* ĭn′ krēs; *v.* ĭn krēs′) -CREASED, -CREASING. (Adding on.) The index and middle fingers of the right "H" hand, palm up, are swung up and over until they come to rest on the index and middle fingers of the left "H" hand, held palm down. *Cf.* ADD 2, ADDITION, GAIN, RAISE.

INDEPENDENCE (ĭn′ dĭ pĕn′ dəns), *n.* (Breaking the bonds.) The "S" hands, crossed in front of the body, swing apart and face out. *Cf.* FREE 1, FREEDOM, INDEPENDENT 1, RESCUE, SAFE, SAVE 1.

INDEPENDENT 1 (ĭn′ dĭ pĕn′ dənt), *adj.* See INDEPENDENCE.

INDEPENDENT 2, *adj.* (Initialized version.) As in INDEPEN-DENCE, the hands swing apart and face out, but here both hands form the letter "I."

INDIVIDUAL 1 (ĭn´ də vĭj ´ ŏŏ əl), *n.* (The shape of an individual.) Both open hands, palms facing each other, move down the sides of the body, tracing its outline to the hips. This is an important suffix sign, that changes a verb to a noun. *E.g.,* TEACH, *v.,* becomes TEACHER, *n.,* by the addition of this sign.

INDIVIDUAL 2, *n.* (The "I" hands; the outline of a person.) The "I" hands, palms facing and little fingers pointing out, are held before the body. They are drawn down a few inches, outlining the shape of an imaginary person standing before the signer.

INFLATION (in flā′ shən), *n.* (The letter "I"; spiraling upwards.) The base of the right "I" hand rests on the left hand. It spirals upward.

INFLUENCE (ĭn′ flŏŏ əns), *n.*, *v.*, -ENCED, -ENCING. (Take something, *influence,* and disseminate it.) The left hand, held limp in front of the body, has its fingers pointing down. The fingers of the right hand, held all together, are placed on the top of the left hand, and then move forward, off the left hand, assuming a "5" position, palm down. *Cf.* ADVICE, ADVISE.

INFORM (ĭn fôrm′), *v.*, -FORMED, -FORMING. (Taking knowledge from the mind and giving it out to all.) The fingertips are positioned on either side of the forehead. Both hands then swing down and out, opening into the upturned "5" position.

Cf. INFORMATION, LET KNOW, NOTIFY.

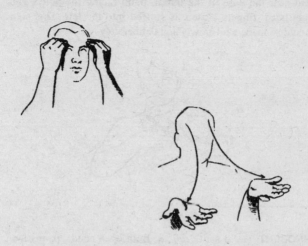

INFORMATION (ĭn′ fər mā′ shən), *n.* See INFORM.

INJURE (ĭn′ jər), *v.,* -JURED, -JURING. (A stabbing pain.) The "D" hands, index fingers pointing to each other, are rotated in elliptical fashion before the chest--simultaneously but in opposite directions. *Cf.* HARM, HURT, INJURY, PAIN.

INJURY (ĭn′ jə rĭ), *n.* See INJURE.

INNER FEELINGS *n.* (Things within.) The left "C" hand is held near the base of the throat, palm facing the body. The right hand, fingers closed, is stuffed into the left. This sign should be made a bit slowly and deliberately.

INNOCENT (ĭn′ ə sənt), *adj., n.* Both open hands, palms facing out, are held in front of the mouth, with the ring fingers bent against the palm. Both hands move out and away from the mouth, describing arcs.

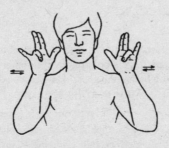

INQUIRE (ĭn kwīr′), *(colloq.), v.,* -QUIRED, -QUIRING. (Fire a question.) The right hand, held in a modified "S" position with palm facing out, assumes a position with the thumb resting on the fingernail of the index finger. The index finger is flicked out and forward, usually directed at the person being asked a question. *Cf.* ASK 2, INTERROGATE, INTERROGATION, QUERY.

INSANE (ĭn sān'), *adj.* (Turning of wheels in the head.) The open right hand is held palm down before the face, fingers spread, bent, and pointing toward the forehead. The fingers move in circles before the forehead. *Cf.* CRAZY 1, INSANITY.

INSANITY (ĭn săn' ə tĭ), *n.* See INSANE.

INSECT (ĭn' sĕkt), *(sl.), n.* (The quivering antennae.) The thumb of the "3" hand rests against the nose, and the index and middle fingers bend slightly and straighten again a number of times.

INSIDE (*prep., adv.* ĭn´ sīd´; *adj.* ĭn´ sīd´). (The natural sign.) The fingers of the right hand are thrust into the left. *Cf.* IN, INTO, WITHIN.

INSPIRE (in spīr´), *v.* (The feelings well up.) Both hands, fingers touching thumbs, are placed against the chest, with palms facing the body. They slide up the chest, opening into the "5" position.

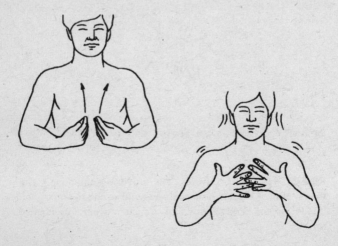

INSTRUCT (ĭn strŭkt´), *v.,* -STRUCTED, -STRUCTING. (Giving forth from the mind.) The fingertips of each hand are placed on the temples. They then swing out and open into the "5"

position. *Cf.* EDUCATE, TEACH.

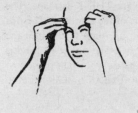

INSULT (ĭn sŭlt′), *v.*, -SULTED, -SULTING. (Directing a barrage of insults or ripostes.) Both index fingers, pointing out from the body, execute continuous alternate forward movements.

INTELLIGENT (in tĕl′ ə jənt), *adj.* (The mind is bright.) The middle finger is placed at the forehead, and then the hand, with an outward flick, turns around so that the palm faces outward. This indicates a brightness flowing from the mind. *Cf.* SMART.

INTEND (ĭn tĕnd′), v., -TENDED, -TENDING. (Relative standing of one's thoughts.) A modified sign for THINK is made: The right index finger touches the middle of the forehead. The tips of the right "V" hand, palm down, are then thrust into the upturned left palm (as in STAND, q.v.). The right "V" hand is then re-thrust into the upturned left palm, with right palm now facing the body. *Cf.* INTENT, INTENTION, MEAN 2, MEANING, PURPOSE, SIGNIFICANCE 2, SIGNIFY.

INTENT (ĭn tĕnt′), n. See INTEND.

INTENTION (ĭn tĕn′ shən), n. See INTEND.

INTEREST 1 (ĭn′ tər ĭst, -trĭst), n., v., -ESTED, -ESTING. (Drawing one out.) The index and middle fingers of both hands, one above the other, are placed on the middle part of the chest. Both hands move forward simultaneously. As they do, the index and middle fingers of each hand come together. *Cf.* FASCINATE, INTERESTED 1, INTERESTING 1.

INTEREST 2, *n.*, *v.* (The tongue is pulled out, causing the mouth to gape.) The curved open right hand is placed at the mouth, with index finger and thumb poised as if to grasp the tongue. The hand moves straight out, assuming the "A" position. *Cf.* INTERESTED 2, INTERESTING 2.

INTERESTED 1 (ĭn' tər ĭs tĭd, -trĭs tĭd, -tə rĕs' tĭd), *adj.* See INTEREST 1.

INTERESTED 2, *adj.* See INTEREST 2.

INTERESTING 1 (ĭn' tər ĭs tĭng, -trĭs tĭng, -tə rĕs' tĭng), *adj.* See INTEREST 1.

INTERESTING 2, *adj.* See INTEREST 2.

INTERFERE (ĭn´ tər fĭr´), *v.*, -FERED, -FERING. (Obstruct, block.) The left hand, fingers together and palm flat, is held before the body, facing somewhat down. The little finger side of the right hand, held with palm flat, makes one or several up-down chopping motions against the left hand, between its thumb and index finger. *Cf.* ANNOY, ANNOYANCE, BOTHER, DIS-TURB, INTERFERENCE, INTERFERE WITH, INTERRUPT, PREVENT, PREVENTION.

INTERFERENCE (ĭn´ tər fĭr´ əns), *n.* See INTERFERE.

INTERFERE WITH *v. phrase.* See INTERFERE.

INTERPRET (ĭn tûr´ prĭt), *v.*, -PRETED, -PRETING. (Changing one language to another.) The "F" hands are held palms facing and thumbs and index fingers in contact with each other. The hands swing around each other, reversing their relative posi-tions.

INTERROGATE (ĭn tĕr´ ə gāt´), *(colloq.)*, *v.* -GATED, -GATING. (Fire a question.) The right hand, held in a modified "S" position with palm facing out, assumes a position with the thumb resting on the fingernail of the index finger. The index finger is flicked out and forward, usually directed at the person being asked a question. *Cf.* ASK 2, INQUIRE, INTERROGATION, QUERY.

INTERROGATION (ïn tĕr´ ə gā´ shən), *(colloq.)*, *n.* See INTER-ROGATE.

INTERRUPT (ĭn´ tə rŭpt´), *v.*, -RUPTED, -RUPTING. (Obstruct, block.) The left hand, fingers together and palm flat, is held before the body, facing somewhat down. The little finger side of the right hand, held with palm flat, makes one or several up-down chopping motions against the left hand, between its thumb and index finger. *Cf.* ANNOY, ANNOYANCE, BOTHER, DISTURB, INTERFERE, INTERFERENCE, INTERFERE WITH, PREVENT, PREVENTION.

INTERSECT (ĭn´ tər sĕkt´), v., -SECTED, -SECTING. (Intersecting lines.) The extended index fingers move toward each other at right angles and cross. *Cf.* INTERSECTION.

INTERSECTION (ĭn´ tər sĕk shən), n. See INTERSECT.

IN THE FUTURE *adv. phrase.* (Something ahead or in the future.) The upright, open right hand, palm facing left, moves straight out and slightly up from a position beside the right temple. *Cf.* FUTURE, LATER 2, LATER ON, WILL, WOULD.

INTO (ĭn´ tōō), *prep.* (The natural sign.) The fingers of the right hand are thrust into the left. *Cf.* IN, INSIDE, WITHIN.

INTOXICATE (ĭn tŏk´ sə kāt´), v., -CATED, -CATING. (The act of drinking.) The thumbtip of the right "Y" hand is tilted toward the mouth, as if it were a drinking glass or bottle. The signer tilts his head back slightly, as if drinking. *Cf.* BEER, DRUNK,

DRUNKARD, DRUNKENNESS, INTOXICATION, LIQUOR.

INTOXICATION (ĭn tŏk´ sə ka´ shən), *n.* See INTOXICATE.

INVITE (ĭn vīt´), *v.*, -VITED, -VITING. (Opening or leading the way toward something.) The open right hand, held up before the body, sweeps down in an arc and over toward the left side of the chest, ending in the palm-up position. Reversing the movement gives the passive form of the verb, except that the hand does not arc upward but rather simply moves outward in a small arc from the body. *Cf.* INVITED, WELCOME.

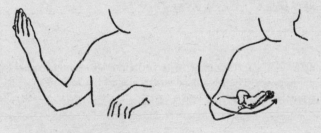

INVITED *passive voice of the verb* INVITE. The upturned right hand, touching the chest, moves straight forward and away from the body.

J

JEALOUS (jĕl′ əs), *adj.* (Biting the finger to suppress the feelings.) The tip of the index finger is bitten. The tip of the finger is sometimes used. *Cf.* ENVIOUS, ENVY, JEALOUSY.

_____

JEALOUSY (jĕl′ ə sĭ), *n.* See JEALOUS.

_____

JOB (jŏb), *n.* (Striking an anvil.) Both "S" hands are held palms down. The right hand strikes against the back of the left a number of times. *Cf.* WORK.

_____

JOIN (join), *v.*, JOINED, JOINING. (Joining together.) Both hands, held in the modified "5" position, palms out, move toward each other. The thumbs and index fingers of both hands then connect. *Cf.* ATTACH, BELONG, CONNECT.

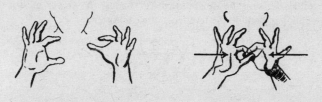

JOY (joi), *n.* (The heart is stirred; the spirits bubble up.) The open right hand, palm facing the body, strikes the heart repeatedly, moving up and off the heart after each strike. *Cf.* GLAD, HAPPY, MERRY.

JUDGE (jŭj), *n.*, *v.*, JUDGED, JUDGING. (The scales move up and down.) The two "F" hands, palms facing each other, move alternately up and down. *Cf.* CONSIDER 3, COURT, EVALUATE 1, IF, JUDGMENT, JUSTICE.

JUDGMENT (jŭj′ mənt), *n.* See JUDGE.

JUMP START *v. phrase.* (Placing the cables on the battery terminals.) Using the downturned "V" hands, the signer mimes clamping them on the terminals of a car battery.

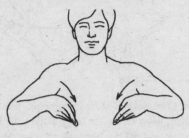

JUNIOR (jōōn' yər), *n.* (College student.) The left index finger taps the palm of the right hand.

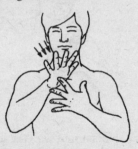

JUST A MOMENT AGO *adv. phrase.* (Time moved backward a bit.) The right "D" hand, palm facing the body, is placed in the palm of the left hand, which is facing right. The right hand swings back a bit toward the body, with the index finger describing an arc. *Cf.* FEW SECONDS AGO, A; WHILE AGO, A 2.

JUSTICE (jŭs′ tĭs), *n*. (The scales move up and down.) The two "F" hands, palms facing each other, move alternately up and down. *Cf.* CONSIDER 3, COURT, EVALUATE 1, IF, JUDGE, JUDGMENT.

K

KANGAROO (kang gə rōō′), *n.* (The shape and movement.) The vertical right arm represents the kangaroo's body, the index and little fingers the ears, and the thumb touching the middle and ring fingers, the snout. With the upturned cupped left hand resting on the right arm near the elbow, to represent the pouch, the signer executes a series of short forward jumping motions.

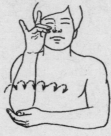

KARATE (kä rä′ tä), *n.* (The chopping motions.) Using both hands and arms, the signer mimes the chopping motions of karate.

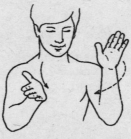

KEEP (kēp), *v.*, KEPT, KEEPING. (Slow, careful movement.) The "K" hands are crossed, the right above the left, little finger edges down. In this position the hands are moved up and down a short distance. *Cf.* CARE 2, CAREFUL 2, MAINTAIN, PRESERVE, TAKE CARE OF.

KEEP A SECRET *colloq. phrase.* (Squeezing the mouth shut.) The right "S" hand is placed thumb side against the lips. It swings to the palm-down position, held tightly against the lips.

KEEP QUIET 1, *v. phrase.* (The natural sign.) The index finger is placed forcefully against the closed lips. The signer frowns or looks stern. *Cf.* KEEP STILL 1.

KEEP QUIET 2, *v. phrase.* (The mouth is sealed; the sign for QUIET.) The downturned open hands are crossed at the lips with the left in front of the right. Both hands are drawn apart and down rather forcefully, while the signer frowns or looks stern. *Cf.* KEEP STILL 2.

 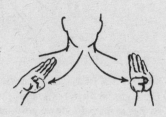

KEEP STILL 1, *v. phrase.* See KEEP QUIET 1.

KEEP STILL 2, *v. phrase.* See KEEP QUIET 2.

KEY (kē), *n.* (The turning of the key.) The right hand, holding an imaginary key, twists it in the open left palm, which is facing right. *Cf.* LOCK 1.

KEYBOARD 1 (kē′ bôrd), *n.* (The shape and function.) The signer types on an imaginary keyboard, and then the down

turned index fingers trace a rectangle, indicating the shape of
the keyboard.

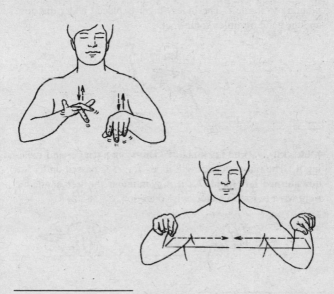

_____

KEYBOARD 2, *n.* (A fingerspelled loan sign.) The letters K-B
are fingerspelled.

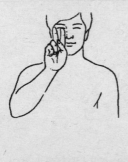

KID (kĭd), *(colloq.)*, *n*. (The running nose.) The index and little fingers of the right hand, held palm down, are extended, pointing to the left. The index finger is placed under the nose and the hand trembles somewhat.

KILL (kĭl), *v*., KILLED, KILLING. (Thrusting a dagger and twisting it.) The outstretched right index finger is passed under the downturned left hand. As it moves under the left hand, the right wrist twists in a clockwise direction. *Cf*. MURDER.

KILOGRAM (kil′ ə gram), *n*. (The letter "K"; weighing.) The right "K" hand is balanced back and forth as it rests on the index finger of the left "G" hand.

KILOMETER (kil ə mē tər), *n*. (The "K" and the "M.") Both hands are first held in the "K" position. They change to the

"M" position, side by side, and move apart.

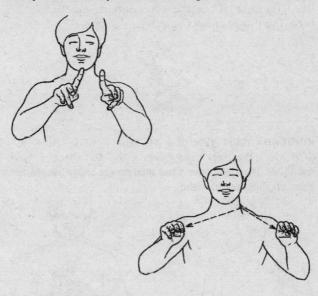

KIND 1 (kind), *adj.* (The heart rolls out.) Both right-angle hands roll over each other as they move down and away from their initial position at the heart. *Cf.* GENEROUS, MERCY.

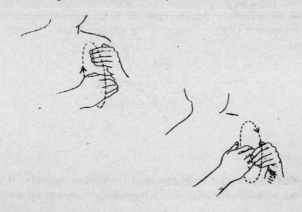

KIND 2, *n.* (The letter "K"; the wholeness or global characteristic.) The right "K" hand revolves once around the left "K" hand. This is used to describe a class or group.

KINDERGARTEN (kin′ dər gär tən), *n.* (The letter "K"; SCHOOL.) The right hand makes a "K" and shakes it back and forth. The right open hand then comes down on the left palm, clapping several times.

KISS (kĭs), *n., v.,* KISSED, KISSING. (Lips touch lips.) With fingers touching their thumbs, both hands are brought together. They tremble slightly, indicating the degree of intensity of the kiss.

KNIFE (nīf), *n.* (Shaving or paring.) The edge of the right "H" hand, resting on the edge of its left counterpart, moves forward several times, as if shaving layers of flesh.

KNOW (nō), *v.*, KNEW, KNOWN, KNOWING. (Patting the head to indicate something of value inside.) The right fingers pat the forehead several times. *Cf.* FAMILIAR, KNOWING, KNOWLEDGE, RECOGNIZE.

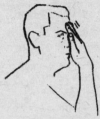

KNOWING (nō′ ĭng), *adj.* See KNOW.

KNOWLEDGE (nŏl′ ĭj), *n.* See KNOW.

L

LADY (lā' dĭ), *n.* (A female with a ruffled bodice; *i.e.,* an elegantly dressed woman, a lady.) The FEMALE root sign is made: The thumb of the right "A" hand moves down along the right jaw, from ear almost to chin. The thumbtip of the right "5" hand, palm facing left, is then placed on the chest, with the other fingers pointing up. Pivoted at the thumb, the hand swings down a bit, so that the other fingers are now pointing out somewhat.

LAMP (lamp), *n.* (The rays come out.) The downturned "8" hand, positioned at the chin, flicks open a number of times. *Cf.* LIGHT 3.

LAND 1 (lănd), *n.* (An expanse of ground.) The sign for SOIL 1 is made: Both hands, held upright before the body, finger imaginary pinches of soil. The downturned open right "5"

hand then sweeps in an arc from right to left.

LAND 2, *n*. (An established area.) The right "N" hand, palm down, executes a clockwise circle above the downturned prone left hand. The tips of the "N" fingers then move straight down and come to rest on the back of the left hand. *Cf.* COUNTRY 2, NATION, REPUBLIC.

LANGUAGE 1 (lăng′ gwĭj), *n*. (A series of letters spelled out on the printed page.) The downturned "F" hands are positioned with thumbs and index fingertips touching. The hands move straight apart to either side in a wavy motion. *Cf.* SENTENCE.

LANGUAGE 2, *n.* (The letter "L.") The sign for LANGUAGE 1 is made, but with the "L" hands.

LANGUAGE OF SIGNS *n.* (LANGUAGE 1 and hand/arm movements.) The "D" hands, palms facing and index fingers pointing back toward the face, describe a series of continuous counterclockwise circles toward and away from the face, imitating the foot motions in bicycling. This is followed by the sign for LANGUAGE 1. *Cf.* SIGN LANGUAGE, SIGNS.

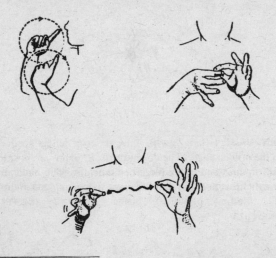

LARGE (lärj), *adj.* (A delineation of something big, modified by the letter "L," which stands for LARGE.) Both "L" hands, palms facing out, are placed before the face, and separate rather widely. *Cf.* BIG 1.

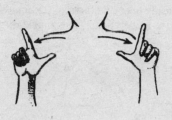

LAST 1 (lăst), *adj.* (The little, *i.e.*, LAST, fingers are indicated.) With the hands in the "I" position, the tip of the right little finger strikes the tip of its left counterpart. The right index finger may be used instead of the right little finger. *Cf.* END 1, FINAL 1, FINALLY 1, LASTLY.

LAST 2, *adj.* (A single little, *i.e.*, LAST, finger is indicated.) The tip of the index finger of the right "D" hand strikes the tip of the little finger of the left "I" hand. *Cf.* END 2, FINAL 2, FINALLY 2, LASTLY.

LAST 3, *v*. (Steady, uninterrupted movement.) The "A" hands are held with palms out, thumbs extended and touching, the right behind the left. In this position the hands move forward in a straight, steady line. *Cf.* CONTINUE, ENDURE 2, EVER 1, LAST-ING, PERMANENT, PERSEVERE, PERSIST, REMAIN, STAY 1, STAY STILL.

LASTING (lăs′ tǐng), *adj*. See LAST 3.

LASTLY (lăst′ lǐ), *adv*. See LAST 1, 2.

LATE (lāt), *adj*. (Hanging back.) The "5" hand and forearm, hanging loosely and straight down from the elbow, move back and forth under the armpit. *Cf.* NOT YET.

LATER 1, *adj*. (A moving on of the minute hand of the clock.) The right "L" hand, its thumb thrust into the palm of the left and acting as a pivot, moves forward a short distance. *Cf.* AFTER A WHILE, AFTERWARD.

LATER 2, *adj., adv.* (Something ahead or in the future.) The upright, open right hand, palm facing left, moves straight out and slightly up from a position beside the right temple. *Cf.* FUTURE, IN THE FUTURE, LATER ON, WILL, WOULD.

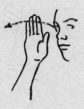

LATER ON *adv. phrase.* See LATER 2.

LAUGH (lăf), *n., v.,* LAUGHED, LAUGHING. (The natural sign.) The fingers of both "D" hands move repeatedly up along the jawline, or up from the corners of the mouth. The signer meanwhile laughs. *Cf.* LAUGHTER 1.

LAUGHTER 1 (lăf′ tər), *n.* See LAUGH.

LAUGHTER 2, *(colloq.), n.* (The shaking of the stomach.) The cupped hands, held at stomach level, palms facing the body, move alternately up and down, describing short arcs. The signer meanwhile laughs.

LAUGHTER 3, *(colloq.), n.* (Literally, rolling in the aisles; the legs are doubled up and the body rolls on the floor.) With index and middle fingers crooked, and its little finger edge or back resting on the upturned left palm, the right hand moves in a continuous counterclockwise circle in the left palm. The signer meanwhile laughs.

LAW (lô), *n.* (A series of LAWS as they appear on the printed page.) The upright right "L" hand, resting palm against palm on the upright left "5" hand, moves down in an arc a short dis tance, coming to rest on the base of the left palm.

LAZINESS (lă′ zĭ nĭs), *n.* (The initial "L" rests against the body; the concept of inactivity.) The right "L" hand is placed against the left shoulder once or a number of times. The palm faces the body. *Cf.* LAZY.

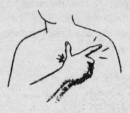

LAZY (lă′ zĭ), *adj.* See LAZINESS.

LEAD (lēd), *v.,* LED, LEADING, *n.* (One hand leads the other.) The right hand grasps the tips of the left fingers and pulls the left hand forward. *Cf.* GUIDE.

LEAF (lēf), *n*. The left "5" hand, palm out, is the tree. The right thumb and index finger trace the shape of a leaf from one of the outstretched left fingers.

LEARN (lûrn), *v.*, LEARNED, LEARNING. (Taking knowledge from a book and placing it in the head.) The downturned fingers of the right hand are placed on the upturned left palm. They close, and then the hand rises and the right fingertips are placed on the forehead.

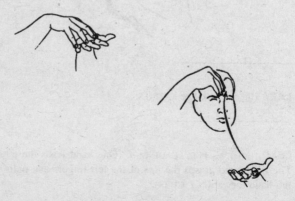

LEATHER (leŧh′ ər), *n., adj.* (The letter "L"; worn on or covering the body.) The thumb of the right "L" hand is placed on the chest and moves down an inch or two several times.

LEAVE (lēv), *v.*, LEFT, LEAVING. (Pulling away.) The down-turned open hands are held in a line, with fingers pointing to the left, the right hand behind the left. Both hands move in unison toward the right. As they do so, they assume the "A" position. *Cf.* DEPART, WITHDRAW 1.

LECTURE (lek′ chər), *n., v.*, -TURED, -TURING. (A gesture of an orator.) The right open hand, palm facing left, is held above and to the right of the head. It pivots on the wrist, forward and backward, several times. *Cf.* SPEECH 2, TALK 2.

LEFT (lĕft), *adj.* (The remainder is left behind.) The "5" hands, palms facing each other and fingers pointing forward, are dropped simultaneously a few inches, as if dropping something on the table. *Cf.* REMAINDER.

LEND 1 (lĕnd), *v.*, LENT, LENDING. (Something kept, *i.e.*, in one's custody, is moved forward to other, temporary, ownership.) The crossed "K" hands, for KEEP, *q.v.*, are moved forward simultaneously, in a short arc. *Cf.* LOAN 1.

LEND 2, *v.* The side of the right index finger is brought up against the right side of the nose. *Cf.* LOAN 2.

LENGTH (lengkth), *n.* (The distance is traced.) The right index finger traces a long line along the left arm from wrist almost to shoulder. *Cf.* LONG.

LESBIAN (lez′ bē ən), *n., adj.* (The letter "L.") The right "L" hand is held palm facing the body, index finger pointing left. In this position the hand is placed against the chin.

LESS (lĕs), *adj.* (The diminishing size or amount.) With palms facing, the right hand is held above the left. The right hand moves slowly down toward the left, but does not touch it. *Cf.* DECREASE, REDUCE.

LESSON (lĕs′ ən), *n.* (A section of a page.) The upturned open left hand represents the page. The little finger edge of the right-angle hand is placed on the left palm near the fingertips. It moves up and over, in an arc, to the base of the left palm.

LET (lĕt), *v.*, LET, LETTING, *n.* (A permissive upswinging of the hands, as if giving in.) Both hands, palms facing and fingers pointing away from the body, are held at chest level, almost a foot apart. With an upward movement, using their wrists as pivots, the hands sweep up until the fingers point almost straight up. *Cf.* ALLOW, GRANT 1, LET'S, LET US, MAY 3, PERMISSION 1, PERMIT 1.

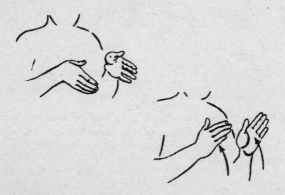

LET KNOW *v. phrase.* (Taking knowledge from the mind and giving it out to all.) The fingertips are positioned on either side of the forehead. Both hands then swing down and out, opening into the upturned "5" position. *Cf.* INFORM, INFORMATION, NOTIFY.

LET'S (lĕts); **LET US** *v. phrase.* See LET.

LETTER (lĕt′ ər), *n.* (The stamp is affixed.) The right thumb is placed on the tongue, and is then pressed into the open left palm. *Cf.* MAIL 1.

LEVEL (lĕv′ əl), *adj., n., v.,* -ELED, -ELING. (Sameness is stressed.) The downturned "B" hands, held at chest height, are brought together repeatedly, so that the index finger edges or fingertips come into contact. *Cf.* EQUAL, EQUIVALENT, EVEN, FAIR.

LIAR (lī′ ər), *n.* (Words diverted instead of coming straight, or truthfully, out.) The index finger of the right "D" hand, pointing to the left, moves along the lips from the right to left. *Cf.* FALSE, FALSEHOOD, LIE 1.

LIBRARY (lī′ brĕr′ ĭ), *n.* (The initial "L.") The right "L" hand, palm out, describes a small clockwise circle.

LICENSE (lī′ səns), *(loc.)*, *n.*, -CENSED, -CENSING. (The "L" hands outline the dimensions of the license form.) The "L" hands, palms out, touch at the thumbtips several times.

LIE 1 (lī), *n., v.,* LIED, LYING. (Words diverted instead of coming straight, or truthfully, out.) The index finger of the right "D" hand, pointing to the left, moves along the lips from right to left. *Cf.* FALSE, FALSEHOOD, LIAR.

LIE 2, *n., v.* (Same rationale as in LIE 1 but more emphatic, as indicated by several fingers.) The index finger edge of the downturned "B" hand moves along the lips (or under the chin) from right to left.

LIFE 1 (līf), *n.* (The fountain [of LIFE, *q.v.*] wells up from within the body.) The upturned thumbs of the "A" hands move in unison up the chest. *Cf.* ADDRESS, ALIVE, LIVE 1, LIVING, RESIDE.

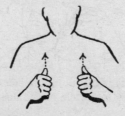

LIFE 2, *n.* (Same rationale as for LIFE 1 with the initials "L.")
The upturned thumbs of the "L" hands move in unison up the
chest. *Cf.* LIVE 2.

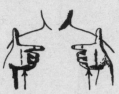

LIGHT 1 (līt), *adj.* (Easily lifted.) The open hands, palms up,
move up and down together in front of the body, as if lifting
something very light.

LIGHT 2, *n.* (The rays come out.) The downturned "8" hand,
positioned near the temple, flicks open a number of times.

LIGHT 3, *n.* (The rays come out.) *Cf.* LAMP.

LIKE 1 (līk), *v.*, LIKED, LIKING. (Drawing out the feelings.) The thumb and index finger of the right open hand, held an inch or two apart, are placed at mid-chest. As the hand moves straight out from the chest the two fingers come together.

LIKE 2, *adj., n.* (Matching fingers are brought together.) The outstretched index fingers are brought together, either once or several times. *Cf.* ALIKE, SAME 1, SIMILAR.

LIKE 3, *v*. (A pleasurable feeling on the heart.) The open right hand is circled on the chest, over the heart. *Cf.* ENJOY, ENJOYMENT, PLEASE, PLEASURE.

LIMIT (lĭm' ĭt), *n., v.*, LIMITED, LIMITING. (The upper and lower limits are defined.) The right-angle hands, palms facing, are held before the body, the right above the left. They swing out 45 degrees simultaneously, pivoted from their wrists. *Cf.* RESTRICT.

LIQUOR (lĭk' ər), *n*. (The act of drinking.) The thumbtip of the right "Y" hand is tilted toward the mouth, as if it were a drinking glass or bottle. The signer tilts his head back slightly, as if drinking. *Cf.* BEER, DRUNK, DRUNKARD, DRUNKENNESS, INTOXICATE, INTOXICATION.

LISTEN (lĭs′ ən), *v.*, -TENDED, -TENING. (Cupping the hand at the ear.) The right hand is placed, usually slightly cupped, behind the right ear.

LITTLE (lĭt′ əl), *adj., adv., n.* (A small or tiny movement.) The right thumbtip is flicked off the index finger several times, as if shooting marbles, although the movement is not so pronounced.

LIVE 1 (lĭv), *v.*, LIVED, LIVING. (The fountain [of LIFE, *q.v.*] wells up from within the body.) The upturned thumbs of the "A" hands move in unison up the chest. *Cf.* ADDRESS, ALIVE, LIFE 1, LIVING.

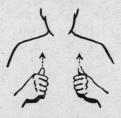

LIVE 2, *v.* See LIFE 2.

LIVING (lĭv′ ĭng), *adj.* See LIVE 1.

LIVING ROOM *n.* (Fine room.) The downturned "5" hand is placed with the thumb touching the chest. It moves repeatedly up and out an inch or two, returning each time to its initial position. This is followed by the sign for ROOM: the open hands, palms facing and fingers pointing out, are dropped an inch or two simultaneously. They then shift their relative positions so that both palms face the body, with one hand, in front of the other. In this new position they again drop an inch or two simultaneously. The "R" hands may be substituted for the open hands.

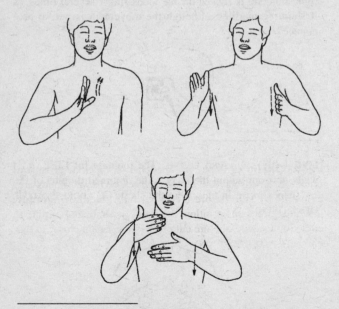

LOAN 1 (lōn), *n.* (Something kept, *i.e.*, in one's custody, is moved forward to other, temporary, ownership.) The crossed "K" hands, for KEEP, *q.v.*, are moved forward simultaneously, in a short arc. *Cf.* LEND 1.

_____

LOAN 2, *(loc.)*, *(colloq.)*, *n.*, *v.*, LOANED, LOANING. The side of the right index finger is brought up against the right side of the nose. *Cf.* LEND 2.

_____

LOCATION (lō kā′ shən), *n.* (The letter "P"; a circle or square is indicated, to show the locale or place.) The "P" hands are held side by side before the body, with middle fingertips touching. From this position, the hands separate and outline a circle (or a square), before coming together again closer to the body. *Cf.* PLACE, POSITION.

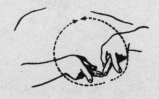

LOCK 1 (lŏk), *n., v.,* LOCKED, LOCKING. (The turning of the key.) The right hand, holding an imaginary key, twists it in the open left palm, which is facing right. *Cf.* KEY.

LOCK 2, *(loc.), v.* (Bind down.) The right "S" hand, palm down, makes a clockwise circle and comes down on the back of the left "S" hand, also held palm down.

LOCKED *(loc.), adj.* (Bound down to custom or habit.) Both "S" hands, palms down, are crossed and brought down in unison before the chest. *Cf.* CONVENTIONAL, CUSTOM, HABIT.

LOCK HORNS *sl. phrase.* (Clashing or banging together.)

Both downturned "Y" hands, representing horns, come together forcefully.

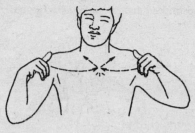

LONE (lōn), *adj.* (One, wandering around in a circle.) The index finger, pointing straight up, palm facing the body (the number *one*), is rotated before the face in a counterclockwise direction. *Cf.* ALONE, ONLY.

LONELY 1 (lōn′ lǐ), *adj.* ("Oneness"; quietness.) The index finger of the right "1" hand moves straight down across the lips once or twice. *Cf.* LONESOME.

LONELY 2, *(colloq.)*, *adj.* ("I" signs; *i.e.*, alone with oneself.) Both "I" hands are held facing the body, the little fingers upright and held an inch or two apart. The little fingers come together and separate repeatedly.

LONESOME (lōn′ səm), *adj.* See LONELY 1.

LONG (lông, lŏng), *adj. n.*, *adv.* (The distance is traced.) The right index finger traces a long line along the left arm from wrist almost to shoulder. *Cf.* LENGTH.

LOOK 1 (lŏŏk), *v.*, LOOKED, LOOKING. (The eyesight is directed forward.) The right "V" hand, palm facing the body, is placed so that the fingertips are just under the eyes. The hand swings around and out, so that the fingertips are now pointing forward. *Cf.* PERCEIVE, PERCEPTION, WATCH 1.

LOOK 2 (lŏŏk), *v.* (Something presented before the eyes.) The open right hand, palm flat and facing out, with fingers together and pointing up, is positioned at shoulder level. Pivoting from the wrist, the hand is swung around so that the palm now faces the eyes. Sometimes the eyes glance at the newly presented palm. *Cf.* SEEM.

LOOK FOR *v. phrase.* (Directing the vision from place to place; the French *chercher.*) The right "C" hand, palm facing left, moves from right to left across the line of vision, in a series of counterclockwise circles. The signer's gaze remains concentrated and his head turns slowly from right to left. *Cf.* EXAMINE, SEARCH, SEEK.

LOSE (lŏŏz), *v.,* LOST, LOSING. (Dropping something.) Both hands, with fingers touching their respective thumbs, are held palms up and with the backs of the fingers almost touching or in contact with one another. The hands drop into an open position, with fingers pointing down. *Cf.* LOST.

LOST (lôst, lŏst), *adj.* See LOSE.

LOUD (loud), *adj.* (Something heard which shakes the surrounding area.) The right index finger touches the ear. The "5" hands, palms down, then move sharply in front of the body, in quick alternate motions, first away from and then back to the body. *Cf.* LOUDLY, LOUD NOISE.

LOUDLY (loud′ lĭ), *adv.* See LOUD.

LOUD NOISE *n. phrase.* See LOUD.

LOUSY (lou′ zĭ), *(sl.), adj.* (A modification of the sign for spitting or thumbing the nose.) The right "3" hand is held with thumbtip against the nose. Then it is thrown sharply forward, and an expression of contempt is assumed.

LOVE (lŭv), *n., v.,* LOVED, LOVING. (Clasping the heart.) The "5" hands are held one atop the other over the heart.

Sometimes the "S" hands are used, in which case they are crossed at the wrists.

LOVER (lŭv' ər), *(colloq.)*, *n.* (Heads nodding toward each other.) The "A" hands are placed together before the body with thumbs up. The thumbs wiggle up and down. *Cf.* SWEETHEART.

LUGGAGE (lŭg' ĭj), *n.* (The natural sign.) The downturned right "S" hand grasps an imaginary piece of luggage and shakes it up and down slightly, as if testing its weight.

M

MACHINE (mə shēn'), *n.* (The meshing gears.) With the knuckles of both hands interlocked, the hands pivot up and down, imitating the meshing of gear teeth. *Cf.* ENGINE, MOTOR 1.

MAD (măd), *adj.* (A violent welling-up of the emotions.) The curved fingers of the right hand are placed in the center of the chest, and fly up suddenly and violently. An expression of anger is worn. *Cf.* ANGER, ANGRY 2, FURY, RAGE.

MAIL 1 (māl), *n.* (The stamp is affixed.) The right thumb is placed on the tongue, and is then pressed into the open left palm. *Cf.* LETTER.

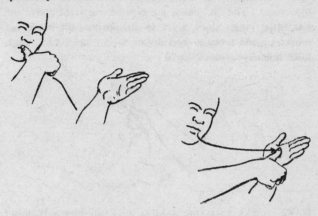

MAIL 2, *v.*, MAILED, MAILING. (Sending a letter.) The sign for LETTER is made: The right thumbtip is licked and placed against the upturned left palm. The right hand, palm out and fingers touching thumb, is then thrown forward, opening into the "5" position, palm out.

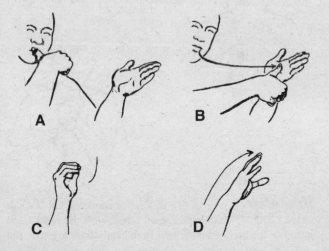

MAINTAIN (măn tān′), *v.*, -TAINED, -TAINING. (Slow, careful movement.) The "K" hands are crossed, the right above the left, little finger edges down. In this position the hands are moved up and down a short distance. *Cf.* CARE 2, CAREFUL 2, KEEP, PRESERVE, TAKE CARE OF.

MAKE (māk), *v.*, MADE, MAKING, *n.* (Fashioning something with the hands.) The right "S" hand, palm facing left, is placed on top of its left counterpart, whose palm faces right. The hands are twisted back and forth, striking each other slightly after each twist. *Cf.* CREATE, MEND, PRODUCE.

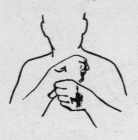

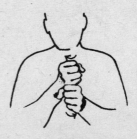

MAKE BRIEF *v. phrase.* (To squeeze or condense into a small space.) The "C" hands face each other, with the right hand nearer to the body than the left. Both hands draw together and

close deliberately, squeezing an imaginary object. *Cf.* SUMMA-
RIZE 1, SUMMARY 1.

MAKE LOVE *(sl.), v. phrase.* (Necks interlocked.) The "S"
hands, palms facing, are crossed at the wrists. They swing up
and down while the wrists remain in contact. *Cf.* NECKING.

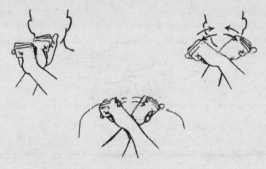

MALE (māl), *n., adj.* (The man's cap.) The thumb and extended fingers of the right hand are brought up to grasp an imaginary cap brim, representing the tipping of caps by men in
olden days. This is a root sign used to modify many others.
Viz.: MALE plus BABY: SON; MALE plus SAME: BROTH-
ER; etc. *Cf.* MAN, MANKIND.

MAN (măn), *n*. See MALE.

MANAGE (măn′ ĭj), *v*., -AGED, -AGING. (Holding the reins over all.) The "A" hands, palms facing, move alternately back and forth, as if grasping and manipulating reins. The left "A" hand, still in position, swings over so that its palm now faces down. The right hand opens to the "5" position, palm down, and swings over the left which moves slightly to the right. *Cf.* CONTROL 1, GOVERN, RULE.

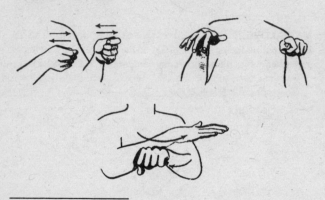

MANKIND (măn′ kīnd′), *n*. See MALE.

MANY (mĕn′ ĭ), *adj*. (*Many* fingers are indicated.) The upturned "S" hands are thrown up, opening into the "5" position, palms up. This may be repeated. *Cf.* NUMEROUS, QUANTITY.

MARBLE (mär′ bəl), *n*. (Flicking a marble ball, as in a child's game.) The signer uses the thumb to "flick" a marble ball forward. The action is repeated. This sign is used for both the ball and the stone used in building and sculpture.

MARRIAGE (măr′ ĭj), *n*. (A clasping of hands, as during the wedding ceremony.) The hands are clasped together, the right on top of the left. *Cf.* MARRY.

MARRY (măr′ ĭ), *v*., -RIED, -RYING. See MARRIAGE.

MATURE (mə tyŏŏr′, -tŏŏr′), *adj., n*. (Growing up.) The index finger edge of the right "M" hand, palm facing down, moves up the outstretched upright left palm.

MAXIMUM (mak′ sə məm), *adj.* Both hands, in the "M" position, are held palms down, fingertips touching. The right hand rises above the left.

MAY 1 (mā), *v.* (Weighing one thing against another.) The upturned open hands move alternately up and down. *Cf.* MAYBE, MIGHT 2, PERHAPS, POSSIBILITY, POSSIBLY, PROBABLE, PROBABLY.

MAY 2, *v.* (An affirmative movement of the hands, likened to a nodding of the head, to indicate ability or power to accomplish something.) Both "A" hands, held palms down, move down in unison a short distance before the chest. *Cf.* CAN, CAPABLE, POSSIBLE.

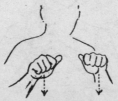

MAY 3, *v.* (A permissive upswinging of the hands, as if giving in.) Both hands, palms facing and fingers pointing away from the body, are held at chest level, almost a foot apart. With an upward movement, using their wrists as pivots, the hands sweep up until the fingers point almost straight up. *Cf.* ALLOW, GRANT 1, LET, LET'S, LET US, PERMISSION 1, PERMIT 1.

MAYBE (mā′ bĭ, -bē), *adv.* See MAY 1.

MAYONNAISE (mā ə nāz′), *n.* (The letter "M"; spreading.) The downturned right "M" hand "spreads" the mayonnaise on the upturned left palm.

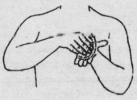

MCDONALD'S (mək don′ ədz), *n.* (The letter "M"; the arches of the well-known hamburger place.) The right "M" hand describes one or two arches along the back of the downturned left hand.

ME (mē; *unstressed* mǐ), *pron.* (The natural sign.) The signer points to himself. *Cf.* I 2.

MEAL (mēl), *n.* (The natural sign.) The closed right hand goes through the natural motion of placing food in the mouth. This movement is repeated. *Cf.* EAT, FEED 1, FOOD.

MEAN 1 (mēn), *adj.* (Striking down against.) Both "A" or "X" hands are held before the chest, the right above the left. The right hand strikes down and out, hitting the left thumb and knuckles with force. *Cf.* CRUEL.

MEAN 2, *v.,* MEANT, MEANING. (Relative standing of one's thoughts.) A modified sign for THINK is made: The right index finger touches the middle of the forehead. The tips of the right "V" hand, palm down, are then thrust into the upturned left palm (as in STAND, *q.v.*). The right "V" hand is then re-thrust into the upturned left palm, with right palm now facing the body. *Cf.* INTEND, INTENT, INTENTION, MEANING, PURPOSE, SIGNIFICANCE 2, SIGNIFY.

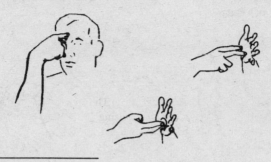

MEANING (mē' nǐng), *n.* See MEAN 2.

MEANTIME (mēn' tīm´), *n., adv.* (Parallel time.) Both "D" hands, palms down, move forward in unison, away from the body. They may move straight forward or may follow a slight upward arc. *Cf.* DURING, WHILE.

MEAT (mēt), *n.* (The fleshy part of the hand.) The right index finger and thumb squeeze the fleshy part of the open left hand, between thumb and index finger.

MEDDLE (med′ 'l), *v.*, -DLED, -DLING. (The nose is poked into something.) The sign for NOSE is formed by touching the tip of the nose with the index finger. The sign for IN, INTO follows: The right hand, fingertips touching the thumb, is thrust into the left "C" hand, which closes a bit over the right fingers as they enter.

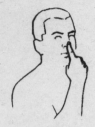

MEDICINE (med′ ə sən), *n.* (Mixing of medicine; rolling a pill.) The ball of the middle fingertip of the right "5" hand describes a small counterclockwise circle in the upturned left palm.

MEET (mēt), *v.*, MET, MEETING. (A coming together of two persons.) Both "D" hands, palms facing each other, are brought together.

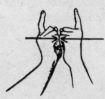

MEETING (mē′ tǐng), *n*. (Assemble all together.) Both "5" hands, palms facing, are held with fingers pointing out from the body. With a sweeping motion they are brought in toward the chest, and all fingertips come together. This is repeated. *Cf.* CONFERENCE, GATHER 2, GATHERING.

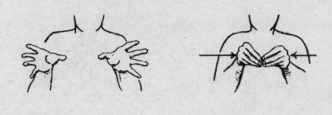

MELT (mĕlt), *v.*, MELTED, MELTING. (Fingering the small pieces resulting from the breaking up of something.) The thumbs rub slowly across the fingertips of the upturned hands, from the little fingers to the index fingers, and then continue to the "A" position, palms up. *Cf.* DISSOLVE.

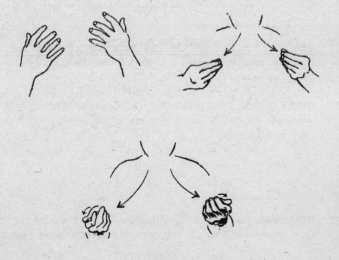

MEMBER 1 (měm′ bər), *n.* (Linked together.) The sign for
JOIN is made: Both hands, held in the modified "5" position,
palms out, move toward each other. The thumbs and index fingers of both hands then connect. This is followed by the sign
for INDIVIDUAL: Both open hands, palms facing each other,
move down the sides of the body, tracing its outline to the
hips.

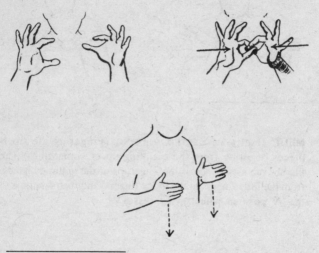

MEMBER 2, *n.* The right "M" hand, palm facing the body and
fingers pointing left, moves from the left shoulder to the right.

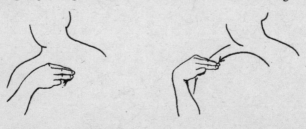

MEMORIAL (mə môr′ ā əl), *n.* (Looking back.) The right "M"
hand, positioned near the right temple, moves straight back

over the shoulder.

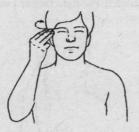

MEMORIZE (mĕm′ ə rīz´), v., -RIZED, -RIZING. (Holding on to knowledge.) The open right hand is placed on the forehead. Then as it is removed straight forward, it is clenched into a fist.

MEND (mĕnd), v., MENDED, MENDING. (Fashioning something with the hands.) The right "S" hand, palm facing left, is placed on top of its left counterpart, whose palm faces right. The hands are twisted back and forth, striking each other slightly after each twist. Cf. CREATE, MAKE, PRODUCE.

MENTAL (měn′ təl), *adj.* (Patting the head to indicate something of value inside.) The right fingers pat the forehead several times. *Cf.* MIND 1.

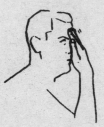

MENTALLY LIMITED *adj.* (The limits, upper and lower, of the mind.) The signer touches the forehead with the right index finger. The two hands are then held palms facing down, the right positioned an inch or so above the left. Both hands move straight forward a short distance.

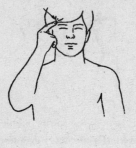

MENTION (měn′ shən), *v.*, -TIONED, -TIONING. (Words tumbling from the mouth.) The right index finger, pointing left, describes a continuous small circle in front of the mouth. *Cf.*

HEARING, SAID, SAY, SPEAK, SPEECH 1, TALK 1, TELL.

MERCY (mûr′ sĭ), *n.* (Feelings from the heart, conferred on others.) The middle fingertip of the open right hand touches the chest over the heart. The same open hand then moves in a small, clockwise circle before the right shoulder, with palm facing forward and fingers pointing up. *Cf.* PITY, SYMPATHY.

MERRY (mĕr′ ĭ), *adj.* (The heart is stirred; the spirits bubble up.) The open right hand, palm facing the body, strikes the heart repeatedly, moving up and off the heart after each strike. *Cf.* GLAD, HAPPY, JOY.

METER (mě′ tər), *n.* (Measuring.) Both "M" hands, palms out and hands touching, move apart a short distance.

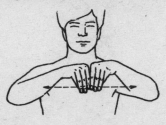

ME TOO *(colloq.).* (Two figures are compared, back and forth.) The right "Y" hand, palm facing left, is moved alternately toward and away from the body. *Cf.* SAME 2.

MICROPHONE (mī′ krə fōn), *n.* (Holding a microphone.) The signer mimes holding a microphone in front of the face.

MIDDAY (mǐd′ dā′), *n.* (The sun is directly overhead.) The right "B" hand, palm facing left, is held upright in a vertical

position, its elbow resting on the back of the open left hand.
Cf. NOON.

MIDDLE (mǐd′ əl), *adj.* (The natural sign.) The downturned
right fingers describe a small clockwise circle and come to rest
in the center of the upturned left palm. *Cf.* CENTER, CENTRAL.

MIDNIGHT (mǐd′ nīt′), *n.* (The sun is directly opposite the
NOON position, *q.v.*) The right "B" hand is held fingers pointing straight down and palm facing left. The left hand, representing the horizon, is held open and fingers together, palm
down, its little finger edge resting against the right arm near
the crook of the elbow.

MIGHT 1 (mīt), *n.* (Flexing the muscles.) With fists clenched, palms facing back, the signer raises both arms and shakes them once, with force. *Cf.* MIGHTY 1, POWER 1, POWERFUL 1, STRONG.

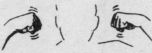

MIGHT 2, *v.* (Weighing one thing against another.) The upturned open hands move alternately up and down. *Cf.* MAY 1, MAYBE, PERHAPS, POSSIBILITY, POSSIBLY, PROBABLE, PROBABLY.

MIGHTY 1 (mī′ tǐ), *adj.* See MIGHT 1.

MIGHTY 2, *adj.* (Strength emanating from the body.) Both "5" hands are placed palms against the chest. They move out and away, forcefully, closing and assuming the "S" position. *Cf.* BRAVE, BRAVERY, HEALTH, HEALTHY, STRENGTH, WELL.

MILK (mǐlk), *n., v.,* MILKED, MILKING. (The act of milking a cow.) Both hands, alternately grasping and releasing imaginary teats, move alternately up and down before the body.

MILLIGRAM (mil′ ə gram), *n*. (The letters "M" and "G";
weighing on a beam balance.) The right "M" hand, positioned
on the knuckle of the lcft index finger, moves forward toward
the left index fingertip, while changing to the "G."

MILLIMETER (mil′ ə mē tər), *n*. (The letters "M.") Both "M"
hands are held with index fingers touching. They move apart a
short distance, dropping down slightly as they do.

MILLION (mĭl′ yən), *n., adj.* (A thousand thousands.) The fingertips of the right "M" hand, palm down, are thrust twice into the upturned left palm, first at the base of the palm and then near the base of the left fingers. (The "M" stands for *mille,* the Latin word for *thousand.*)

MIND 1 (mīnd), *n.* (Patting the head to indicate something of value inside.) The right fingers pat the forehead several times. *Cf.* MENTAL.

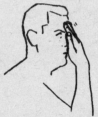

MIND 2, *n.* (Directing one's attention forward; applying oneself; concentrating.) Both hands, fingers pointing up and together, are held at the sides of the face. They move straight out from the face. *Cf.* CONCENTRATE, CONCENTRATION, FOCUS, PAY ATTENTION (TO).

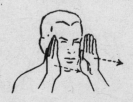

MINE (mīn), *pron.* (Pressing something to one's bosom.) The "5" hand is brought up against the chest. *Cf.* MY.

MINGLE (mǐng′ gəl), *v.*, -GLED, -GLING. (Mingling with.) Both hands are held in modified "A" positions, thumbs out. The left hand is positioned with its thumb pointing straight up, and the right hand, with its thumb pointing down, revolves above the left thumb in a clockwise direction. *Cf.* EACH OTHER, ONE ANOTHER.

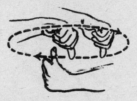

MINIMUM (min′ ē əm), *adj., n.* (The space limitations; the letter "M.") Both "M" hands are held one above the other, palms facing down. The top hand moves down to rest on the back of the bottom hand.

MINUTE (mĭn' ĭt), *n.* (The minute hand of a clock.) The right "D" hand is held with its index finger edge against the palm of the left "5" hand, which faces right. The right index finger moves forward in a short arc. *Cf.* MOMENT.

MISSING (mĭs' ĭng), *adj.* The extended right index finger strikes against the downturned middle finger of the left hand, which is held with palm down and other fingers pointing right.

MISTAKE (mĭs tāk'), *n.* (Rationale obscure; the thumb and little finger are said to represent, respectively, right and wrong, with the head poised between the two.) The right "Y" hand, palm facing the body, is brought up to the chin. *Cf.* ERROR, WRONG.

MISUNDERSTAND (mĭs´ ŭn dər stănd´), v., -STOOD, -STAND-
ING. (The thought is twisted around.) The right "V" hand is
positioned with index and middle fingers touching the right
side of the forehead. The hand swings around so that the palm
now faces out, with the two fingers still on the forehead.

MIX (mĭks), n., v., MIXED, MIXING. (Scrambling or mixing up.)
The downturned right hand is positioned above the upturned
left. The fingers of both are curved. Both hands move in opposite horizontal circles. Cf. COMPLICATE, CONFUSE, CONFUSED,
CONFUSION, MIXED, MIXED UP, MIX-UP.

MIXED (mĭkst), adj. See MIX.

MIXED UP adj. phrase. See MIX.

MIX-UP (mĭks´ ŭp´), n. See MIX.

MOB (mob), *n.* (Many people spread out.) The downturned claw hands move straight forward. *Cf.* CROWD.

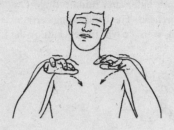

MODERN (mod' ərn), *adj.* (A new leaf is turned.) With both hands held palm up before the body, the right hand sweeps in an arc into the left, and continues up a bit.

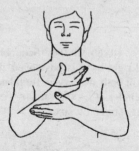

MOMENT (mō' mənt), *n.* (The minute hand of a clock.) The right "D" hand is held with its index finger edge against the palm of the left "5" hand, which faces right. The right index finger moves forward in a short arc. *Cf.* MINUTE.

MONEY 1 (mŭn′ ĭ), *n.* (Slapping of paper money in the palm.) The upturned right hand, grasping some imaginary bills, is brought down into the upturned left palm a number of times.

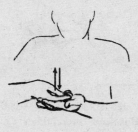

MONEY 2, *n.* (Fingering the money.) The thumb rubs over the index and middle fingers of the upturned hand, as if fingering money.

MONSTER (mon′ stər), *n.* (The characteristic gestures of children trying to frighten others.) Both claw hands are held palms out in a threatening way. The signer grimaces and shows the teeth.

MONTH (mŭnth), *n.* (The tip and three joints represent the four weeks of a month.) The extended right index finger moves down along the upturned, extended left index finger.

MONTHLY (mŭnth′ lĭ), *adj., adv.* (Month after month.) The sign for MONTH is made several times. *Cf.* RENT.

MOON (mōōn), *n.* (The face only.) The right "C" hand indicates the face of the moon.

MORE (mōr), *adj., n., adv.* (One hand is added to the other; an addition.) Both hands, palms facing, are held fingers together, the left a bit above the right. The right hand is brought up to the left until their fingertips touch.

MORNING (môr' nǐng), *n.* (The sun comes over the horizon.) The little finger edge of the left hand rests in the crook of the right elbow. The left arm, held horizontally, represents the horizon. The open right hand, fingers together and pointing up, with palm facing the body, rises slowly to an almost upright angle.

MOTHER 1 (mŭth' ər), *n.* (A female who carries a baby.) The FEMALE root sign is made: The thumb of the right "A" hand moves down along the line of the right jaw, from ear almost to chin. Both hands are then held open and palms facing up, as if holding a baby. This is the formal sign.

MOTHER 2, (*colloq.*), *n.* (Derived from the FEMALE root sign.) The thumb of the right "5" hand rests on the right cheek or on the right chin bone. The other fingers wiggle slightly. Or the thumb is thrust repeatedly into the right side of the face, and the rest of the hand remains open and in the "5" position, palm facing out. This latter modification is used for MAMA.

MOTIVATE (mō′ tə vāt′), *v.*, -VATED, -VATING. (Pushing forward.) Both "5" hands are held, palms out, the right fingers facing right and the left fingers left. The hands move straight forward in a series of short movements. *Cf.* ENCOURAGE, MOTIVATION, URGE 1.

MOTIVATION (mō′ tə vā′ shən), *n.* See MOTIVATE.

MOTOR 1 (mō′ tər), *n.* (The meshing gears.) With the knuckles of both hands interlocked, the hands pivot up and down, imitating the meshing of gear teeth. *Cf.* ENGINE, MACHINE.

MOTOR 2 , *n.* (The pistons moving.) Both upturned fists move alternately up and down.

MOVE (mōōv), *n., v.,* MOVED, MOVING. (Moving from one place to another.) The downturned hands, fingers touching their respective thumbs, move in unison from left to right. *Cf.* PUT.

MOVIE(S) (mōō′ vĭ), *n.* (The frames of the film speeding through the projector.) The left "5" hand, palm facing right and thumb pointing up, is the projector. The right "5" hand is placed against the left, and moves back and forth quickly. *Cf.* FILM, MOVING PICTURE.

MOVING PICTURE See MOVIE(S).

_____

MOW (mō), *v.* (The clipping blades.) The downturned right "5" hand rests on its downturned left counterpart. Both hands move quickly back and forth over each other, imitating opposite moving blades for cutting grass or hair.

_____

MUCH (mŭch), *adj., adv.* (A large amount.) The "5" hands face each other, fingers curved and touching. They move apart rather quickly. *Cf.* EXPAND, GREAT 1.

_____

MUG (mug), *n.* (Holding the handle and tipping the mug to the mouth.) The little finger of the right "Y" hand rests on the upturned left palm. The "Y" hand moves up to the mouth, as if tipping the contents of the mug into the mouth.

MULL OVER *v. phrase.* (Many thoughts turn over in the mind.) The right hand makes a continuous counterclockwise circle in front of the head. Meanwhile, the fingers wriggle continuously.

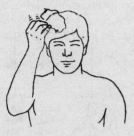

MULTIPLY (mŭl′ tə plī′), *v.,* -PLIED, -PLYING. (A multiplying.) The "V" hands, palms facing the body, alternately cross and separate, several times. *Cf.* FIGURE 1.

MURDER (mûr′ dər), *n.* (Thrusting a dagger and twisting it.) The outstretched right index finger is passed under the downturned left hand. As it moves under the left hand, the right wrist twists in a clockwise direction. *Cf.* KILL.

MUSEUM (myo͞o zē′ əm), *n.* (The letter "M"; a house or building.) With both hands forming the letter "M," the signer traces the outline of the roof and walls.

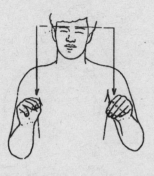

MUSHROOM (mush′ ro͞om), *n.* (The stem and cap.) The downturned right claw hand is positioned on top of the left index finger.

MUSIC (mū′ zĭk), *n.* (A rhythmic, wavy movement of the hand, to indicate a melody; the movement of a conductor's hand in directing a musical performance.) The right "5" hand, palm facing left, is waved back and forth next to the left hand, in a series of elongated figure-eights. *Cf.* SING, SONG.

MUST (mŭst), *aux. v.* (Being pinned down.) The right hand, in the "X" position, palm down, moves forcefully up and down once or twice. An expression of determination is frequently assumed. *Cf.* HAVE TO, NECESSARY 1, NECESSITY, NEED 1, OUGHT TO, SHOULD.

MY (mī), *pron.* (Pressing something to one's bosom.) The "5" hand is brought up against the chest. *Cf.* MINE.

MYSELF (mĭ sĕlf′), *pron.* (The thumb represents the self.) The upturned thumb of the right "A" hand is brought up against the chest.

N

NAG (năg), *v.*, NAGGED, NAGGING. (The hen's beak pecks.) The index finger and thumb of the right hand, held together, are brought against the index finger of the left "D" hand a number of times. *Cf.* PICK ON.

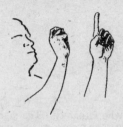

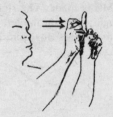

NAKED (nā′ kĭd), *adj.* (Devoid of everything on the surface.) The middle finger of the downturned right "5" hand sweeps over the back of the downturned left "A" or "S" hand, from wrist to knuckles, and continues beyond a bit. *Cf.* NUDE.

NAME (nām), *n., v.,* NAMED, NAMING. (The "X" used by illiterates in writing their names. This sign is indicative of widespread illiteracy when the language of signs first began to evolve as an instructional medium in deaf education.) The right "H" hand, palm facing left, is brought down on the left "H" hand, palm facing right.

NAMED *v.* (NAME, indicating who is named.) The sign for NAME is made: The right "H" hand, palm facing left, is brought down on the left "H" hand, palm facing right. The hands, in this position, move forward a few inches. *Cf.* CALLED.

NARRATE (nă rāt′, năr′ ăt), *v.,* -RATED, -RATING. (The unraveling or stretching out of words or sentences.) Both open hands are held close to each other, with fingers open and palms facing and almost touching. As the hands are drawn apart, the thumb and index finger of each hand come together to form circles. This is repeated several times. *Cf.* NARRATIVE, STORY, TALE.

NARRATIVE (năr′ ə tĭv), *n*. See NARRATE.

NATION (nā′ shən), *n*. (An established area.) The right "N" hand, palm down, executes a clockwise circle above the down-turned prone left hand. The tips of the "N" fingers then move straight down and come to rest on the back of the left hand. *Cf.* COUNTRY 2, LAND 2, REPUBLIC.

NEAR (nĭr), *adv., prep.* (One hand is near the other.) The left hand, cupped, fingers together, is held before the chest, palm facing the body. The right hand, also cupped, fingers together, moves a very short distance back and forth, as it is held in front of the left. *Cf.* CLOSE (TO) 2.

NECESSARY (něs′ ə sěr′ ĭ), *adj.* (Being pinned down.) The right hand, in the "X" position, palm down, moves forcefully up and down once or twice. An expression of determination is frequently assumed. *Cf.* HAVE TO, MUST, NECESSITY, NEED 1, OUGHT TO, SHOULD.

NECESSITY (nə sĕs′ ə tĭ), *n.* See NECESSARY.

NECKING (nĕk′ ĭng), *(sl.), n.* (Necks interlocked.) The "S" hands, palms facing, are crossed at the wrists. They swing up and down while the wrists remain in contact. *Cf.* MAKE LOVE.

NEED 1 (nēd), *n., v.,* NEEDED, NEEDING. (Being pinned down.) The right hand, in the "X" position, palm down, moves forcefully up and down once or twice. An expression of determination is frequently assumed. *Cf.* HAVE TO, MUST, NECESSARY, NECESSITY, OUGHT TO, SHOULD, VITAL 2.

NEED 2, *n.* (Grasping something and pulling it in.) The upturned "5" hands, held side by side before the chest, close slightly into a grasping position as they move in toward the body. *Cf.* DESIRE, WANT, WISH 1.

NEEDLE (nĕd′ l), *n.* (The natural sign.) The signer mimes threading a needle and pulling the thread through the hole.

NEPHEW (nĕf′ ū), *n.* (The initial "N"; the upper or masculine portion of the head.) The right "N" hand, held near the right temple, shakes slightly or pivots at the wrist.

NERVOUS (nûr′ vəs), *adj.* (The trembling fingers.) Both "5" hands, held palm down, tremble noticeably.

NETWORK(ING) (net´ wûrk), *n., v.* (Remaining in contact.)
The middle fingers of both "5" hands touch and both hands
move together in a large counterclockwise circle.

NEVER (nĕv´ ər), *adv.* The open right hand, fingers together
and palm facing out, moves in a short arc from left to right,
and then straight down. The movement is likened to forming a
question mark or an "S" in the air.

NEVERTHELESS (nĕv´ ər ŧħə lĕs´), *adv.* Both hands, in the
"5" position, are held before the chest, fingertips facing each

other. With an alternate back-forth movement, the fingertips are made to strike each other. *Cf.* HOWEVER.

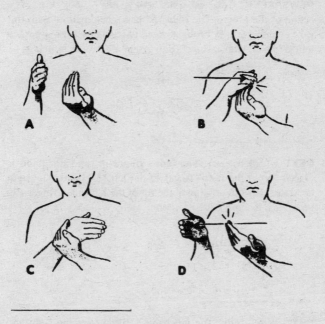

NEW (nū, nōō), *adj.* (Turning over a new leaf.) With both hands held palm up before the body, the right hand sweeps in an arc into the left, and continues up a bit. *Cf.* NEWS.

NEWS (nūz, n$\overline{oo}$z), *n.* See NEW.

NEWSPAPER (nūz′ pā´ pər, n$\overline{oo}$z′-, nūs′-, n$\overline{oo}$s′-), *n.* (The action of the press.) The right "5" hand, held palm down, fingers pointing left, is brought down twice against the upturned left "5" hand, whose fingers point right. *Cf.* PAPER, PUBLISH.

NEXT 1 (někst), *adj.* The index finger of the right hand is placed across the index finger of the left "L" hand. The right hand then flips over, around the tip of the left index finger and up against its underside.

NEXT 2, *adj., adv.* The left hand is lifted over the right and placed down in front of the right palm.

NEXT WEEK *adv. phrase.* The upright, right "D" hand is placed palm-to-palm against the left "5" hand, whose palm faces right. The right "D" hand moves along the left palm from base to fingertips and then beyond in an arc.

NEXT YEAR *adv. phrase.* (A year in the future.) The right "S" hand, palm facing left, is brought forcefully down to rest on the upturned thumb edge of the left "S" hand, which is held with palm facing right. (*Cf.* YEAR.) From this position the right hand moves forward with index finger extended and pointing ahead.

NIBBLE (nib′ əl), *v., n.* (Small bites.) The right fingertips make a series of small "bites" against the index finger edge of the downturned left hand.

NICE (nīs), *adj.* (Everything is wiped off the hand, to emphasize an uncluttered or clean condition.) The right hand slowly
wipes the upturned left palm, from wrist to fingertips. *Cf.*
CLEAN, PLAIN 2, PURE, PURITY.

NIECE (nēs), *n.* (The initial "N"; the lower or feminine portion of the head.) The right "N" hand, held near the right side
of the jaw, shakes slightly, or pivots at the wrist.

NIGHT (nīt), *n.* (The sun drops beneath the horizon.) The left
hand, palm down, is positioned at chest height. The downturned right hand, held an inch or so above the left, moves
over the left hand in an arc, as the sun setting beneath the horizon.

NIGHTMARE (nīt′ mâr), *n.* (Bad dream.) The sign for BAD is
made: the tips of the right "B" hand are placed at the lips and
then the hand is thrown down. This is followed by the sign for
DREAM: the right curved index finger opens and closes

quickly and continuously as it leaves its initial position on the forehead and moves up into the air.

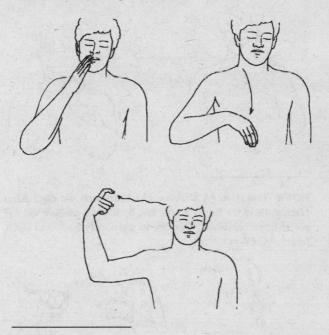

NO (nō), *interj.* (The letters "N" and "O".) The index and middle fingers of the right "N" hand are held raised, and are then lowered against the extended right thumb, in a modified "O" position.

NO GOOD (nō gŏŏd'), *phrase.* (A fingerspelled loan sign.) The letters "N-G" are fingerspelled.

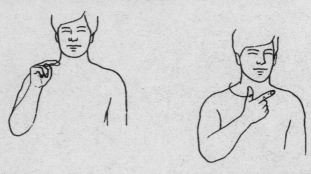

NOISE (noiz), *n.* (A shaking which disturbs the ear.) After placing the index finger on the ear, both hands assume the "S" position, palms down. They move alternately back and forth, forcefully. *Cf.* NOISY.

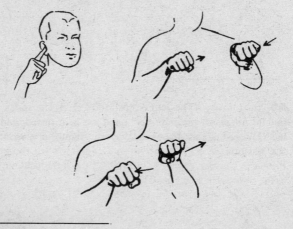

NOISY (noi′ zǐ), *adj.* See NOISE.

NOMINATE (nom′ ə nāt), *v.* (The "N" letters; offering something up front.) The "N" hands, palms up, move forward alternately, tracing continuous elliptical paths.

NONE 1 (nŭn), *adj.* (The zeros.) Both "O" hands, palms facing, are thrown out and down into the "5" position. *Cf.* NOTH-ING 1.

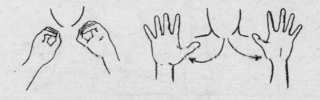

NONE 2, *adj.* (The "O" hands.) Both "O" hands are crossed at the wrists before the chest, thumb edges toward the body. From this position the hands draw apart, the right hand moving to the right and the left hand to the left.

 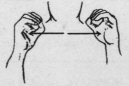

NONSENSE (nŏn′ sĕns), *n.* (Thoughts flickering back and forth.) The right "Y" hand, thumb almost touching the forehead, is shaken back and forth across the forehead several times. *Cf.* FOOLISH, RIDICULOUS, SILLY.

NOON (no͞on), *n.* (The sun is directly overhead.) The right "B" hand, palm facing left, is held upright in a vertical position, its elbow resting on the back of the open left hand. *Cf.* MIDDAY.

NOSY (nŏ′ zĭ), *(sl.), adj.* (A big nose.) The right index finger, after resting on the tip of the nose, moves forward and then back to the nose, in an oval, as if tracing a long extension of the nose.

NOT 1 (not), *adv.* (Crossing the hands a negative gesture.) The downturned open hands are crossed. They are drawn apart rather quickly.

NOT 2, *adv.* The right "A" hand is placed with the tip of the upturned thumb under the chin. The hand draws out and forward in a slight arc.

NOTHING 1 (nŭth′ ĭng), *n.* (The zeros.) Both "O" hands, palms facing, are thrown out and down into the "5" position. *Cf.* NONE 1.

NOTHING 2, *n.* (The zeros.) Both "O" hands, palms facing, move back and forth a number of times, the right hand to the right and the left hand to the left.

NOTIFY (nō′ tə fī′), *v.*, -FIED, -FYING. (Taking knowledge from the mind and giving it out to all.) The fingertips are positioned on either side of the forehead. Both hands then swing down and out, opening into the upturned "5" position. *Cf.* INFORM, INFORMATION, LET KNOW.

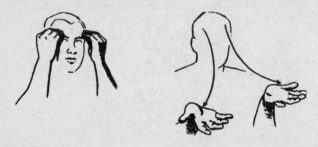

NOT YET *phrase.* (Hanging back.) The "5" hand and forearm, hanging loosely and straight down from the elbow, move back and forth under the armpit. *Cf.* LATE.

NOW (nou), *adv.* (Something right in front of you.) The upturned right-angle hands drop down rather sharply. The "Y" hands may also be used. *Cf.* PRESENT 3.

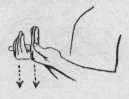

NOW AND THEN *adv. phrase.* (Forward in slow, deliberate movements.) The right hand, palm facing the signer, fingers pointing left, makes a series of small forward movements, describing a small arc each time. *Cf.* FROM TIME TO TIME, ONCE IN A WHILE.

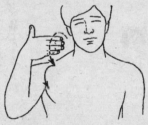

NUCLEAR (nōō′ klē ər), *adj.* (The letter "N"; around the world.) The right "N" hand makes a circle around the left "S" hand.

NUDE (nūd, nōōd), *adj.* (Devoid of everything on the surface.) The middle finger of the downturned right "5" hand sweeps over the back of the downturned left "A" or "S" hand, from wrist to knuckles, and continues beyond a bit. *Cf.* NAKED.

NUMEROUS (nū′ mər əs, nōō′-), *adj.* (Many fingers are indicated.) The upturned "S" hands are thrown up, opening into the "5" position, palms up. This may be repeated. *Cf.* MANY, QUANTITY.

O

OBEDIENCE (ō bē′ dǐ əns), *n.* (The hands are thrown open as an act of obeisance.) Both "A" hands, palms facing, are positioned at either side of the head. They are thrown open and out, ending in the "5" position, palms up. The head is bowed slightly at the same time. *Cf.* OBEDIENT, OBEY.

OBEDIENT (ō bē′ dǐ ənt), *adj.* See OBEDIENCE.

OBEY (ō bā′), *v.,* OBEYING, OBEYED. See OBEDIENCE.

OBJECT (əb jĕkt′), *v.,* -JECTED, -JECTING. (The hand is thrust into the chest to force a complaint out.) The curved fingers of the right hand are thrust forcefully into the chest. *Cf.* COMPLAIN, COMPLAINT, OBJECTION, PROTEST.

OBJECTION (əb jĕk′ shən), *n.* See OBJECT.

OBSERVE 1 (əb zûrv′), *v.*, -SERVED, -SERVING. (The vision is directed forward.) The tips of the right "V" fingers point to the eyes. The right hand is then swung around and forward a bit.

OBSERVE 2, *v.* (The vision is directed all over.) Both "V" hands, pointing out, are moved alternately in different directions.

OBVIOUS (ŏb′ vĭ əs), *adj.* (Rays of light clearing the way.) Both hands are held at chest height, palms out, all fingertips together. They open into the "5" position in unison, the right hand moving toward the right and the left toward the left. The palms of both hands remain facing out. *Cf.* CLEAR, EVIDENT, PLAIN 1.

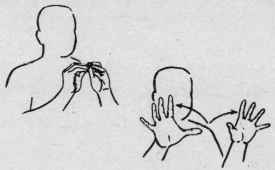

OCCASIONAL (ə kā′ zhən əl), *adj.* (The "1" finger is brought up very slowly.) The right index finger, resting in the open left palm, which is facing right, swings up slowly from its position to one in which it is pointing straight up. The movement is repeated slowly, after a pause. *Cf.* OCCASIONALLY, ONCE IN A WHILE, SOMETIME(S).

OCCASIONALLY (ə kā′ zhən ə lĭ), *adv.* See OCCASIONAL.

ODD (ŏd), *adj.* (Something which distorts the vision.) The "C" hand describes a small arc in front of the face. *Cf.* CURIOUS 1, STRANGE, WEIRD.

ODOR (ō′ dər), *n.* (Bringing something up to the nose.) The upturned right hand moves slowly up to and past the nose, and the signer breathes in as the hand sweeps by. *Cf.* SMELL.

OFFER (ôf′ ər), *v.*, -FERED, -FERING. (An offering; a presenting.) Both hands, slightly cupped, palms up, are held close to the chest. They move up and out in unison, describing a very slight arc. *Cf.* OFFERING, PRESENT 1, PROPOSE, SUGGEST.

OFFERING (ôf′ ər ĭng), *n.* See OFFER.

OFF THE SUBJECT *phrase.* (Deviating.) The left index finger is held either straight up or pointing forward. The right index finger moves sharply off to the left, striking the left index as it does.

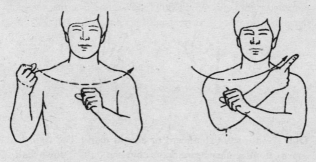

OFTEN (ôf′ ən, ŏf′ ən), *adv.* The left hand, open in the "5" position, palm up, is held before the chest. The right hand, in the right-angle position, fingers pointing up, arches over and into the left palm. This is repeated several times. *Cf.* FREQUENT.

O.K. 1 (ō′ kā′), *adj., adv.* (Λ straightening out.) The right hand, fingers together and palm facing left, is placed in the upturned left palm, whose fingers point away from the body. The right hand slides straight out along the left palm, over the left fingers, and stops with its heel resting on the left finger-tips. *Cf.* ALL RIGHT, RIGHT 1, YOU'RE WELCOME 2.

O.K. 2 (*adj., adv.* ō´ kā´; *v., n.* ō´ kā ´), *(colloq.), phrase.* The letters "O" and "K" are fingerspelled.

OLD (ōld), *adj.* (The beard of an old man.) The right hand grasps an imaginary beard at the chin and pulls it downward.

OLYMPICS (ō lim´ pikz), *n.* (The interlocking circles of the Olympic logo.) The thumbs and index fingers of both hands interlock several times.

ON (ŏn, ôn), *prep.* (Placing one hand on the other.) The right hand is placed on the back of the downturned left hand.

ONCE IN A WHILE *adv. phrase.* (The "1" finger is brought up very slowly.) The right index finger, resting in the open left palm, which is facing right, swings up slowly from its position to one in which it is pointing straight up. The movement is repeated slowly, after a pause. *Cf.* FROM TIME TO TIME, NOW AND THEN, OCCASIONAL, OCCASIONALLY, SOMETIME(S).

ONE ANOTHER *pron. phrase.* (Mingling with.) Both hands are held in modified "A" positions, thumbs out. The left hand is positioned with its thumb pointing straight up, and the right hand, with its thumb pointing down, revolves above the left thumb in a clockwise direction. *Cf.* EACH OTHER, MINGLE.

ONE MORE *colloq. phrase.* (One finger beckons.) The right hand is held palm up, with the index finger making very small and rapid beckoning movements.

ONLY (ŏn′ lĭ), *adv.* (One, wandering around in a circle.) The index finger, pointing straight up, palm facing the body (the number *one*), is rotated before the face in a counterclockwise direction. *Cf.* ALONE, LONE.

ON THE CONTRARY *adv. phrase.* (Opposites.) With index fingertips touching initially, both hands move away from each other.

OPEN (ō′ pən), *adj., v.,* OPENED, OPENING. (The natural sign.) The "B" hands, palms out, are held with index finger edges touching. They swing apart so that the palms now face each other.

_____

OPEN THE DOOR *v. phrase.* (The opening and closing of the door.) The "B" hands, palms out and edges touching, are drawn apart and then come together again. *Cf.* DOOR, DOORWAY.

_____

OPEN THE WINDOW *phrase.* (The opening of the window.) With both palms facing the body, the little finger edge of the right hand rests atop the index finger edge of the left hand. The right hand then moves straight up. *Cf.* WINDOW.

OPERA 1 (ŏp′ ər ə), *n.* (The rhythmic movement.) The right "5" hand, palm facing left, is waved back and forth over the downturned left hand. The mouth may be held open in song. *Cf.* SING, SONG.

OPERA 2, *n.* (A variation of OPERA 1, above.) The letter "O" is substituted for the "5."

OPERATION 1 (ŏp′ ə rā′ shən), *n.* (The action of the scalpel.) The thumb of the right "A" hand is drawn straight down across the upright left palm.

OPERATION 2, *n.* (The action of a scalpel.) The thumbtip of
the right "A" hand, palm facing down, moves a short distance
across the lower chest or stomach region.

OPINION (ə pǐn′ yən), *n.* (The "O" hand, circling in the
head.) The right "O" hand circles before the forehead several
times.

OPPONENT (ɔ pō′ nənt), *n.* (At sword's point.) The two
index fingers, after pointing to each other, are drawn sharply
apart. This is followed by the sign for INDIVIDUAL: Both
open hands, palms facing each other, move down the sides of
the body, tracing its outline to the hips. *Cf.* ENEMY, RIVAL 1.

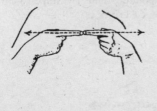

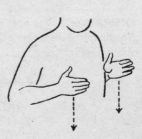

OPPORTUNITY (ŏp´ ər tū´ nə tĭ), *n.* (The letters "O" and "P"; pushing through.) Both "O" hands are held palms down, side by side. They swing up a bit as they assume the "P" position.

OPPOSE (ə´ pōz), *v.*, OPPOSED, OPPOSING. (Opposed to; restraint.) The tips of the right fingers, held together, are thrust purposefully into the open left palm, whose fingers are also together and pointing forward. *Cf.* AGAINST.

OPPOSITE (ŏp´ ə zĭt), *adj., n.* (Separateness.) The tips of the extended index fingers touch before the chest, the right finger pointing left and the left finger pointing right. The fingers then draw apart sharply to either side. *Cf.* CONTRAST.

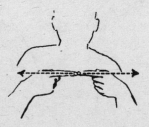

OR (ôr; *unstressed* ər), *conj.* (Considering one thing against another.) The "A" hands, palms facing and thumbs pointing straight up, move alternately up and down before the chest. *Cf.* EITHER 3, WHETHER, WHICH.

ORANGE 1 (ôr′ ĭnj, ŏr′-), *n., adj.* (The action of squeezing an orange to get its juice into the mouth.) The right "C" hand is held at the mouth. It opens and closes deliberately, as if squeezing an orange.

ORANGE 2, *n.* (The peeling of the fruit.) The thumbtip of the right "Y" hand moves over the back of the left "S" hand, which is held palm down or palm facing the body.

ORDER 1 (ôr′ dər), *n.*, *v.*, -DERED, -DERING. (An issuance from the mouth.) The tip of the index finger of the "D" hand, palm facing the body, is placed at the closed lips. It moves around and out, rather forcefully.

ORDER 2, *n.*, *v.* (Placing things in order.) The hands, palms facing, fingers together and pointing away from the body, are positioned at the left side and held about a foot apart. With a slight up-down motion, as if describing waves, the hands travel in unison from left to right. *Cf.* ARRANGE, ARRANGEMENT, PLAN, PREPARE 1, PUT IN ORDER, READY 1.

ORGANIZATION 1 (ôr′ gən ə zā′ shən), *n.* (A grouping together.) Both "C" hands, palms facing, are held a few inches apart at chest height. They are swung around in unison, so that the palms now face the body. *Cf.* CLASS, CLASSED, COMPANY, GROUP 1.

ORGANIZATION 2, *n*. (The letter "O"; a group or class.) Both "O" hands are held with palms facing out and thumb edges touching. The hands swing apart, around, and come together again with little finger edges touching.

ORIGIN (ŏr′ ə jĭn, ôr′-), *n*. (Turning a key to open up a new venture.) The right index finger, resting between the left index and middle fingers, executes a half turn, once or twice. *Cf.* BEGIN, START.

ORPHAN (ôr′ fən), *n*. (The letter "O"; female and male.) The right "O" hand is placed first at the chin and then at the temple.

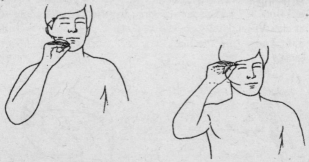

OTHER (ŭth′ ər), *adj.* (Moving over to another position.) The right "A" hand, thumb up, is pivoted from the wrist and swung over to the right, so that the thumb now points to the right. *Cf.* ANOTHER.

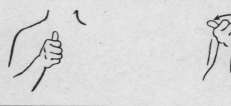

OUGHT TO (ôt), *aux. v.* (Being pinned down.) The right hand, in the "X" position, palm down, moves forcefully up and down once or twice. An expression of determination is frequently assumed. *Cf.* HAVE TO, MUST, NECESSARY, NECESSITY, NEED 1, SHOULD.

OUR (our), *pron.* (An encompassing, including oneself and others.) The right hand, palm facing left, is placed at the right shoulder. It swings around to the left shoulder, its palm now facing right.

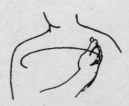

OURSELVES (our sĕlvz'), *pron. pl.* (An encompassing; the thumb representing *self, i.e.,* oneness.) The right "A" hand, thumb held straight up, is placed at the right shoulder. It executes the same movement as in OUR.

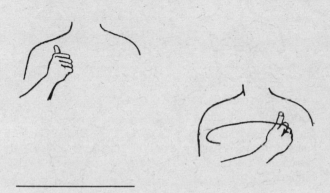

OUT (out), *adv.* (The natural motion of withdrawing, *i.e.,* taking *out,* of the hand.) The downturned open right hand, grasped loosely by the left, is drawn up and out of the left hand's grasp. As it does so, the fingers come together with the thumb. The left hand, meanwhile, closes into the "O" position, palm facing right.

OUTFIT (out′ fit), *n.* (Matching top and bottom.) The thumb of the right "Y" hand is placed at midchest, and then the hand travels down so that the little finger of the same "Y" hand touches the trousers or skirt.

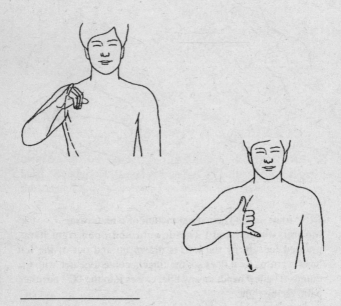

OVER (ō′ vər), *prep.* (A crossing over.) The left hand is held before the chest, palm down and fingers together. The right hand, fingers together, glides over the left, with the right little finger touching the top of the left hand. *Cf.* ACROSS, CROSS.

OVER AGAIN *phrase.* (Turning over a new leaf.) The left hand, in the "5" position, palm up, is held before the chest. The right hand, in the right-angle position, fingers pointing up, arches up and over into the left palm.

OVERCOME (ō´ vər kŭm´), *v.,* -CAME, -COME, -COMING. (Forcing the head into a bowed position.) The right "S" hand, placed across the left "S" hand, moves over and down a bit. *Cf.* BEAT, DEFEAT.

OVERHEAD PROJECTOR *n.* (Projecting something behind a speaker.) The right hand, thumb resting against all the other fingers, moves over the right shoulder, as all fingers open into the "5" position.

 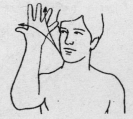

OVER MY HEAD *sl. phrase*. Both index fingers flick out as the "S" hands, palms facing backwards, are thrown over the head.

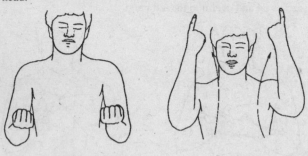

OWE (ō), *v.*, OWED, OWING. (Pointing where the money should be placed.) The index finger of one hand is thrust into the upturned palm of the other several times. *Cf.* DUE.

OWN (ōn), *v., adj.* (Holding something to oneself.) The down-turned right hand, fingers open, is brought up to the chest, where the fingers come together.

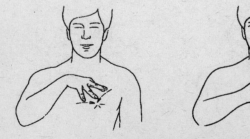

OXYGEN (ok′ sə jin), *n.* (The symbol for oxygen.) The signer fingerspells "O-2," dropping the hand a bit for the "2."

P

PACKAGE (păk' ĭj), *n., v.,* -AGED, -AGING. (The dimensions are indicated.) The open hands, palms facing and fingers pointing out, are dropped an inch or two simultaneously. They then shift their relative positions so that both palms face the body, with one hand in front of the other. In this new position they again drop an inch or two simultaneously. *Cf.* BOX, ROOM 1.

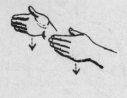 

PAGEANT (paj' ənt), *n.* (The sash worn by a contestant.) The curved thumb and index finger of the right hand trace an imaginary ribbon from the left shoulder to the right side of the waist. The letter "P" may be substituted for the thumb and index.

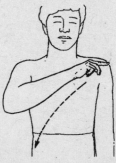

PAIL (pāl), *n.* (The shape and grasping the handle.) The left hand holds an imaginary pail. The right index finger describes a downturned arc as it moves from the left wrist to the elbow.

PAIN (pān), *n.* (A stabbing pain.) The "D" hands, index fingers pointing to each other, are rotated in elliptical fashion before the chest--simultaneously but in opposite directions. *Cf.* ACHE, HARM, HURT, INJURE, INJURY.

PAJAMAS (pə jä′ məz), *n.* (A fingerspelled loan sign.) The signer fingerspells "P-J".

PAL (pal) *n.* The right index finger and thumb form a "C". The right thumbtip moves across the chin, from left to right.

PALE (pāl) *adj., v.,* PALED, PALING. The sign for WHITE is made: The fingertips of the "5" hand are placed against the chest. The hand moves straight out from the chest, while the fingers and thumb all come together. Then both hands, fingers spread, rise up and over the cheeks.

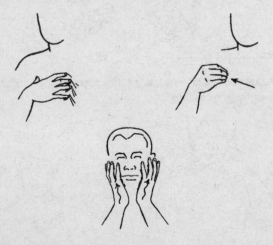

PANDA (pan' də), *n.* (The letter "P"; emphasizing the panda's markings.) The right "P" hand makes a counterclockwise circle around the face.

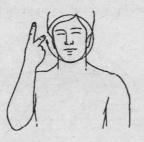

PANTS (pănts), *n. pl.* (The natural sign.) The open hands are drawn up along the thighs, starting at the knees.

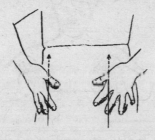

PAPER (pā′ pər), *n.* (The action of the press.) The right "5" hand, held palm down, fingers pointing left, is brought down twice against the upturned left "5" hand, whose fingers point right. *Cf.* NEWSPAPER, PUBLISH.

PAPER CLIP (pā′ pər klip), *n.* (Affixing the clip.) Using the downturned right index finger and thumb, the signer slides an imaginary paper clip over the fingers of the left hand.

PARALLELOGRAM (par ə lel′ ə gram), *n.* With the left hand in the "P" position and the right in the "R" position, the signer traces a rectangle in the air.

PARDON (pär′ dən), *n.* (A wiped-off and cleaned slate.) The right hand wipes off the left palm several times. *Cf.* APOLOGIZE 2, APOLOGY 2, EXCUSE, FORGIVE.

PARENTS 1 (pâr′ əntz), *n.* (Mother and father.) Using the right "5" hand, the right thumbtip first touches the right side of the chin, then moves up to touch the right temple.

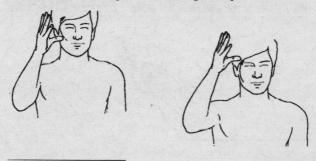

PARENTS 2, *n.* Same as for PARENTS 1 above, but the letter "P" is used.

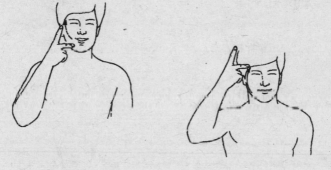

PARROT (par′ ət), *n.* (The curved beak.) The curved index finger moves away from and down from the nose.

PART (pärt), *n., adj.* (Cutting off or designating a part.) The little finger edge of the open right hand moves straight down the middle of the upturned left palm. *Cf.* PIECE, PORTION, SOME.

PARTNER (pärt′ nər), *n.* (Sharing.) The little finger edge of the right hand sweeps back and forth over the index finger edge of the left hand. This is followed by the sign for INDIVIDUAL.

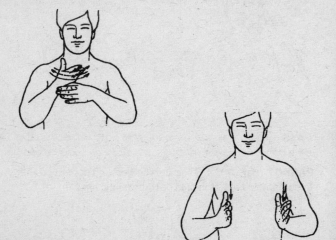

PARTY 1 (pär′ tĭ), *n.* (The swinging of tambourines.) Both open hands, held somewhat above the head, are pivoted back and forth repeatedly, as if swinging a pair of tambourines.

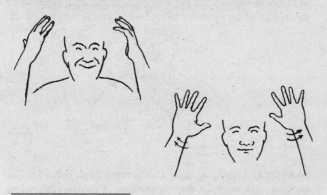

PARTY 2, *n.* (The rhythmic swaying of the feet.) The down-turned index and middle fingers of the right "V" hand swing rhythmically back and forth over the upturned left palm. *Cf.* DANCE.

PASS (păs), *v.,* PASSED, PASSING. (One hand passes the other.) Both "A" hands, palms facing each other, are held before the body, the right behind the left. The right hand moves forward, its knuckles brushing those of the left, and continues forward a bit beyond the left.

PASSOVER (pas′ ō vər), *n.* (The letter "P"; passing over.) The right "P" hand passes over the downturned left hand.

PAST (păst), *adj., n., adv.* (Something past, behind.) The upraised right hand, in the "5" position with palm facing the body, is held just above the right shoulder and is thrown back over it. *Cf.* PREVIOUS, PREVIOUSLY, WAS, WERE.

PATIENT (pā′ shənt), *n.* (The letter "P"; the red cross on the hospital gown's sleeve.) The thumb and middle fingers of the right "P" hand trace a small cross on the upper left arm.

PATRONIZE (pā' trən īz), *v.* (Offering unwanted sympathy.)
The middle fingers of both "5" hands move forward in small
circles together. The signer's expression is one of condescension. This sign indicates patronizing someone. To be patron-
ized, the hands swing around so that the middle fingers point
to the signer. The same expression is used.

PAY 1 (pā), *v.*, PAID, PAYING. (Giving forth of money.) The
right index finger, resting in the upturned left palm, swings
forward and up a bit.

PAY 2, *v.* (Peeling off a bill.) The right hand, grasping several
imaginary bills, "peels off" one as it moves forward.

PAY ATTENTION (TO) *v. phrase.* (Directing one's attention forward; applying oneself; concentrating.) Both hands, fingers pointing up and together, are held at the sides of the face. They move straight out from the face. *Cf.* CONCENTRATE, CONCENTRATION, FOCUS, MIND 2.

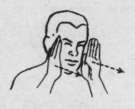

PAY TO *v.* See PAY 1

PEACE (pēs), *n.* (The hands are clasped as a gesture of harmony or *peace*; the opening signifies quiet or calmness.) The hands are clasped both ways, and then open and separate, assuming the "5" position, palms down.

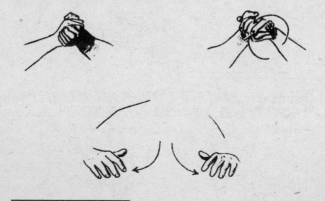

PEACOCK (pē' kok), *n.* (The letter "P"; the fan tail.) The right "P" hand is first positioned at the left elbow; then it moves down the arm, opening into a wide fan, with fingers spread apart.

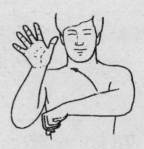

PENALTY (pĕn' əl tĭ), *n.* (Nicking into one.) The knuckle of the right "X" finger is nicked against the palm of the left hand, held in the "5" position, palm facing right. *Cf.* COST, EXPENSE, FINE 2, PRICE, TAX, TAXATION.

PENGUIN (pen' gwin), *n.* (The characteristic gait.) Both downturned hands, fingers touching, are held at the sides of the body. The signer rocks alternately back and forth.

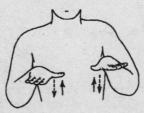

PEOPLE (pē′ pəl), *n. pl.* (The letter "P" in continuous motion, to indicate plurality.) The "P" hands, side by side, are moved alternately toward the body in continuous counterclockwise circles.

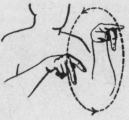

PERCEIVE (pər sēv′), *v.,* -CEIVED, -CEIVING. (The eyesight is directed forward.) The right "V" hand, palm facing the body, is placed so that the fingertips are just under the eyes. The hand swings around and out, so that the fingertips are now pointing forward. *Cf.* LOOK 1, PERCEPTION, WATCH 1.

PERCENT (pər sent′), *n.* (The symbol.) The right "O" hand draws a percent symbol (%) in the air.

PERCEPTION (pər sĕp′ shən), *n.* See PERCEIVE.

PERFECT (*adj., n.* pûr′ fĭkt; *v.* pər fĕkt′), -FECTED, -FECTING. (The letter "P"; the hands come into precise contact.) The "P" hands face each other. The right executes a clockwise circle above the stationary left, and then moves down so that the thumb and middle fingers of each hand come into precise contact.

PERFORM 1 (pər fôrm′), *v.,* -FORMED, -FORMING. (An activity.) Both open hands, palms down, are swung right and left before the chest. *Cf.* DO.

PERFORM 2, *v.* (Motion or movement, modified by the letter "A" for act.) Both "A" hands, palms out, are held at shoulder height and rotate alternately toward the head. *Cf.* ACT, PLAY 2, SHOW 2.

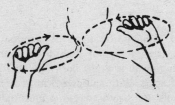

PERFORMANCE 1 (pər fôr′ məns), *n.* See PERFORM 1.

_____

PERFORMANCE 2, *n.* See PERFORM 2.

_____

PERHAPS (pər hăps′), *adv.* (Weighing one thing against another.) The upturned open hands move alternately up and down. *Cf.* MAY 1, MAYBE, MIGHT 2, POSSIBILITY, POSSIBLY, PROBABLE, PROBABLY.

_____

PERMANENT (pûr′ mə nənt), *adj.* (Steady, uninterrupted movement.) The "A" hands are held with palms out, thumbs extended and touching, the right behind the left. In this position the hands move forward in a straight, steady line. *Cf.* CONTINUE, ENDURE 2, EVER 1, LAST 3, LASTING, PERSEVERE, PERSIST, REMAIN, STAY 1, STAY STILL.

_____

PERMISSION 1 (pər mĭsh′ ən), *n.* (A permissive upswinging of the hands, as if giving in.) Both hands, palms facing and fingers pointing away from the body, are held at chest level, almost a foot apart. With an upward movement, using their wrists as pivots, the hands sweep up until the fingers point

almost straight up. *Cf.* ALLOW, GRANT 1, LET, LET'S, LET US, MAY
3, PERMIT 1.

PERMISSION 2, *n.* (The "P" hands are used.) The same sign as
in PERMISSION 1 is used, except with the "P" hands. *Cf.* PER-
MIT 2.

PERMIT 1 (pər mit'), *v.*, -MITTED, -MITTING. See PERMISSION 1.

PERMIT 2, *n., v.* See PERMISSION 2.

PERPENDICULAR 1 (pûr pən dik' yə lər), *adj.* (The letter
"P".) The right index finger touches the middle finger of the
left "P" hand.

PERPENDICULAR 2, *adj.* (The shape.) The little finger edge of the right hand rests upright and perpendicular in the upturned left palm. It may wave back and forth slightly, as if achieving balance.

PERSEVERE (pûr´ sə vîr´), *v.*, -VERED, -VERING. (Steady, uninterrupted movement.) The "A" hands are held with palms out, thumbs extended and touching, the right behind the left. In this position the hands move forward in a straight, steady line. *Cf.* CONTINUE, ENDURE 2, EVER 1, LAST 3, LASTING, PERMANENT, PERSIST, REMAIN, STAY 1, STAY STILL.

PERSIST (pər sĭst´, -zĭst´), *v.*, -SISTED, -SISTING. (Steady, uninterrupted movement.) The "A" hands are held with palms out, thumbs extended and touching, the right behind the left. In this position the hands move forward in a straight, steady line. *Cf.* CONTINUE, ENDURE 2, EVER 1, LAST 3, LASTING, PERMANENT, PERSEVERE, REMAIN, STAY 1, STAY STILL.

PERSON (pûr′ sən), *n.* (The letter "P"; an individual is indicated.) The "P" hands, side by side, move straight down a short distance, as if outlining the sides of an unseen individual.

"PERSON" ENDING Both open hands, palms facing each other, move down the sides of the body, tracing its outline to the hips.

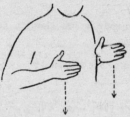

PERSONAL (pûr′ sən əl), *adj.* (The lips are sealed, as in a secret or something personal.) The back of the right thumb is pressed against the lips.

PERSONAL COMPUTER *n.* (A fingerspelled loan sign.) The signer fingerspells "P-C".

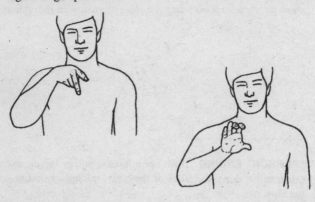

PERSPIRATION 1 (pûr´ spə rā´ shən), *n.* See PERSPIRE 1.

PERSPIRATION 2, *n.* See PERSPIRE 2.

PERSPIRE 1 (pər spīr´), *v.,* -SPIRED, -SPIRING. (Wiping the brow.) The bent right index finger is drawn across the forehead from left to right and then shaken to the side, as if getting rid of the sweat. *Cf.* PERSPIRATION 1.

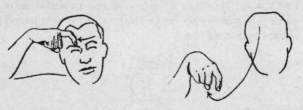

PERSPIRE 2, *v.* (Perspiration dripping from the brow.) The index finger edge of the open right hand wipes across the brow, and the same open hand then continues forcefully downward off the brow, its fingers wiggling, as if shaking off the perspiration gathered. *Cf.* PERSPIRATION 2.

PERSUADE (pər swād′), *v.*, -SUADED, -SUADING. (Shaking someone, to implant one's will into another.) Both "A" hands, palms facing, are held before the chest, the left slightly in front of the right. In this position the hands move back and forth a short distance. *Cf.* PERSUASION, URGE 2.

PERSUASION (pər swā′ zhən), *n.* See PERSUADE.

PHEW! *interj.* The "5" hand, palm facing the body, is shaken up and down several times.

PHONE (fōn), *n., v.,* PHONED, PHONING. (The natural sign.) The right "Y" hand is placed at the right side of the head with the thumb touching the ear and the little finger touching the lips. This is the more modern telephone receiver. *Cf.* TELE-PHONE.

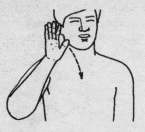

PHOOEY! *interj.* (A look of derision.) With a look of derision, the signer throws one hand down and out, as if ridding himself of something. *Cf.* BAH!

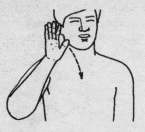

PHOTOGRAPH (fō′ tə grăf′), *n., v.,* -GRAPHED, -GRAPHING. (Recording an image.) The right "C" hand is held in front of the face, with thumb edge near the face and palm facing left. The hand is then brought sharply around in front of the open left hand and is struck firmly against the left palm, which is held facing forward with fingers pointing up. *Cf.* PICTURE.

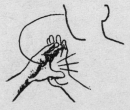

PICK 1 (pĭk), *v.*, PICKED, PICKING. (The natural motion of selecting something from the hand.) The thumb and index fingers of the outstretched right hand grasp an imaginary object on the upturned left palm. The right hand then moves straight up. *Cf.* FIND, SELECT 1.

PICK 2, *v.* (The natural sign.) The fingertips and thumbtip of the downturned open right hand come together, and the hand moves up a short distance, as if picking something. *Cf.* PICK UP 2.

PICK ON (pĭk), *v. phrase.* (The hen's beak pecks.) The index finger and thumb of the right hand, held together, are brought against the index finger of the left "D" hand a number of times. *Cf.* NAG.

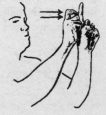

PICK UP 1, *v. phrase*. (To take up.) Both hands, held palms down in the "5" position, are at chest level. With a grasping upward movement, both close into "S" positions before the face. *Cf.* ASSUME, TAKE UP.

PICK UP 2, *v. phrase*. See PICK 2.

PICTURE (pĭk′ chər), *n., v.,* -TURED, -TURING. (Recording an image.) The right "C" hand is held in front of the face, with thumb edge near the face and palm facing left. The hand is then brought sharply around in front of the open left hand and is struck firmly against the left palm, which is held facing forward with fingers pointing up. *Cf.* PHOTOGRAPH.

PIE (pī), *n.* (Slicing a wedge-shaped piece of pie.) The upturned left hand represents the pie. The little finger edge of the open right hand goes through the motions of slicing a wedge-shaped piece from the pie.

PIECE (pēs), *n.*, *v.*, PIECED, PIECING. (Cutting off or designating a part.) The little finger edge of the open right hand moves straight down the middle of the upturned left palm. *Cf.* PART 1, PORTION, SOME.

PIG (pĭg), *n.* (The snout digs into the trough.) The downturned right prone hand is placed under the chin, fingers pointing forward. The hand, in this position, swings alternately up and down.

PILGRIM (pĭl′ grĭm), *n.* (The letter "P"; the wide collar.) Both "P" hands trace a wide collar around the neck, beginning in the back and moving around to the front.

PIONEER (pī ə nir'), *n.* (The first finger, *i.e.,* first explorers.) The middle finger of the right "P" hand touches the tip of the left thumb, the hand's first finger.

PITY (pĭt' ĭ), *n., v.,* PITIED, PITYING. (Feelings from the heart, conferred on others.) The middle fingertip of the open right hand touches the chest over the heart. The same open hand then moves in a small, clockwise circle before the right shoulder, with palm facing forward and fingers pointing up. *Cf.* MERCY, SYMPATHY.

PIZZA 1 (pēt' sə), *n.* (Eating a slice.) The signer mimes eating a slice of pizza.

PIZZA 2, *n.* (The letter "P"; the drawing of a "Z" in the air.) The right "P" hand draws a "Z" in the air.

PIZZA 3, *n.* (The double "Z" in the spelling.) The curved index and middle fingers draw a "Z" in the air.

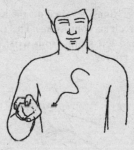

PLACE (plās), *n.* (The letter "P"; a circle or square is indicated, to show the locale or place.) The "P" hands are held side by side before the body, with middle fingertips touching. From this position, the hands separate and outline a circle (or a square), before coming together again closer to the body. *Cf.* LOCATION, POSITION.

PLAIN 1 (plān), *adj.* (Rays of light clearing the way.) Both hands are held at chest height, palms out, all fingertips together. They open into the "5" position in unison, the right hand moving toward the right and the left toward the left. The palms of both hands remain facing out. *Cf.* CLEAR, EVIDENT, OBVIOUS.

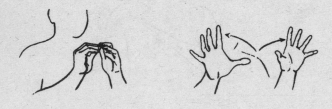

PLAIN 2, *adj.* (Everything is wiped off the hand, to emphasize an uncluttered or clean condition.) The right hand slowly wipes the upturned left palm, from wrist to fingertips. *Cf.* CLEAN, NICE, PURE, PURITY.

PLAIN 3, *n.* (The letters "P"; the space.) Both "P" hands draw a circle toward the chest.

PLAN (plăn), *n., v.,* PLANNED, PLANNING. (Placing things in order.) The hands, palms facing, fingers together and pointing away from the body, are positioned at the left side and held about a foot apart. With a slight up-down motion, as if describing waves, the hands travel in unison from left to right. *Cf.* ARRANGE, ARRANGEMENT, ORDER 2, PREPARE 1, PUT IN ORDER, READY 1.

PLANE 1 (plăn), *n.* (The wings of the airplane.) The "Y" hand, palm down and drawn up near the shoulder, moves forward, up and away from the body. Either hand may be used. *Cf.* AIRPLANE, FLY 1.

PLANE 2, *n.* (The wings and fuselage of the airplane.) The hand assumes the same position as in PLANE 1, but the index finger is also extended, to represent the fuselage of the airplane. Either hand may be used, and the movement is the same as in PLANE 1. *Cf.* FLY 2.

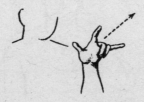

PLANET (plăn′ ĭt), *n.* (The letter "P"; around the world.) The right "P" hand moves around the left fist.

PLASTIC (plas′ tik), *n., adj.* (Pliable.) The right hand grasps the middle finger of the left "P" hand and bends it back and forth.

PLATEAU (pla tō′), *n.* (The flatness.) The right "P" hand, palm down, moves in a circle.

PLATTER (plat′ ər), *n.* (The shape and function.) Both upturned hands, side by side, describe a circle as they move outward from the body.

PLAY 1 (plā), *v.*, PLAYED, PLAYING. (Shaking tambourines.) The "Y" hands, held aloft, are shaken back and forth, pivoted at the wrists.

PLAY 2, *n.* (Motion or movement, modified by the letter "A" for "act.") Both "A" hands, palms out, are held at shoulder height and rotate alternately toward the head. *Cf.* ACT, PERFORM 2, PERFORMANCE 2, SHOW 2.

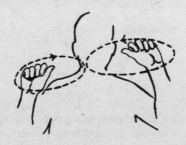

PLEASANT (plĕz' ənt), *adj.* (A crinkling-up of the face.) Both hands, in the "5" position, palms facing back, are placed on either side of the face. The fingers wiggle back and forth, while a pleasant, happy expression is worn. *Cf.* CHEERFUL, FRIENDLY.

_____

PLEASE (plēz), *v.*, PLEASED, PLEASING. (A pleasurable feeling on the heart.) The open right hand is circled on the chest, over the heart. *Cf.* ENJOY, ENJOYMENT, LIKE 3, PLEASURE.

_____

PLEASURE (plĕzh' ər), *n.* See PLEASE.

_____

PLENTY (plĕn' tĭ), *n., adj., adv.* (A full cup.) The left hand, in the "S" position, is held palm facing right. The right "5" hand, palm down, is brushed outward several times over the top of

the left, indicating a wiping off of the top of a cup. *Cf.*
ENOUGH.

PLUS (plŭs), *prep., n.* (A mathematical symbol.) The two
index fingers are crossed at right angles. *Cf.* POSITIVE.

POISON (poi′ zən), *n.* (The crossed bones.) Both "S" hands
are crossed and held against the chest. The signer bares the
teeth, in imitation of a skull.

POLAR BEAR *n.* (A white bear.) The sign for BEAR is made: Both claw hands, crossed, scratch the shoulders several times. This is followed by WHITE: The right "5" hand is placed against the chest, palm facing the body. The hand moves forward once or twice; each time the fingertips come together.

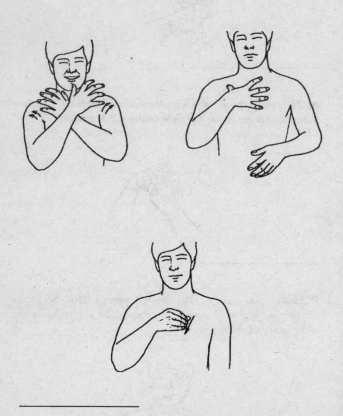

POLICE (pə lēs'), *n., v.,* -LICED, -LICING. (The letter "C" for "cop"; the shape and position of the badge.) The right "C"

hand, palm facing left, is placed against the heart. *Cf.* COP.

POLITE (pə līt′), *adj.* (The ruffled shirt front of a gentleman of old.) The thumb of the right "5" hand is thrust into the chest. The hand then pivots down, with thumb remaining in place. This latter part of the sign, however, is optional.

POLLUTE 1 (pə lōōt′), *v.* (Spreading poison.) The middle finger of the right "P" hand makes a small clockwise circle in the upturned left palm. This is a sign for POISON. The downturned hand then spreads out in a counterclockwise arc.

POLLUTE 2, *v.* (Spreading dirt.) The downturned open hand is placed under the chin, where the fingers wriggle. This is the sign for DIRT. The downturned hand then spreads out in a counterclockwise arc.

POLO (pō′ lō), *n.* (The polo playing.) The signer, holding a pair of imaginary reins and moving as if on horseback, swings an imaginary polo mallet, hitting a ball on the ground.

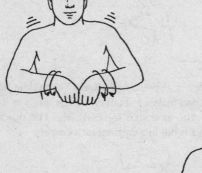

POND (pond), *n.* (The letter "P"; the space and shimmering water.) The right "P" hand describes a counterclockwise circle, while the hand trembles slightly, as if reflecting the shimmering water.

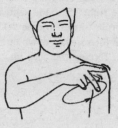

POOL (pŏol), *n.* (The game of pool.) The signer, hunched over an imaginary cue stick, mimes striking the ball. *Cf.* BILLIARDS.

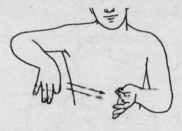

POOR (pŏor), *adj.* (Ragged elbows.) The open right hand is placed at the left elbow. It moves down and off, closing into the "O" position.

POP (pŏp), *n.* (Corking a bottle.) The left "O" hand is held with thumb edge up, representing a bottle. The thumb and index finger of the right "5" hand represent a cork, and are inserted into the circle formed by the "O" hand. The palm of the open right hand then strikes down on the upturned edge of the "O" hand, as if forcing the cork into the bottle. *Cf.* SODA POP, SODA WATER.

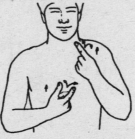 

POPCORN (pop' kôrn), *n.* (The popping.) The index fingers alternately flick up.

POPSICLE (pop' si kəl), *n.* (Licking the popsicle.) The index and middle fingers of either hand, held together, are brought up repeatedly to the outstretched tongue.

POPULATION (pop yə lā′ shən), *n.* (Running through many individuals.) The left "5" hand is held palm facing the body. The right "P" hand sweeps over the outstretched left fingers, starting at the little finger.

POP UP (*colloq.*), *v.* (Popping up before the eyes.) The right index finger, pointing up, pops up between the index and middle fingers of the left hand, whose palm faces down. *Cf.* APPEAR.

PORCUPINE (pôr′ kyə pĭn), *n.* (The outstretched quills.) The right "S" hand rests on the back of the left "S" hand. The right hand, moving down to the fingers of the left, opens wide, the fingers representing outstretched quills.

PORTION (pōr' shən), *n.* (Cutting off or designating a part.) The little finger edge of the open right hand moves straight down the middle of the upturned left palm. *Cf.* PART 1, PIECE, SOME.

POSITION (pə zĭsh' ən), *n.* (The letter "P"; a circle or square is indicated, to show the locale or place.) The "P" hands are held side by side before the body, with middle fingertips touching. From this position, the hands separate and outline a circle (or a square), before coming together again closer to the body. *Cf.* LOCATION, PLACE.

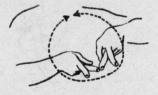

POSITIVE (pŏz' ə tĭv), *adj.* (A mathematical symbol.) The two index fingers are crossed at right angles in the sign for PLUS. *Cf.* PLUS.

POSSIBILITY (pŏs´ ə bĭl' ə tĭ), *n.* (Weighing one thing against another.) The upturned open hands move alternately up and

down. *Cf.* MAY 1, MAYBE, MIGHT 2, PERHAPS, POSSIBLY, PROBA-
BLE, PROBABLY.

 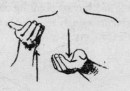

POSSIBLE (pŏs′ ə bəl), *adj.* (An affirmative movement of the
hands, likened to a nodding of the head, to indicate ability or
power to accomplish something.) Both "A" hands, held palms
down, move down in unison a short distance before the chest.
Cf. CAN, CAPABLE, MAY 2.

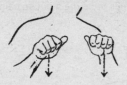

POSSIBLY (pŏs′ ə blĭ), *adv.* See POSSIBILITY.

POST OFFICE *n.* (A fingerspelled loan sign.) The signer fingerspells "P-O."

 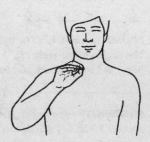

POSTPONE (pōst pōn'), *v.*, -PONED, -PONING. (Putting off; moving things forward repeatedly.) The "F" hands, palms facing and fingers pointing out from the body, are moved forward simultaneously in a series of short movements. *Cf.* DELAY, PROCRASTINATE, PUT OFF.

POTATO CHIP (pə tā' tō chĭp) *n.* (Breaking a chip with the teeth.) The sign for POTATO is made: the downturned right index and middle fingers are thrust repeatedly onto the left fist. The signer then mimes breaking a potato chip with the teeth.

POUND (pound), *n.* (The balancing of the scale is described.) The fingers of the right "H" hand are centered on the left index finger and rocked back and forth. *Cf.* WEIGH, WEIGHT.

POVERTY (pŏv′ ər tĭ), *n.* (The knuckles are rubbed, to indicate a condition of being worn down.) The knuckles of the
curved index and middle fingers of both hands are rubbed up
and down against each other. Instead of the up-down rubbing,
they may rub against each other in an alternate clockwise-
counterclockwise manner. *Cf.* DIFFICULT 1, DIFFICULTY, HARD 1,
HARDSHIP, PROBLEM 2.

POWER 1 (pou′ ər), *n.* (Flexing the muscles.) With fists
clenched, palms facing back, the signer raises both arms and
shakes them once, with force. *Cf.* MIGHT 1, MIGHTY 1, POWER-
FUL 1, STRONG.

POWER 2, *n.* (The curve of the flexed biceps is indicated.)
The left hand, clenched into a fist, is held up, palm facing the
body. The index finger of the right "D" hand moves in an arc
over the left biceps muscle, from shoulder to crook of the
elbow. *Cf.* POWERFUL 2.

POWERFUL 1 (pou′ ər fəl), *adj*. See POWER 1.

POWERFUL 2, *adj*. See POWER 2.

PRACTICE (prăk′ tĭs), *n., v.*, -TICED, -TICING. (Polishing or sharpening up.) The knuckles of the downturned right "A" hand are rubbed briskly back and forth over the side of the hand and index finger of the left "D" hand. *Cf*. TRAIN 2.

PRAISE (prāz), *n., v.*, PRAISED, PRAISING. (Good words coming from the mouth; clapping hands.) The fingertips of the right hand, palm flat and facing the body, are brought up to the lips so that they touch (part of the sign for GOOD, *q.v.*). The hands are then clapped together several times. *Cf*. APPLAUD, APPLAUSE, CONGRATULATE 1, CONGRATULATIONS 1.

PRECISE (prĭ sīs′), *adj*. (The fingers come together precisely.) The thumb and index finger of each hand, palms facing, the right above the left, form circles. They are brought together with a deliberate movement, so that the fingers and thumbs now touch. Sometimes the right hand, before coming together

with the left, executes a slow clockwise circle above the left.
Cf. EXACT, EXACTLY, SPECIFIC 1.

PREFER (prĭ fûr'), *v.*, -FERRED, -FERRING. (More good.) The
fingertips of one hand are placed at the lips, as if tasting something (see GOOD). Then the hand is moved up to a position
just above the head, where it assumes the "Λ" position, thumb
up. *Cf.* BETTER.

PREGNANT (preg' nənt), *adj.* One or both open hands are
placed on the stomach and move forward an inch or two, to
indicate the swollen belly..

PREPARE 1 (prĭ pâr′), *v.*, -PARED, -PARING. (Placing things in order.) The hands, palms facing, fingers together and pointing away from the body, are positioned at the left side and held about a foot apart. With a slight up-down motion, as if describing waves, the hands travel in unison from left to right. *Cf.* ARRANGE, ARRANGEMENT, ORDER 3, PLAN 1, PUT IN ORDER, READY 1.

PREPARE 2, *v.* (Set out.) The "A" hands are crossed, with the right resting on top of the left. The right palm faces left and the left palm faces right. Both hands suddenly open and swing apart to the palm-down position. *Cf.* READY 3.

PRESENT 1 (prĕz′ ənt), *n.* (An offering; a presenting.) Both hands, slightly cupped, palms up, are held close to the chest. They move up and out in unison, describing a very slight arc. *Cf.* OFFER, OFFERING, PROPOSE, SUGGEST.

PRESENT 2 (*n.* prĕz′ ənt; *v.* prĭ zĕnt′), -SENTED, -SENTING. (A giving of something.) Both "A" hands, with index fingers somewhat draped over the tips of the thumbs, are held palms facing in front of the chest. They are pivoted forward and down in unison, from the wrists. *Cf.* CONTRIBUTE, GIFT.

PRESENT 3, *adj.* (Something right in front of you.) The upturned right-angle hands drop down rather sharply. The "Y" hands may also be used. *Cf.* NOW.

PRESERVE (prĭ zûrv′), *v.,* -SERVED, -SERVING. (Slow, careful movement.) The "K" hands are crossed, the right above the left, little finger edges down. In this position the hands are moved up and down a short distance. *Cf.* CARE 2, CAREFUL 2, KEEP, MAINTAIN, TAKE CARE OF.

PRESIDENT (prĕz′ ə dənt), *n.* The "C" hands, held palms out at either temple, are drawn out and up from the head into the "S" position.

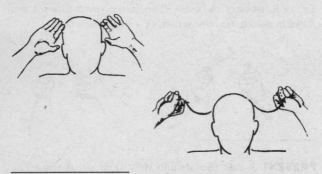

PRETTY (prĭt′ ĭ), *adj.* (Literally, a good face.) The right hand, fingers closed over the thumb, is placed at or just below the lips (indicating a tasting of something GOOD, *q.v.*). It then describes a counterclockwise circle around the face, opening into the "5" position, to indicate the whole face. At the completion of the circling movement the hand comes to rest in its initial position, at or just below the lips. *Cf.* BEAUTIFUL, BEAUTY.

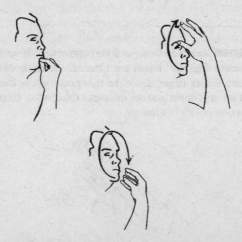

PRETZEL (pret′ səl), *n.* (The shape.) Both "R" hands trace the twisted shape of a pretzel.

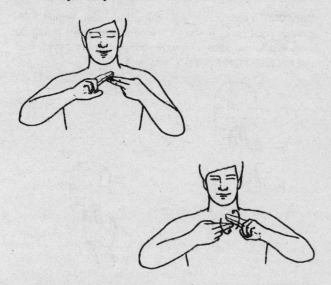

PREVENT (prĭ vĕnt′), *v.,* -VENTED, -VENTING. (Obstruct, block.) The left hand, fingers together and palm flat, is held before the body, facing somewhat down. The little finger side of the right hand, held with palm flat, makes one or several up-down chopping motions against the left hand, between its thumb and index finger. *Cf.* ANNOY, ANNOYANCE, BOTHER, DISTURB, INTERFERE, INTERFERENCE, INTERFERE WITH, INTERRUPT, PREVENTION.

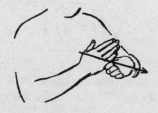

PREVENTION (pri věn′ shən), *n.* See PREVENT.

PREVIOUS (prē′ vǐ əs), *adj.* (Something past, behind.) The upraised right hand, in the "5" position with palm facing the body, is held just above the right shoulder and is thrown back over it. *Cf.* PAST, PREVIOUSLY, WAS, WERE.

PREVIOUSLY *adv.* See PREVIOUS.

PRICE (prīs), *n., v.,* PRICED, PRICING. (Nicking into one.) The knuckle of the right "X" finger is nicked against the palm of the left hand, held in the "5" position, palm facing right. *Cf.* COST, EXPENSE, FINE 2, PENALTY, TAX, TAXATION.

PRIDE (prīd), *n., v.,* PRIDED, PRIDING. (The feelings rise up.) The thumb of the right "A" hand, palm down, moves up along

the right side of the chest. A haughty expression is assumed.
Cf. PROUD.

PRINCE (prins), *n.* (The male root sign; tracing the royal
sash.) The right hand grasps an imaginary cap brim, and then
the signer, using the right "P" hand, traces an imaginary sash
from left shoulder to right hip.

PRINCESS (prin' sis), *n.* (The female root sign; tracing the
royal sash.) The right thumb moves down the line of the right
jaw, and then, as above for PRINCE, the royal sash is traced.

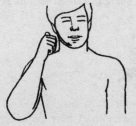

PRINCIPLE (prĭn′ sə pəl), *n.* (A collection or listing is indicated by the open palm, representing a page.) The right "P" hand is placed against the upper part of the open left hand, which faces right, fingers pointing upward. The right "P" hand swings down to the lower part of the left palm.

PRINT (prĭnt), *v.*, PRINTED, PRINTING. (The act of printing block letters.) The right index finger traces letters in the upturned left palm.

PRIVACY (prī′ və sĭ), *n.* (The sealing of the lips; keeping the words back.) The back of the thumb of the right "A" hand is placed firmly against the closed lips. The thumb, in this position, may move off the lips slightly and return again to the lips. As an optional addition, the thumb may swing down under the downturned cupped left hand, after being placed on the lips as above. *Cf.* PRIVATE 1.

PRIVATE 1 (prī′ vĭt), *adj*. See PRIVACY.

PRIVATE 2, *(colloq.)*, *adj*. (Closed.) Both open hands are held before the body, fingers pointing out, right palm facing left and left facing right. The right hand, held above the left, comes down against the index finger edge of the left a number of times.

PROBABLE (prŏb′ ə bəl), *adj*. (Weighing one thing against another.) The upturned open hands move alternately up and down. *Cf.* MAY 1, MAYBE, MIGHT 2, PERHAPS, POSSIBILITY, POSSIBLY, PROBABLY.

PROBABLY (prŏ′ ə blĭ), *adv*. See PROBABLE.

PROBLEM 1 (prŏb′ ləm), *n.* (A clouding over; a troubling.) Both "B" hands, palms facing each other, are rotated alternately before the forehead. *Cf.* TROUBLE, WORRIED, WORRY 1.

PROBLEM 2, *n.* (The knuckles are rubbed, to indicate a condition of being worn down.) The knuckles of the curved index and middle fingers of both hands are rubbed up and down against each other. Instead of the up-down rubbing, they may rub against each other in an alternate clockwise-counterclockwise manner. *Cf.* DIFFICULT 1, DIFFICULTY, HARD 1, HARDSHIP, POVERTY.

PROCEED (prə sēd′), *v.*, -CEEDED, -CEEDING. (Moving forward.) Both right-angle hands, palms facing each other and knuckles facing forward, move forward simultaneously. *Cf.* GO AHEAD.

PROCRASTINATE (prō krǎs′ tə nāt′), v., -NATED, -NATING. (Putting off; moving things forward repeatedly.) The "F" hands, palms facing and fingers pointing out from the body, are moved forward simultaneously in a series of short movements. *Cf.* DELAY, POSTPONE, PUT OFF.

PRODUCE (prə dūs′), v., -DUCED, -DUCING. (Fashioning something with the hands.) The right "S" hand, palm facing left, is placed on top of its left counterpart, whose palm faces right. The hands are twisted back and forth, striking each other slightly after each twist. *Cf.* CREATE, MAKE, MEND.

PROGRAM (prō′ grǎm, -grəm), n. (The letter "P"; a listing on both sides of the page.) The thumb side of the right "P" hand is placed against the palm of the open left hand, which is facing right. The right "P" hand moves down the left palm. The left hand then swings around so that its palm faces the body. The right "P" hand then moves over and down the back of the left hand.

PROGRESS (*n*. prŏg' rĕs; *v*. prə grĕs'), -GRESSED, -GRESSING. (Moving forward, step by step.) Both hands, in the right angle position, palms facing, are held before the chest, a few inches apart, with the right hand slightly behind the left. The right hand is brought up, over and forward, so that it is now ahead of the left. The left hand then follows suit, so that it is now ahead of the right.

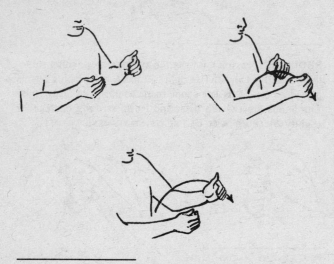

PROHIBIT (prŏ hĭb' ĭt), *v*., -ITED, -ITING. (A modification of LAW, *q.v.*; "against the law.") The downturned right "D" or "L" hand is thrust forcefully into the left palm. *Cf.* FORBID 1, FORBIDDEN 1.

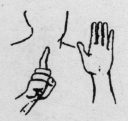

PROJECT (proj′ ekt), *n.* (The letters "P" and "J.") The middle finger of the right "P" hand moves down the left palm, held facing the body. Then the right "J" hand moves down the back of the left hand.

PROMINENT (prŏm′ ə nənt), *adj.* (One's fame radiates far and wide.) The extended index fingers rest on the lips (or on the temples). Moving in small, continuous spirals, they move up and to either side of the head. *Cf.* FAME, FAMOUS.

PROMISE (prŏm' ĭs), *n., v.,* -ISED, -ISING. (The arm is raised.) The right index finger is placed at the lips. The right arm is then raised, palm out and elbow resting on the back of the left hand. *Cf.* SWEAR 1.

PROMOTE (prə mōt'), *v.,* -MOTED, -MOTING. (Something high up.) Both hands, in the right angle position, are held before the face, about a foot apart, palms facing. They are raised abruptly about a foot, in a slight outward curving movement. *Cf.* HIGH 1, PROMOTION.

PROMOTION (prə mō' shən), *n.* See PROMOTE.

PROOF (prōōf), *n.* (Laying out the proof for all to see.) The back of the open right hand is placed with a flourish on the

open left palm. The index finger may first touch the lips. *Cf.*
PROVE.

PROPER (prŏp′ ər), *adj.* The right index finger, held above
the left index finger, comes down rather forcefully so that the
bottom of the right hand comes to rest on top of the left thumb
joint. *Cf.* CORRECT 1, RIGHT 3.

PROPOSE (prə pōz′), *v.*, -POSED, -POSING. (An offering; a presenting.) Both hands, slightly cupped, palms up, are held close
to the chest. They move up and out in unison, describing a
very slight arc. *Cf.* OFFER, OFFERING, PRESENT 1, SUGGEST.

PROTECT (prə tĕkt′), *v.*, -TECTED, -TECTING. (Hold down firmly; cover and strengthen.) The "S" hands, downturned, are held side by side in front of the body, the arms almost horizontal, and the left hand in front of the right. Both arms move a short distance forward and slightly downward. *Cf.* DEFEND, DEFENSE, GUARD, PROTECTION, SHIELD.

PROTECTION (prə tĕk′ shən), *n.* See PROTECT.

PROTEST (*n.* prō′ tĕst; *v.* prə tĕst′), -TESTED, -TESTING. (The hand is thrust into the chest to force a complaint out.) The curved fingers of the right hand are thrust forcefully into the chest. *Cf.* COMPLAIN, COMPLAINT, OBJECT, OBJECTION.

PROUD (proud), *adj.* (The feelings rise up.) The thumb of the right "A" hand, palm down, moves up along the right side of the chest. A haughty expression is assumed. *Cf.* PRIDE.

PROVE (prōōv), *v.*, PROVED, PROVEN, PROVING. See PROOF.

PROVIDE (prə vīd'), *v.*, -VIDED, -VIDING. (Handing over.) The "AND" hands are held upright with palms toward the body. From this position they swing forward and down, opening up as if giving something out.

PUBLIC RELATIONS (pŭb' lĭk rĭ lā' shəns), *n.* (The abbreviation; a fingerspelled loan sign.) The letters "P" and "R" are fingerspelled. This may be confused with "Puerto Rico," so one must rely on context.

PUBLISH (pŭb' lĭsh), *v.*, -LISHED, -LISHING. (The action of the press.) The right "5" hand, held palm down, fingers pointing left, is brought down twice against the upturned left "5" hand, whose fingers point right. *Cf.* NEWSPAPER, PAPER.

PUNCH 1 (pŭnch), *n.*, *v.*, PUNCHED, PUNCHING. (The natural sign.) The right "S" hand strikes its knuckles forcefully against the open left palm, which is held facing right. *Cf.* HIT 1, STRIKE.

PUNCH 2, *n.*, *v.* (The natural sign.) The right fist strikes the chin.

PUNISH (pŭn' ĭsh), *v.*, -ISHED, -ISHING. (A striking movement.) The right index finger strikes the left elbow with a glancing blow.

PURE (pyŏŏr), *adj.* (Everything is wiped off the hand, to emphasize an uncluttered or clean condition.) The right hand slowly wipes the upturned left palm, from wrist to fingertips. *Cf.* CLEAN, NICE, PLAIN 2, PURITY.

PURITY (pyŏŏr' ə tĭ), *n.* See PURE.

PURPOSE (pûr′ pəs), *n.* (Relative standing of one's thoughts.) A modified sign for THINK is made: The right index finger touches the middle of the forehead. The tips of the right "V" hand, palm down, are then thrust into the upturned left palm (as in STAND, *q.v.*). The right "V" hand is then re-thrust into the upturned left palm, with right palm now facing the body. *Cf.* INTEND, INTENT, INTENTION, MEAN 2, MEANING, SIGNIFICANCE 2, SIGNIFY.

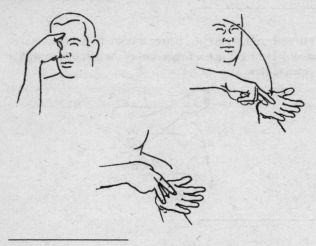

PUT (po͝ot), *v.,* PUT, PUTTING. (Moving from one place to another.) The downturned hands, fingers touching their respective thumbs, move in unison from left to right. *Cf.* MOVE.

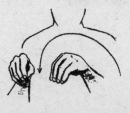

PUT IN ORDER *v. phrase.* (Placing things in order.) The hands, palms facing, fingers together and pointing away from the body, are positioned at the left side and held about a foot apart. With a slight up-down motion, as if describing waves, the hands travel in unison from left to right. *Cf.* ARRANGE, ARRANGEMENT, ORDER 2, PLAN, PREPARE 1, READY 1.

PUT OFF *v. phrase.* (Putting off; moving things forward repeatedly.) The "F" hands, palms facing and fingers pointing out from the body, are moved forward simultaneously in a series of short movements. *Cf.* DELAY, POSTPONE, PROCRASTI-NATE.

Q

QUANTITY (kwŏn' tə, tǐ), *n.* (Many fingers are indicated.) The upturned "S" hands are thrown up, opening into the "5" position, palms up. This may be repeated. *Cf.* MANY, NUMEROUS.

QUARREL (kwôr' əl, kwŏr'-), *n., v.* -RELED, -RELING. (Repeated rejoinders.) Both "D" hands are held with index fingers pointing toward each other. The hands move up and down alternately, each pivoting in turn at the wrist.

QUART (kwôrt), *n.* The "Q" hand, palm down, shakes slightly.

QUERY (kwĭr′ ĭ), *n., v.,* -RIED, -RYING. (Firing questions.) The index fingers of both "D" hands repeatedly curve and straighten out as the hands are alternately flung forward and back, as if firing questions. *Cf.* EXAMINATION 2, QUIZ.

QUESTION 1 (kwĕs′ chən), *n.* (The natural sign.) The right index finger draws a question mark in the air. *Cf.* QUESTION MARK.

QUESTION 2 *n.* See QUERY.

QUESTION MARK *n.* See QUESTION 1.

QUICK (kwĭk), *adj.* (A quick movement.) The thumbtip of the upright right hand is flicked quickly off the tip of the curved right index finger, as if shooting marbles. *Cf.* FAST, IMMEDIATELY, QUICKNESS, SPEED, SPEEDY.

QUICKNESS *n.* See QUICK.

QUIET 1 (kwī′ ət), *n.*, *adj.*, *interj.*, *v.*, QUIETED, QUIETING. (The natural sign.) The index finger is brought up against the pursed lips. *Cf.* BE QUIET 1, SILENCE 1, SILENT.

QUIET 2, *n.*, *adj.*, *interj.*, *v.* (Quiet and peace.) The open hands are crossed before the mouth, the right palm facing left, left facing right. Then both hands, held palms down, move down from the mouth, curving outward to either side of the body. *Cf.* BE QUIET 2, BE STILL, CALM, SILENCE 2.

QUIT (kwĭt), *v.*, QUIT, QUITTING. (Pulling out.) The index and middle fingers of the right "H" hand are grasped by the left hand. The right hand pulls out of the left. *Cf.* RESIGN, WITHDRAW 2.

QUIZ (kwĭz), v., QUIZZED, QUIZZING, n. (Firing questions.) The index fingers of both "D" hands repeatedly curve and straighten out as the hands are alternately flung forward and back, as if firing questions. *Cf.* EXAMINATION 2, QUERY.

QUOTATION (kwŏ tā′ shən), n. (The quotation marks are indicated.) The curved index and middle fingers of both hands, held palms out, move slightly to either side of the body, as if drawing quotation marks in the air. *Cf.* QUOTE, SO-CALLED, SUBJECT, TITLE, TOPIC.

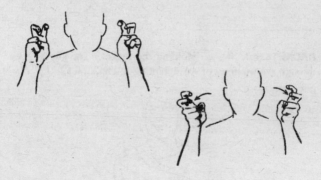

QUOTE (kwŏt), n., v., QUOTED, QUOTING. See QUOTATION.

R

RACE (rās), *n.*, *v.*, RACED, RACING. (Opposing objects.) The "A" hands are held side by side before the chest, palms facing each other and thumbs pointing forward. In this position the hands move alternately back and forth, toward and away from the body. *Cf.* COMPETE 2, COMPETITION 2.

RACKET (rak' it), *n.* (Holding the racket.) The signer goes through the motions of manipulating a tennis racket. *Cf.* TENNIS.

RAGE (rāj), *n.*, *v.*, RAGED, RAGING. (A violent welling-up of the emotions.) The curved fingers of the right hand are placed in the center of the chest, and fly up suddenly and violently.

An expression of anger is worn. *Cf.* ANGER, ANGRY 2, FURY, MAD.

RAILROAD (rāl′ rōd′), *n.* (The letter "R".) The right "R" hand, palm down, moves down an inch or two, and moves to the right in a small arc.

RAINBOW (rān′ bō), *n.* (Tracing the colors across the sky.) The right "4" hand, palm facing the signer, describes an arc in the air, from left to right.

RAISE (rāz), *n.*, *v.*, RAISED, RAISING. (Adding on.) The index and middle fingers of the right "H" hand, palm up, are swung up and over until they come to rest on the index and middle fingers of the left "H" hand, held palm down. *Cf.* ADD 2, ADDITION, GAIN, INCREASE.

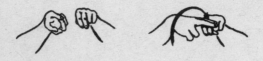

RAISINS (rā′ zənz), *n.* (The letter "R"; a cluster of grapes.) The right "R" fingers move down the back of the prone left hand, tapping as they go.

RAMP (ramp), *n.* (The incline.) The downturned right hand, fingers pointing forward, moves up an imaginary incline. Both hands may also be used, with one leading the other.

RANCH (ranch), *n.* (The letter "R"; the stubbled chin of a rough cowboy.) The right "R" hand, palm facing left, slides from the left chin to the right.

RASH (rash), *n.* (Spots on the body.) Both claw hands make dots all over the chest and/or face.

REACTION (rĭ ăk′shən), *n.* (The letter "R"; coming out of the mouth.) Both "R" hands are held before the face, with the right "R" hand at the lips and behind the left "R" hand. Both hands move forward simultaneously, describing a small upward arc. *Cf.* RESPONSE 2.

READ (rĕd), *v.*, READ, READING. (The eyes scan the page.) The left hand is held before the body, palm up and fingers pointing to the right. This represents the page. The right "V" hand then moves down as if scanning the page.

READY 1 (rĕd' ĭ), *adj.*, *v.*, READIED, READYING. (Placing things in order.) The hands, palms facing, fingers together and pointing away from the body, are positioned at the left side and held about a foot apart. With a slight updown motion, as if describing waves, the hands travel in unison from left to right. *Cf.* ARRANGE, ARRANGEMENT, ORDER 2, PLAN, PREPARE 1, PUT IN ORDER.

READY 2, *adj.*, *adv.* (The "R" hands.) The same sign as for READY 1, *q.v.*, is made, except that the "R" hands are used. With palms facing down, they move simultaneously from left to right.

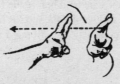

READY 3, *adj.*, *v.* (Set out.) The "A" hands are crossed, with the right resting on top of the left. The right palm faces left and the left palm faces right. Both hands suddenly open and swing apart to the palm-down position. *Cf.* PREPARE 2.

REAL (rē′ əl, rēl), *adj.* (Coming forth directly from the lips; true.) The index finger of the right "D" hand, palm facing left, is placed against the lips. It moves up an inch or two and then describes a small arc forward and away from the lips. *Cf.* REALLY, SURE, SURELY, TRUE, TRULY, TRUTH.

REALLY (rē′ ə lĭ, rē′ lĭ), *adv.* See REAL.

REASON (rē′ zən), *n.* (The letter "R"; the thought.) The fingertips of the right "R" hand describe a small counterclockwise circle in the middle of the forehead.

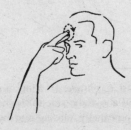

RECALL (rĭ kôl′), *v.*, -CALLED, -CALLING. (Knowledge which remains.) The sign for KNOW is made: The right fingertips are placed on the forehead. The sign for REMAIN then follows: The "A" hands are held with palms toward the body, thumbs extended and touching, the right behind the left. In this position the hands move forward in a straight, steady line, or straight down. *Cf.* REMEMBER.

RECEIVE (rĭ sēv′), *v.*, -CEIVED, -CEIVING. (A grasping and bringing forward to oneself.) Both hands, in the "5" position, fingers curved, are crossed at the wrists, with the left palm facing right and the right palm facing left. They are brought in toward the chest, while closing into a grasping "S" position. *Cf.* GET.

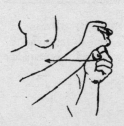

RECEIVE REGULARLY *phrase.* (Pulling in repeatedly.) The right claw hand, held above the side of the head, palm facing left, is pulled down repeatedly, closing into the "S" shape each time. This is an appropriate sign for "subscription," "benefits," such as Social Security, and "earnings" or "salary."

RECENT (rē′ sənt), *adj*. (The slight movement represents a slight amount of time.) With the closed right hand held with knuckles against the right cheek, the thumbtip flicks off the tip of the curved index finger a number of times. The eyes squint a bit and the lips are drawn out in a slight smile. The hand remains against the cheek during the flicking movement. Sometimes, instead of the flicking movement, the tip of the curved index finger scratches slightly up and down against the cheek. In this case, the palm faces back toward the shoulder. The same expression is used as in the flicking movement. *Cf.* RECENTLY, WHILE AGO, A 1.

RECENTLY *adv*. See RECENT.

RECTANGLE (rek' tang gəl), *n.* (The letter "R"; the shape.) Both "R" hands describe a rectangle in the air.

RED (rĕd), *adj., n.* (The lips, which are red, are indicated.) The tip of the right index finger moves down across the lips. The "R" hand may also be used.

REDUCE (rĭ dūs', -dōōs'), *v.,* -DUCED, -DUCING. (The diminishing size or amount.) With palms facing, the right hand is held above the left. The right hand moves slowly down toward the left, but does not touch it. *Cf.* DECREASE, LESS.

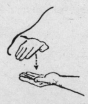

REFLECT (ri flekt'), *v.* (The image reflects back.) The right

"R" fingers, held up, touch the outstretched left palm, and move forward slowly and deliberately. The signer may cause the right hand to tremble slightly as it moves forward.

REFUSE (rĭ fūz′), v., -FUSED, -FUSING. (Holding back.) The right "A" hand, palm facing left, moves up sharply to a position above the right shoulder. *Cf.* WON'T.

REGRET (rĭ grĕt′), n., v., -GRETTED, -GRETTING. (The heart is circled, to indicate feeling, modified by the letter "S," for SORRY.) The right "S" hand, palm facing the body, is rotated several times over the area of the heart. *Cf.* APOLOGIZE 1, APOLOGY 1, REGRETFUL, SORROW, SORROWFUL 2, SORRY.

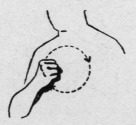

REGRETFUL (rǐ grět′ fəl), *adj*. See REGRET.

REGULAR (rĕg′ yə lər), *adj*. (Coming together with regular frequency.) Both "D" hands are held with index fingers pointing forward, the right hand above the left. The right "D" hand is brought down on the left several times in rhythmic succession as both hands move forward.

REJOICE (rǐ jois′), *v*., -JOICED, -JOICING. (Waving of flags.) Both upright hands, grasping imaginary flags, wave them in small circles. *Cf*. CELEBRATE, CELEBRATION, CHEER, VICTORY 1, WIN 1.

RELAX 1 (rǐ lăks′), *v*., -LAXED, -LAXING. (The folded arms; a position of rest.) With palms facing the body, the arms are folded across the chest. *Cf*. REST 1, RESTFUL 1.

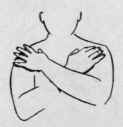

RELAX 2, *n.* (The "R" hands.) The sign for REST 1, *q.v.*, is made, but with the crossed "R" hands. *Cf.* REST 2, RESTFUL 2.

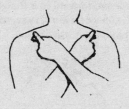

RELAY (rē' lā), *n., v.* (Back and forth movement.) Both "R" hands pass each other repeatedly as they move back and forth.

RELY (rǐ lī'), *v.*, -LIED, -LYING. (Hanging on to.) With the right index finger resting across its left counterpart, both hands drop down a bit. *Cf.* DEPEND, DEPENDABLE.

REMAIN (rĭ mān'), *v.*, -MAINED, -MAINING. (Steady, uninterrupted movement.) The "A" hands are held with palms out, thumbs extended and touching, the right behind the left. In this position the hands move forward in a straight, steady line. *Cf.* CONTINUE, ENDURE 2, EVER 1, LAST 3, LASTING, PERMANENT, PERSEVERE, PERSIST, STAY 1, STAY STILL.

REMAINDER (rĭ mān' dər), *n.* (The remainder is left behind.) The "5" hands, palms facing each other and fingers pointing forward, are dropped simultaneously a few inches, as if dropping something on the table. *Cf.* LEFT.

REMEMBER (rĭ mĕm' bər), *v.*, -BERED, -BERING. (Knowledge which remains.) The sign for KNOW is made: The right fingertips are placed on the forehead. The sign for REMAIN then follows: The "A" hands are held with palms toward the body, thumbs extended and touching, the right behind the left. In this position the hands move forward in a straight, steady line, or straight down. *Cf.* RECALL.

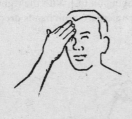

REMOVE (rĭ mŏov'), v., -MOVED, -MOVING. (Removing.) The right "A" hand, resting in the palm of the left "5" hand, moves slightly up and away, describing a small arc. It is then cast downward, opening into the "5" position, palm down, as if removing something from the left hand and casting it down. *Cf.* DEDUCT, ELIMINATE, SUBTRACT, SUBTRACTION.

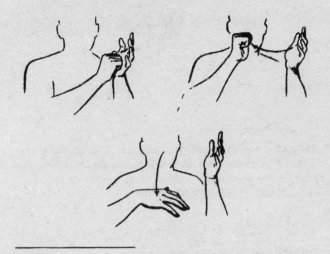

RENT (rent), n., v. (Monthly.) The sign for MONTH is made: The extended right index finger moves down along the upturned extended left index finger. This movement is repeated several times. *Cf.* MONTHLY.

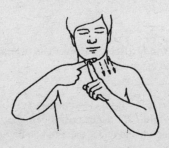

REPAIR WHAT WAS SAID (Grammatical device in ASL.)
The right index finger is brought firmly up against the tightly
closed lips. The eyes may be closed and the head may shake
slightly. The English gloss here may be "Excuse me, I didn't
mean that;" "Let me correct myself." Also known as "repairs"
in ASL grammar.

REPEAT (rĭ pēt′), *v.*, -PEATED, -PEATING. The left hand, open
in the "5" position, palm up, is held before the chest. The right
hand, in the right angle position, fingers pointing up, arches
over and into the left palm. *Cf.* AGAIN.

REPEATEDLY *adv.* (Repeating over and over again.) The sign
for REPEAT is made several times.

REPLACE (rĭ plās′), *v.*, -PLACED, -PLACING. (Exchanging
places.) The right "A" hand, positioned above the left "A"
hand, swings down and under the left, coming up a bit in front

of it. *Cf.* EXCHANGE, SUBSTITUTE, TRADE.

REPLY (rĭ plī′), *n., v.,* -PLIED, -PLYING. (Directing a reply from the mouth to someone.) The tip of the right index finger, held in the "D" position, palm facing the body, is placed on the lips, while the left "D" hand, palm also facing the body, is held about a foot in front of the right hand. The right index finger, swinging around, moves toward and stops in a pointing position a few inches from the left index fingertip. *Cf.* ANSWER, RESPOND, RESPONSE 1.

REPRESENT (rĕp´ rĭ zĕnt´), *v.*, -SENTED, -SENTING. (Directing the attention to something, and bringing it forward.) The right index finger points into the left palm, held facing out before the body. The left palm moves straight out. *Cf.* DEMONSTRATE, DISPLAY, EXAMPLE, EXHIBIT, EXHIBITION, SHOW 1, SIGNIFY 1.

REPUBLIC (ri pub´ lik), *n.* (The letter "R"; NATION.) The tips of the right "R" fingers make a clockwise circle above the downturned left hand and come down to rest on the back of the left fist. *Cf.* COUNTRY 2, LAND 2, NATION.

REQUEST (rĭ kwĕst´), *n., v.*, -QUESTED, -QUESTING. (Pray tell.) Both hands, held upright about a foot in front of the chest, with palms facing and fingers pointing straight up, are positioned about a foot apart. Moving toward the chest, they come togeth er until they touch, as if in prayer. *Cf.* ASK 1.

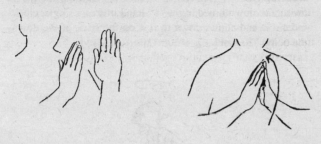

REQUIRE (rĭ kwīr′), *v.*, -QUIRED, -QUIRING. (Something specific is moved in toward oneself.) The palm of the left "5" hand faces right. The right index finger is thrust into the left palm, and both hands are drawn sharply in toward the chest. *Cf.* DEMAND.

RESCUE (rĕs′ kū), *v.*, -CUED, -CUING, *n.* (Breaking the bonds.) The "S" hands, crossed in front of the body, swing apart and face out. *Cf.* FREE 1, FREEDOM, INDEPENDENCE, INDEPENDENT 1, SAFE, SAVE 1.

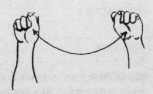

RESERVATION 1 (rĕz´ ər vā´ shən), *n.* (Binding the hands down.) The downturned, right "S" hand makes a single, clockwise circle and comes down to rest on the back of the downturned, left "S" hand. *Cf.* APPOINTMENT, RESERVE.

RESERVATION 2, *n.* (Tying down.) Both hands are held in the downturned "A" or "S" position. The right hand makes a clockwise circle, coming down to rest on the back of the left.

RESERVE (rĭ zûrv´), *v.* -SERVED, -SERVING. See

RESERVATION 1.

RESIDENCE (rĕz´ ə dəns), *n.* (The letter "R"; LIVE.) Both "R" hands move up together against the body. This is an initialized version of LIVE.

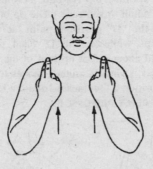

RESIGN (rĭ zīn′), v., -SIGNED, -SIGNING. (Pulling out.) The index and middle fingers of the right "H" hand are grasped by the left hand. The right hand pulls out of the left. *Cf.* QUIT, WITHDRAW 2.

RESPECT (rĭ spĕkt′), n., v., -SPECTED, -SPECTING. (The letter "R"; bowing the head.) The right "R" hand swings up in an arc toward the head, which bows somewhat as the hand moves up toward it. The hand's movement is sometimes reversed, moving down and away from the head in an arc, while the head bows.

RESPOND (rĭ spŏnd'), *v.*, -PONDED, -PONDING. (Directing a reply from the mouth to someone.) The tip of the right index finger, held in the "D" position, palm facing the body, is placed on the lips, while the left "D" hand, palm also facing the body, is held about a foot in front of the right hand. The right index finger, swinging around, moves toward and stops in a pointing position a few inches from the left index fingertip. *Cf.* ANSWER, REPLY, RESPONSE 1.

RESPONSE 1 (rĭ spŏns'), *n.* See RESPOND.

RESPONSE 2, *n.* (The letter "R"; coming out of the mouth.) Both "R" hands are held before the face, with the right "R" hand at the lips and behind the left "R" hand. Both hands move forward simultaneously, describing a small upward arc. *Cf.* REACTION.

RESPONSIBILITY 1 (rĭ spŏn´ sə bĭl' ə tĭ), *n.* (Something which weighs down or burdens one with responsibility.) The fingertips of both hands, placed on the right shoulder, bear down. *Cf.* RESPONSIBLE 1.

RESPONSIBILITY 2, *n.* (Something which weighs down or burdens, modified by the letter "R," for "responsibility.") The "R" hands bear down on the right shoulder in the same manner as RESPONSIBILITY 1. *Cf.* RESPONSIBLE 2.

RESPONSIBLE 1 (ri spŏn′ sə bəl), *adj.* See RESPONSIBILITY 1.

RESPONSIBLE 2, *adj.* See RESPONSIBILITY 2.

REST 1 (rĕst), *n.* (The folded arms; a position of rest.) With palms facing the body, the arms are folded across the chest. *Cf.* RELAX 1, RESTFUL 1.

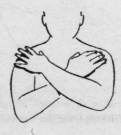

REST 2, *n.* (The "R" hands.) The sign for REST 1 is made, but with the crossed "R" hands. *Cf.* RELAX 2, RESTFUL 2.

RESTFUL 1 (rĕst′ fəl), *adj.* See REST 1.

RESTFUL 2, *adj.* See REST 2.

RESTRICT (rĭ strĭkt′), *v.*, -STRICTED, -STRICTING. (The upper and lower limits are defined.) The right-angle hands, palms facing, are held before the body, the right above the left. They swing out 45 degrees simultaneously, pivoted from their wrists. *Cf.* LIMIT.

RESUME (rez′ ŏŏ mā), *n.* (The letter "R"; the shape of a piece of paper.) Both "R" hands trace the top and sides of an imaginary piece of paper.

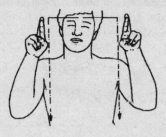

RETALIATE (rĭ tăl′ ĭ āt′), *v.*, -ATED, -ATING. (Birds pecking back and forth at each other.) The right index finger and thumb, pressed together, strike their counterparts with force. *Cf.* RETALIATION, REVENGE.

RETALIATION (rĭ tăl′ ĭ ā′ shən), *n.* See RETALIATE.

RETIRE (rĭ tīr′), *v.*, -TIRED, -TIRING. (A position of idleness.) With thumbs tucked in the armpits, the remaining fingers of both hands wiggle. *Cf.* VACATION.

REVENGE (rĭ vĕnj′), *n., v.,* -VENGED, -VENGING. (Birds peck-ing back and forth at each other.) The right index finger and thumb, pressed together, strike their left counterparts with force. *Cf.* RETALIATE, RETALIATION.

REVERSE ROLES *phrase.* (Changing places.) The right "V" hand, palm up, fingers pointing left, turns over to the palm down position.

REVOLUTION 1 (rev ə lōō′ shən), *n.* (The letter "R"; a whirl-wind.) Both "R" hands, fingertips pointing at each other, are held with the right above the left. The "R" fingers spin around each other in a sudden and dramatic movement.

REVOLUTION 2, *n*. (The letter "R"; turning around or rebelling.) The upturned right "R" hand, held palm back at shoulder height, twists around suddenly with a dramatic flourish to the palm out position.

RHINOCEROS (rī nos' ər əs), *n*. (The horn.) The right "I" hand, palm facing left and thumb tucked under the fingers, is placed on the nose. The hand moves forward and up in an arc, tracing the characteristic shape of the horn.

RICH (rĭch), *adj.* (A pile of money.) The sign for MONEY is made: The back of the upturned right hand, whose thumb and fingertips are all touching, is placed in the upturned left palm. The right hand then moves straight up, as it opens into the "5" position, palm facing down and fingers somewhat curved. *Cf.* WEALTH, WEALTHY.

RIDICULOUS (rĭ dĭk′ yə ləs), *adj.* (Thoughts flickering back and forth.) The right "Y" hand, thumb almost touching the forehead, is shaken back and forth across the forehead several times. *Cf.* FOOLISH, NONSENSE, SILLY.

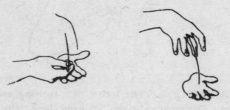

RIGHT 1 (rīt), *adj.* (A straightening out.) The right hand, fingers together and palm facing left, is placed in the upturned left palm, whose fingers point away from the body. The right hand slides straight out along the left palm, over the left fingers, and stops with its heel resting on the left fingertips. *Cf.* ALL RIGHT, O.K. 1, YOU'RE WELCOME 2.

RIGHT 2, *adj., adv.* (The letter "R"; the movement.) The right "R" hand moves toward the right.

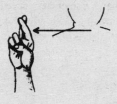

RIGHT 3, *adj., adv.* The right index finger, held above the left index finger, comes down rather forcefully so that the bottom of the right hand comes to rest on top of the left thumb joint. *Cf.* CORRECT 1, PROPER.

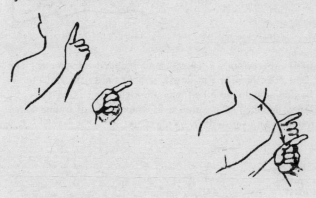

ROAD (rōd), *n.* (The winding movement.) Both hands, palms facing and fingers together and extended straight out, move in unison away from the body, in a winding manner. *Cf.* STREET.

ROB 1 (rŏb), *v.,* ROBBED, ROBBING. (The hand, partly concealed, takes something surreptitiously.) The index and middle
fingers of the right hand, somewhat curved, are placed under
the left elbow. As they move slowly along the left forearm
toward the left wrist, they close a bit. *Cf.* STEAL 1, THEFT 1,
THIEF, THIEVERY.

ROB 2, (*colloq.*), *v.* (A sly, underhanded movement.) The
right open hand, palm down, is held under the left elbow.
Beginning with the little finger, the right hand closes finger by
finger into the "A" position, as if wrapping itself around something, and moves to the right. *Cf.* STEAL 2.

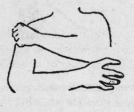

ROB 3, *v.* (A mustachioed thief.) The fingertips of both "H"
hands, palms facing the body, are placed above the lips and are
drawn slowly apart, describing a mustache. Sometimes one

hand only is used. *Cf.* CROOK, THEFT 2.

ROBOT (rō′ bət), *n*. (The robot's mechanical gait.) The signer mimes the mechanical walk of a fiction-type robot, with the stiff movements of the hands and legs.

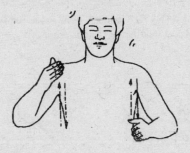

ROCKING CHAIR *n*. (The "R" hands; retire or loaf.) The thumbs of both "R" hands are tucked into the arm pits and the signer imitates the forward backward motion of a rocking chair.

ROOM 1 (rōōm, rŏŏm), *n*. (The dimensions are indicated.)
The open hands, palms facing and fingers pointing out, are
dropped an inch or two simultaneously. They then shift their
relative positions so that both palms face the body, with one
hand in front of the other. In this new position they again drop
an inch or two simultaneously. *Cf.* BOX 1, PACKAGE.

ROOM 2, *n*. (The "R" hands.) This is the same sign as for
ROOM 1, except that the "R" hands are used.

ROOMY (rōō′ mē), *adj*. (Lots of elbow room.) The "S" hands,
palms facing, are positioned at chest height. As the elbows
move apart the palms move down.

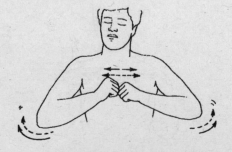

ROUGH (rŭf), *adj.* (The "roughness," in the form of ridges, described.) The tips of the curved right fingers trace imaginary ridges over the upright left palm, from the base of the hand to the fingertips. The action is repeated several times. *Cf.* RUDE, RUDENESS, SCOLD 1.

RUDE (rōōd), *adj.* (The "roughness," of words is described.) The tips of the curved right fingers trace imaginary ridges over the upright left palm, from the base of the hand to the fingertips. The action is repeated several times. *Cf.* ROUGH, RUDENESS, SCOLD 1.

RUDENESS (rōōd' nĭs), *n.* See RUDE.

RUG (rŭg), *n.* (The "R"; covering a flat surface.) The right "R" hand is placed on the upturned left palm, with the right thumb underneath the left hand. The right hand moves straight forward from the heel.

RUIN (rōō 'ĭn), *n.* (Wiping off.) The left "5" hand, palm up, is held slightly above the right "5" hand, held palm down. The right hand swings up, just brushing over the left palm. Both hands close into the "S" position, and the right is brought back with force to its initial position, striking a glancing blow against the left knuckles as it returns. *Cf.* DESTROY.

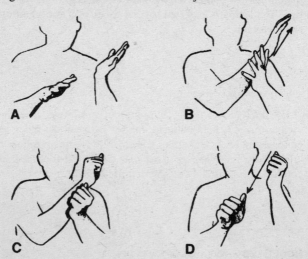

RULE (ro͞ol), *n.*, *v.*, RULED, RULING. (Holding the reins over all.) The "A" hands, palms facing, move alternately back and forth, as if grasping and manipulating reins. The left "A" hand, still in position, swings over so that its palm now faces down. The right hand opens to the "5" position, palm down, and swings over the left, which moves slightly to the right. *Cf.* CONTROL 1, GOVERN, MANAGE.

RUN (rŭn), *v.*, RAN, RUN, RUNNING. The open left hand is held pointing out, palm down. The open right hand is held beneath it, facing up. The right hand is thrown forward rather quickly so the palm brushes repeatedly across the palm of the left.

RUN AWAY *v. phrase.* (Slipping out and away.) The right index finger is held pointing upward between the index and middle fingers of the prone left hand. From this position the right index finger moves to the right, slipping out of the grasp of the left fingers and away from the left hand.

S

SAD (săd), *adj.* (The facial features drop.) Both "5" hands, palms facing the eyes and fingers slightly curved, drop simultaneously to a level with the mouth. The head drops slightly as the hands move down, and an expression of sadness is assumed. *Cf.* GLOOM, GLOOMY, GRIEF, SORROWFUL 1.

SAFE (săf), *adj., n.* (Breaking the bonds.) The "S" hands, crossed in front of the body, swing apart and face out. *Cf.* FREE 1, FREEDOM, INDEPENDENCE, INDEPENDENT 1, RESCUE, SAVE 1.

SAFETY PIN (săf' tē pin), *n.* (Closing the pin.) The right index and thumb come together against the left chest.

SAID (sĕd), *v.* (Words tumbling from the mouth.) The right index finger, pointing left, describes a continuous small circle in front of the mouth. *Cf.* HEARING, MENTION, SAY, SPEAK, SPEECH 1, TALK 1, TELL.

SAILOR (sā′ lər), *n.* (The bell bottoms.) Both hands, fingers pointing straight down, indicate the flare of bell bottom pants, first above the left leg and then the right.

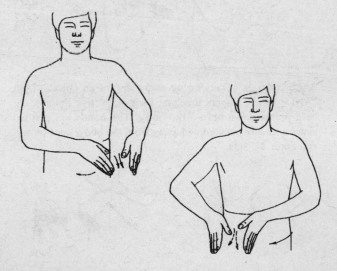

SALARY (săl′ ə rĭ), *n.* (EARN, MONEY.) The sign for EARN is made: the right "5" hand, its little finger edge resting on the upturned left palm, moves toward the left and closes into the "S" position. This is followed by MONEY: The upturned right fingertips, grasping a wad of imaginary dollar bills, slaps down on the left palm.

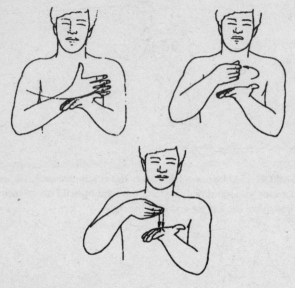

SALE (săl), *n.* (Transferring ownership of an object.) Both "AND" hands, fingers touching their respective thumbs, are held palms down before the body. The hands are pivoted simultaneously outward and away from the body, once or several times. *Cf.* SELL.

SALOON (sə loon'), *n.* (Raising the beer stein or mug.) The thumb of the right "A" or "Y" hand is brought up to the mouth. *Cf.* BAR.

SALT (sôlt), *n.* (The act of tapping the salt from a knife edge.) Both "H" hands, palms down, are held before the chest. The fingers of the right "H" hand tap those of the left several times.

SAME 1 (sām), *adj.* (Matching fingers are brought together.) The outstretched index fingers are brought together, either once or several times. *Cf.* ALIKE, LIKE 2, SIMILAR.

SAME 2, (*colloq.*), *adj.* (Two figures are compared, back and forth.) The right "Y" hand, palm facing left, is moved alternately toward and away from the body. *Cf.* ME TOO.

SANDAL (săn′ dəl), *n.* (The crossed straps or thongs.) The downturned right "4" hand crosses the downturned left hand from little finger edge to thumb. It then turns around to the palm up position and crosses the left hand from wrist to fingertips.

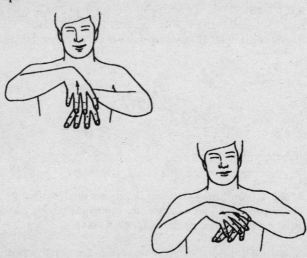

SANDWICH (sănd′ wĭch, săn′-), *n.* (In between slices.) The fingers of the upturned right hand are tucked between the middle and third fingers of the left hand, whose palm faces the signer. The motion may be repeated.

SATISFACTION (săt´ ĭs făk´ shən), *n.* (The inner feelings settle down.) Both "B" hands (or "5" hands, fingers together) are placed palms down against the chest, the right above the left. Both move down simultaneously a few inches. *Cf.* CONTENT, CONTENTED, SATISFIED, SATISFY 1.

SATISFIED *adj.* See SATISFACTION.

SATISFY 1 (săt´ ĭs fī), *v.*, -FIED, -FYING. See SATISFACTION.

SATISFY 2, *v.* This is the same sign as for SATISFY 1 but with only one hand used.

SAVE 1 (sāv), *v.*, SAVED, SAVING. (Breaking the bonds.) The "S" hands, crossed in front of the body, swing apart and face out. *Cf.* FREE 1, FREEDOM, INDEPENDENCE, INDEPENDENT 1, RESCUE, SAFE.

SAVE 2, *v.* (Holding back.) The right "V" fingers are tapped once or twice across the back of their left counterparts. Both palms face the chest.

SAY (sā), *v.*, SAID, SAYING. (Words tumbling from the mouth.) The right index finger, pointing left, describes a continuous small circle in front of the mouth. *Cf.* HEARING, MENTION, SAID, SPEAK, SPEECH 1, TALK 1, TELL.

SCARE(D) (skâr), *v.*, SCARED, SCARING, *n.* (The heart is suddenly covered with fear.) Both hands, fingers together, are placed side by side, palms facing the chest. They quickly open and come together over the heart, one on top of the other. *Cf.* AFRAID, FEAR 1, FRIGHT, FRIGHTEN, TERROR 1.

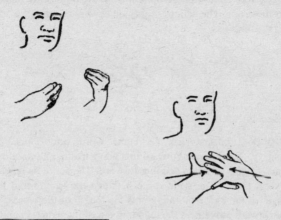

SCHOOL (skōōl), *n.* (The teachers hands are clapped for attention.) The hands are clapped together several times.

SCIENCE (sī' əns), *n.* (Pouring alternately from test tubes.) The upright thumbs of both "A" hands swing over alternately in elliptical fashion, as if pouring out the contents of a pair of test tubes. .

SCOLD 1 (skōld), *(colloq.)*, *v.*, SCOLDED, SCOLDING. (Rough language.) The tips of the curved right fingers trace imaginary ridges over the upright left palm, from the base of the hand to the fingertips. The action is repeated several times. *Cf.* ROUGH, RUDE, RUDENESS.

SCOLD 2, *(sl.)*, *v.* (Big, *i.e.*, curse, words tumble out.) The right "Y" hand moves forward in a wavy manner along the left index finger, which is pointing forward. The action is repeated several times. The wide space between the thumb and little finger of the "Y" hand represents the length of the words, and the forward movement the tumbling out of the words in anger.

SCOTCH TAPE *n., v.* (Spreading the tape.) Both downturned thumbs, tips touching, move apart in opposite directions, as if smoothing on a piece of tape.

SCREAM (skrēm), *v.*, SCREAMED, SCREAMING. (Harsh words thrown out.) The right hand, as in CURSE 1, appears to claw words out of the mouth. This time, however, it turns and throws them out, ending in the "5" position. *Cf.* CURSE 2, SHOUT.

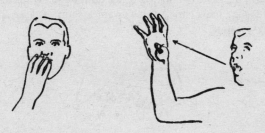

SCREW (skrōō), *n., v.* (The movement.) The right index finger makes a clockwise turn in the left palm.

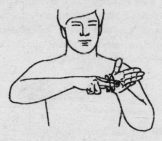

SEARCH (sûrch), *v.*, SEARCHED, SEARCHING. (Directing the vision from place to place.) The right "C" hand, palm facing left, moves from right to left across the line of vision, in a series of counterclockwise circles. The signer's gaze remains concentrated and his head turns slowly from right to left. *Cf.* EXAMINE, LOOK FOR, SEEK.

SEAT (sēt), *n.*, *v.*, SEATED, SEATING. (The act of sitting.) The extended right index and middle fingers are draped across the back of the same two fingers of the downturned left hand. The hands then move straight downward a short distance. *Cf.* BE SEATED, CHAIR, SIT.

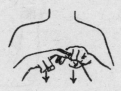

SECOND 1 (sĕk′ ənd), *adj.* (The second finger is indicated.) The tip of the index finger of the right "D" hand is placed on the tip of the middle finger of the left "V" hand. The right hand then executes a short pivotal movement in a clockwise direction. The left "L" hand may be substituted for the left "V" hand, with the right index fingertip placed on the left index fingertip. *Cf.* SECONDARY, SECONDLY.

SECOND 2, *n.* (The ticking off of seconds on the clock.) The index finger of the right "D" hand executes a series of very short movements in a clockwise manner as it rests against the left "S" hand, which is facing right.

SECONDARY (sĕk′ ən dĕr′ ĭ), *adj.* See SECOND 1.

SECONDLY (sĕk′ ənd lǐ), *adv.* See SECOND 1.

SEE (sē), *v.,* SAW, SEEN, SEEING. (The eyesight is directed for-ward.) The right "V" hand, palm facing the body, is placed so that the fingertips are just under the eyes. The hand swings straight out. *Cf.* SIGHT.

SEEK (sēk), *v.,* SOUGHT, SEEKING. (Directing the vision from place to place.) The right "C" hand, palm facing left, moves from right to left across the line of vision, in a series of coun-terclockwise circles. The signers gaze remains concentrated and his head turns slowly from right to left. *Cf.* EXAMINE, LOOK FOR, SEARCH.

SEEM (sēm), *v.*, SEEMED, SEEMING. (Something presented before the eyes.) The open right hand, palm flat and facing out, with fingers together and pointing up, is positioned at shoulder level. Pivoting from the wrist, the hand is swung around so that the palm now faces the eyes. Sometimes the eyes glance at the newly presented palm. *Cf.* LOOK 2.

SEE-SAW (sē′ sô), *n.* (The up-and-down movement.) Both downturned "H" hands are held with index and middle fingers touching. They move alternately up and down, always maintaining contact.

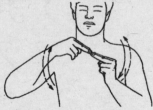

SEETHE (sēth), *v.* (A slow boil.) The right hand, palm up, is placed beneath the palm down left hand. The right fingers wriggle under the left palm.

SELECT 1 (sǐ lěkt'), *v.*, -LECTED, -LECTING. (The natural motion of selecting something from the hand.) The thumb and index fingers of the outstretched right hand grasp an imaginary object on the upturned left palm. The right hand then moves straight up. *Cf.* FIND, PICK 1.

SELECT 2, *v.* (Taking unto oneself.) The right hand, palm out, is extended before the chest, index finger and thumb in an open position, the other fingers separated and pointing up. The hand is drawn in toward the chest, and the index and thumb close at the same time, indicating something taken to oneself. *Cf.* CHOOSE, TAKE.

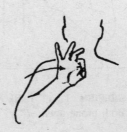

-SELF (sĕlf), *n.* used with a gender prefix as a reflexive and intensive pronoun; *adj.* (The individual is indicated with the thumb.) The right hand, held in the "A" position, thumb up, moves several times in the direction of the person indicated: *myself, yourself, himself, herself, itself, oneself, ourselves, yourselves, themselves. Cf.* YOURSELF.

SELF-CENTERED (self' sen tərd), *adj. phrase.* (SELF and CENTER.) The sign for SELF is made: The right "A" hand, thumb pointing up, is brought against the chest. The sign for CENTER follows: The downturned right fingers describe a small clockwise circle and come to rest in the upturned left palm.

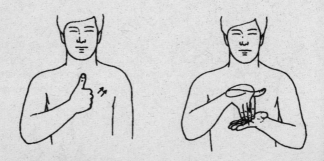

SELFISH 1 (sĕl' fĭsh), *adj.* (Pulling things toward oneself.) Both prone open or "V" hands are held in front of the body with fingers bent. The hands are then drawn quickly and forcefully inward, as if raking things toward oneself. *Cf.* GREEDY 1, STINGY 1.

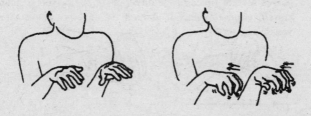

SELFISH 2, *adj.* (Scratching the palm in greed.) The right fingers scratch the upturned left palm several times. A frowning expression is often used. *Cf.* GREEDY 2, STINGY 2.

SELL (sĕl), *v.*, SOLD, SELLING. (Transferring ownership of an object.) Both "AND" hands, fingers touching their respective thumbs, are held palms down before the body. The hands are pivoted simultaneously outward and away from the body, once or several times. *Cf.* SALE.

SEND 1 (sĕnd), *v.*, SENT, SENDING. (Sending away from.) The right fingertips tap the back of the downturned, left "S" hand and then swing forward, away from the hand.

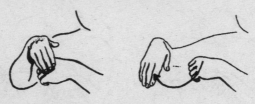

SEND 2, *v.* (Sending something forth.) The right "AND" hand is held palm out. It then opens and moves forcefully outward, in a throwing motion.

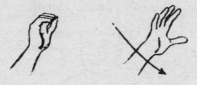

SENIOR (sēn′ yər), *n., adj.* (College student.) The right index finger touches the thumbtip of the left hand. Also, the open "5" hand, palm down, may rest on the left thumbtip. *Cf.* TOP DOG.

SENSITIVE (sĕn′ sə tĭv), *adj.* (A nimble touch.) The middle finger of the right hand touches the chest over the heart very briefly and lightly, and is then flicked off. *Cf.* SENSITIVITY.

SENSITIVITY (sĕn´ sə tǐv´ ɔ tǐ), *n.* See SENSITIVE.

SENTENCE (sĕn´ təns), *n., v.,* -TENCED, -TENCING. (A series of letters spelled out on the printed page.) The downturned "F" hands are positioned with thumbs and index fingertips touching. The hands move straight apart to either side in a wavy or straight motion. *Cf.* LANGUAGE 1.

 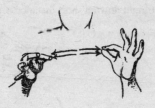

SEPARATE 1 (sĕp´ ə rāt´), -RATED, -RATING. (The hands are moved apart.) Both hands, in the "A" position, thumbs up, are held together, with knuckles touching. With a deliberate movement they come apart. *Cf.* APART, DIVORCE 1.

SEPARATE 2, *v., adj., n.* (Separating to classify.) Both hands, in the right angle position, are placed palms down before the body, knuckles to knuckles. They pull apart or separate, once or a number of times.

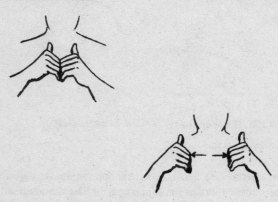

SETTLE (set′ l), *v.* (Settle down.) Both open hands are held palms down and fingers pointing forward. The hands move straight down a short distance. *Cf.* SIT DOWN.

SEVERAL (sĕv′ ər əl), *adj.* (The fingers are presented in order, to convey the concept of "several.") The right "A" hand is held palm facing up. One by one the fingers open, beginning with the index finger and ending with the little finger. Some use only the index and middle fingers. *Cf.* FEW.

SEWING MACHINE *n.* (The needle moves over the cloth.) The left index finger points straight forward. The right thumb and index, forming a somewhat elongated circle, moves forward repeatedly over the left index, from knuckle to tip, imitating the up-down movement of the needle.

SEXUAL INTERCOURSE *n. phrase.* (The motions of the legs during the sexual act.) The upturned left "V" hand remains motionless, while the downturned right "V" hand comes down repeatedly on the left.

SHADE (shād), *n.* (The natural sign.) The signer mimes pulling down a window shade.

SHAME 1 (shām), *n., v.,* SHAMED, SHAMING. (The color rises in the cheek; an attempt is made to hide the head.) The backs of the fingers of the right hand, held in the right angle position, are placed against the right cheek. The hand moves up along the cheek, pivoting at the wrist, so that the fingers finally point to the rear. *Cf.* ASHAMED, BASHFUL, SHAMEFUL, SHAME ON YOU, SHY 1.

SHAME 2, *n.* Similar to SHAME 1, but both hands are used, at either cheek. *Cf.* SHY 2.

SHAMEFUL (shām' fəl), *adj.* See SHAME 1.

SHAME ON YOU *phrase.* See SHAME 1.

SHAPE (shăp), *n.*, *v.*, SHAPED, SHAPING. (Contours are indicated or outlined.) Both "A" hands, held about a foot apart before the face, with palms facing each other, move down simultaneously in a wavy, undulating motion. *Cf.* FIGURE 2, FORM 1, STATUE.

SHARK (shärk), *n.* (The dorsal fin.) The upturned fingers of the right "B" hand protrude straight up between the left middle and ring fingers. The right fingers move off and away, in a wavy, meandering path.

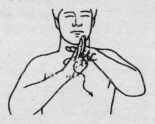

SHE (shē), *pron.* (Pointing at a female.) The FEMALE prefix sign is made: The right "A" hand's thumb moves down along the line of the right jaw, from ear almost to chin. The right index finger then points at an imaginary female. If in context the gender is clear, the prefix sign is usually omitted. *Cf.* HER.

SHIELD (shēld), *n., v.,* SHIELDED, SHIELDING. (Hold down firmly; cover and strengthen.) The "S" hands, downturned, are held side by side in front of the body, the arms almost horizontal, and the left hand in front of the right. Both arms move a short distance forward and slightly downward. *Cf.* DEFEND, DEFENSE, GUARD, PROTECT, PROTECTION.

SHINE (shīn), *v.,* SHINED, SHINING, SHONE. (Reflected glistening of light rays.) The left hand, held supinely before the chest, palm down, represents the object from which the rays glisten. The right hand, in the "5" position, touches the back of the left lightly and moves up toward the right, pivoting slightly at the wrist, with fingers wiggling. *Cf.* SHINING.

SHINING *adj.* See SHINE.

SHIRT (shûrt), *n.* (Draping the clothes on the body.) With fingertips resting on the chest, both hands move down simultane ously. The action is repeated. *Cf.* CLOTHES, CLOTHING, DRESS, WEAR.

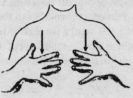

SHIVER (shĭv' ər), *v.*, -ERED, -ERING. (The trembling from cold.) Both "S" hands, palms facing, are placed at the sides of the body. In this position the arms and hands shiver. *Cf.* COLD 1, WINTER 1.

SHOCKED (shŏkt), *v.* (The mind is frozen; the thought is frozen.) The index finger of the right "D" hand, palm facing the body, touches the forehead (modified THINK sign, *q.v.*). Both hands, in the "5" position, palms down, are then suddenly and deliberately dropped down in front of the body. A look of surprise is assumed at this point, and the head jerks back slightly.

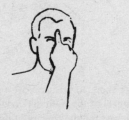

SHOP (shŏp), *n.*, *v.*, SHOPPED, SHOPPING. (Paying out money.) The right hand, palm up and all fingertips touching the thumb, is placed in the upturned left hand. From this position it moves forward and off the left hand a number of times. The right fingers usually remain against the thumb, but they may be opened very slightly each time the right hand moves forward. *Cf.* SHOPPING.

SHOPPING (shŏp′ ĭng), *n.* See SHOP.

SHOPPING CENTER *n.* (SHOP, CENTER.) The sign for SHOPPING is made: the right hand, palm up and all fingers touching the thumb, is placed in the upturned left hand. The right hand moves forward and off the left hand several times. This is followed by CENTER: the downturned right fingers make a clockwise circle over the upturned open left hand, coming down to stand on the left palm.

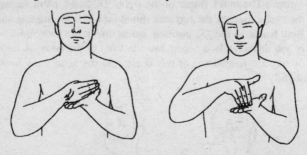

SHORT 1 (shôrt), *adj.* (To make short; to measure off a short space.) The index and middle fingers of the right "H" hand are placed across the top of the index and middle fingers of the left

"H" hand, and move a short distance back and forth, along the length of the left index finger. *Cf.* BRIEF, SHORTEN.

SHORT 2, *adj.* (A shortness of height is indicated.) The right hand, in right-angle position, pats an imaginary head at approximately chest level. *Cf.* SMALL 2.

SHORTEN (shôr′ tən), *v.*, -ENED, -ENING. See SHORT 1.

SHORTS (shôrtz), *n.* (The length is indicated.) The signer indicates the hem of a pair of shorts on the legs. Indicate the length of the shorts by crossing the thighs.

SHOULD (sho͝od), *v.* (Being pinned down.) The right hand, in the "X" position, palm down, moves forcefully up and down once or twice. An expression of determination is frequently assumed. *Cf.* HAVE TO, MUST, NECESSARY, NECESSITY, NEED 1, OUGHT TO.

SHOUT (shout), *v.*, SHOUTED, SHOUTING. (Harsh words thrown out.) The right hand, as in CURSE 1, appears to claw words out of the mouth. This time, however, it turns and throws them out, ending in the "5" position. *Cf.* CURSE 2, SCREAM.

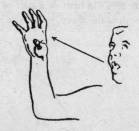

SHOVEL (shŭv′ əl), *v.*, -ELED, -ELING. (Turning over the earth.) The upturned right palm, cupped, acts like a scoop for

the earth, turning it over to the left. The upturned left palm
may act as a foil.

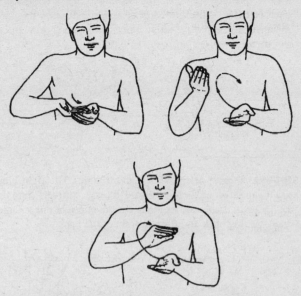

SHOW 1 (shō), *n., v.,* SHOWED, SHOWING. (Directing the attention to something, and bringing it forward.) The right index finger points into the left palm, held facing out before the body.
The left palm moves straight out. For the passive form of this
verb, *i.e.,* BE SHOWN, the movement is reversed: The left hand,
palm facing in, is moved in toward the body, while the right
index finger remains pointing into the left palm. *Cf.* DEMON-
STRATE, DISPLAY, EXAMPLE, EXHIBIT, EXHIBITION, REPRESENT.

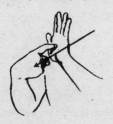

SHOW 2, *n*. (Motion or movement, modified by the letter "A" for "act.") Both "A" hands, palms out, are held at shoulder height and rotate alternately toward the head. *Cf.* ACT, PERFORM 2, PERFORMANCE 2, PLAY 2.

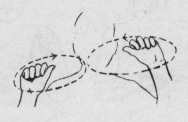

SHRIVEL (shrĭv′ əl), *v*. (The natural sign.) The right claw hand, palm down or facing forward, slowly "shrivels" into the "S." The sign is sometimes made with the upright index finger simply waving back and forth in front of the lips.

SHUT (shŭt), *adj., v.,* SHUT, SHUTTING. (The act of closing.) Both "B" hands, held palms out before the body, come together with some force. *Cf.* CLOSE 1.

SHY 1 (shī), *adj.* (The color rises in the cheek; an attempt is made to hide the head.) The backs of the fingers of the right hand, held in the right angle position, are placed against the right cheek. The hand moves up along the cheek, pivoting at the wrist, so that the fingers finally point to the rear. *Cf.* ASHAMED, BASHFUL, SHAME 1, SHAMEFUL, SHAME ON YOU.

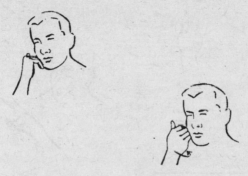

SHY 2, *adj.* Similar to SHY 1, but both hands are used, at either cheek. *Cf.* SHAME 2.

SICK (sĭk), *adj., adv.* (The sick parts of the anatomy are indicated.) The right middle finger rests on the forehead, and its left counterpart is placed against the stomach. The signer assumes an expression of sadness or physical distress. *Cf.* ILL.

SIGHT (sīt), *n.,* SAW, SEEN, SEEING. (The eyesight is directed forward.) The right "V" hand, palm facing the body, is placed so that the fingertips are just under the eyes. The hand swings straight out. *Cf.* SEE.

SIGNIFICANCE 1 (sĭg nĭf′ ə kəns), *n.* Both "F" hands, palms facing each other, move apart, up, and together in a smooth elliptical fashion, coming together at the tips of the thumbs and index fingers of both hands. *Cf.* IMPORTANT, SIGNIFICANT, VALUABLE, VALUE, WORTH, WORTHWHILE, WORTHY.

SIGNIFICANCE 2, *n.* (Relative standing of one's thoughts.) A modified sign for THINK is made: The right index finger touches the middle of the forehead. The tips of the right "V" hand, palm down, are then thrust into the upturned left palm (as in STAND, *q.v.*). The right "V" hand is then re-thrust into the upturned left palm, with right palm now facing the body. *Cf.* INTEND, INTENT, INTENTION, MEAN 2, MEANING, PURPOSE, SIGNIFY.

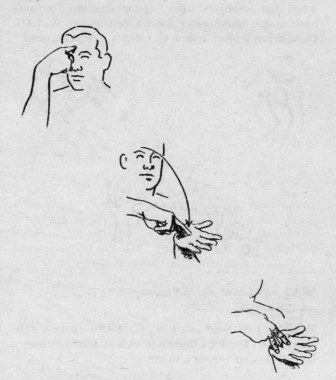

SIGNIFICANT (sĭg nĭf′ ə kəns), *adj.* See SIGNIFICANCE 1.

SIGNIFY (sĭg′ nə fī′), *v.*, -FIED, -FYING. See SIGNIFICANCE 2.

SIGN LANGUAGE *n.* (LANGUAGE 1, *q.v.*, and hand/arm movements.) The "D" hands, palms facing and index fingers pointing back toward the face, describe a series of continuous counterclockwise circles toward and away from the face, imitating the foot motions in bicycling. This is followed by the sign for LANGUAGE: The downturned "F" hands are positioned with thumbs and index fingertips touching. The hands move straight apart to either side in a wavy motion. The LANGUAGE part is often omitted. *Cf.* LANGUAGE OF SIGNS, SIGNS.

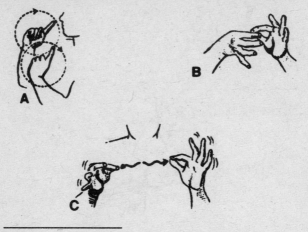

SIGNS (sīnz), *n. pl.* See SIGN LANGUAGE.

SILENCE 1 (sī′ ləns), *interj., n., v.,* -LENCED, -LENCING. (The natural sign.) The index finger is brought up against the pursed lips. *Cf.* BE QUIET 1, QUIET 1, SILENT.

SILENCE 2, *n., interj., v.* (Quiet and peace.) The open hands are crossed before the mouth, the right palm facing left, the left facing right. Then both hands, held palms down, move down from the mouth, curving outward to either side of the body. *Cf.* BE QUIET 2, BE STILL, CALM, QUIET 2.

SILENT (sī′ lənt), *adj.* See SILENCE 1.

SILLY (sĭl′ ĭ), *adj.* (Thoughts flickering back and forth.) The right "Y" hand, thumb almost touching the forehead, is shaken back and forth across the forehead several times. *Cf.* FOOLISH, NONSENSE, RIDICULOUS.

SIMILAR (sĭm′ ĭ lər), *adj.* (Matching fingers are brought together.) The outstretched index fingers are brought together, either once or several times. *Cf.* ALIKE, LIKE 2, SAME 1.

SIMPLE 1 (sĭm′ pəl), *adj.* (The fingertips are easily moved.) The right fingertips brush repeatedly over their upturned left counterparts, causing them to move. *Cf.* EASY 1.

SIMPLE 2, *adj.* Both hands are held in the "F" position, fingers pointing out and palms facing each other. The right hand comes down past the left, its index finger and thumb smartly striking their left counterparts. The signer often assumes a pursed lips expression.

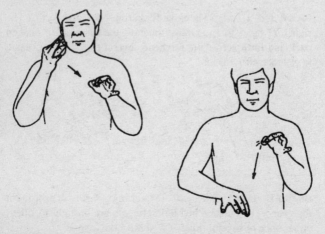

SINCE 1 (sĭns), *adv., prep., conj.* (From a point up and over.) In the "D" position, palms down, both index fingers touch the right shoulder and then are brought up and over, ending in a palm-up position, pointing straight ahead of the body. *Cf.* ALL

ALONG, EVER SINCE, SO FAR, THUS FAR.

SINCE 2, *conj.* (A thought or knowledge uppermost in the mind.) The fingers of the right hand, or the index finger, are placed on the center of the forehead, and then the hand is brought strongly up above the head, assuming the "A" position, thumb pointing up. *Cf.* BECAUSE, FOR 2.

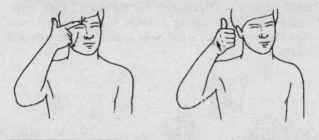

SINCERE (sĭn sĭr′), *adj.* (The letter "H," for HONEST; a straight and true path.) The index and middle fingers of the right "H" hand, whose palm faces left, move straight forward along the upturned left palm. *Cf.* HONEST, HONESTY.

SING (sĭng), v., SANG or SUNG, SUNG, SINGING, n. (A rhythmic, wavy movement of the hand, to indicate a melody; the movement of a conductor's hand in directing a musical performance.) The right "5" hand, palm facing left, is waved back and forth next to the left hand, in a series of elongated figure-eights. Cf. MUSIC, SONG.

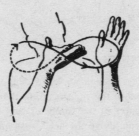

SINK (singk), n. (The faucets and the shape.) Both down-turned hands mime turning a pair of faucets. The upturned open hands then trace the outline of a sink, from the bottom to the sides.

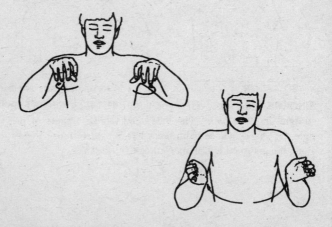

SISTER (sĭs′ tər), n. (Female root sign: SAME. Meaning a female from the same family.) The FEMALE root sign is made: The thumb of the right "A" hand moves down along the right jawbone, almost to the chin. This is followed by the sign for SAME: The outstretched index fingers are brought together, either once or several times.

SIT (sĭt), *v.*, SAT, SITTING. (The act of sitting.) The extended right index and middle fingers are draped across the back of the same two fingers of the downturned left hand. The hands then move straight downward a short distance. *Cf.* BE SEATED, CHAIR, SEAT.

SIT DOWN *v.* (The natural sign.) Both open hands are held palms down and fingers pointing forward. The hands move straight down a short distance. *Cf.* SETTLE.

SITUATION (sich oo ā' shən), *n.* (The letter "S"; an encircling environment.) The right "S" hand makes a counterclockwise circle around the upturned left index finger.

SKATEBOARD (skāt' bord), *n.* The right index and middle fingers "stand" on the tips of their left counterparts. Both hands, thus connected, move forward in a swaying motion, imitating the rhythms of riding on a skateboard.

SKEPTIC (skĕp' tĭk), *n.* (Warding off.) The sign for SKEPTICAL is formed. This is followed by the sign for INDIVIDUAL.

SKEPTICAL (skĕp' tə kəl), *adj.* (Throwing the fist.) The right "S" hand is held before the right shoulder, elbow bent out to

the side. The hand is then thrown forward several times, as if
striking at someone.

SKI 1 (skē), *v.* (The ski poles.) The signer, holding an imaginary pair of ski poles, pushes down on them in order to create
forward motion.

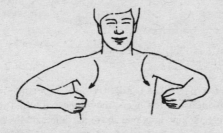

SKI 2, *v.* (Downhill movement.) Both "X" hands, palms up,
move downward as if sliding downhill.

SKILL (skĭl), *n*. (A sharp-edged hand.) The right hand grasps the little finger edge of the left firmly. As it leaves this position, moving down and out, it assumes the "A" position, palm facing left. *Cf*. EXPERIENCE 1, EXPERT, SKILLFUL.

SKILLFUL (skĭl' fəl), *adj*. See SKILL.

SKINNY (skĭn' ĭ), (*sl*.), *adj*. (A thin, tapering object is described with the little fingers, the thinnest of all.) The tips of the little fingers, touching, one above the other, are drawn apart. The cheeks may also be drawn in for emphasis. *Cf*. THIN 2.

SLED (sled), *n*. (The handlebars.) The signer mimes manipulating a sleds handlebars back and forth. The head should be hanging down, as if the body were belly-down on a sled.

SLEEP 1 (slēp), *v.*, SLEPT, SLEEPING, *n.* (The eyes are closed.) The fingers of the right open hand, facing the forehead, are placed on the forehead. The hand moves down and away from the head, with the fingers closing so that they all touch. The eyes meanwhile close, and the head bows slightly, as in sleep. *Cf.* ASLEEP.

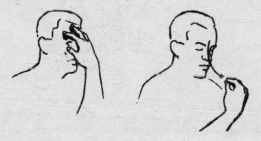

SLEEP 2, *n., v.* (The natural sign.) The signer's head leans to the right and rests in the upturned palm of the open right hand.

SLEEPY (slē′ pĭ), *adj.* (Drooping eyelids.) The right fingers are wiggled in front of the face, and the head is bowed forward.

SLIDE (slīd), *n.* (Slide being inserted in projector.) The right "H" hand, palm facing the signer and fingertips pointing left, moves into the left palm.

SLOW (slō), *adj.* (The movement indicates the slowness.) The right hand is drawn slowly over the back of the downturned left hand, from fingertips to wrist.

SMALL 1 (smôl), *adj.* (Indicating a small mass.) The extended right thumb and index finger are held slightly spread. They are then moved slowly toward each other until they almost touch. *Cf.* TINY.

SMALL 2, *adj.* (A shortness of height is indicated.) The right hand, in right-angle position, pats an imaginary head at approximately chest level. *Cf.* SHORT 2.

SMART (smärt), *adj.* (The mind is bright.) The middle finger is placed at the forehead, and then the hand, with an outward flick, turns around so that the palm faces outward. This indicates a brightness flowing from the mind. *Cf.* INTELLIGENT.

SMELL (smĕl), *v.*, SMELLED, SMELLING, *n.* (Bringing something up to the nose.) The upturned right hand moves slowly up to and past the nose, and the signer breathes in as the hand sweeps by. *Cf.* ODOR.

SMILE (smīl), *v.*, SMILED, SMILING, *n.* (Drawing the lips into a smile.) The right index finger is drawn back over the lips, toward the ear. As the finger moves back, the signer breaks into a smile. (Both index fingers may also be used.)

SNAIL (snāl), *n.* (The shape and function.) The downturned bent right "V" hand is concealed by the downturned cupped left hand. The right "V" fingers protrude from the left as both hands move slowly forward.

SNAPS (snapz), *n.* (Fastening snaps on clothes.) The signer mimes closing snaps on the shirt.

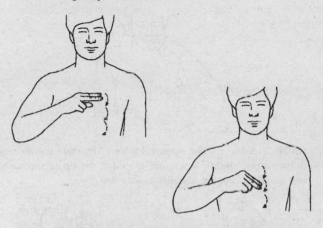

SNATCH UP *(colloq.), v.* (Sleight of hand.) The downturned open hand is positioned at chest height, with the middle finger hanging farther down than the rest of the fingers. With a quick and sudden movement, the hand moves up into the "A" position. For maximum impact, the signer's tongue is visible, sticking out from the pursed lips. As the hand moves up the tongue is suddenly sucked into the mouth.

SNEEZE (snēz), *v., n.* (Stifling a sneeze.) The index finger is pressed lengthwise under the nose.

SNOB (snob), *n.* (The upturned nose.) The right thumb and index finger, slightly open, are placed at the tip of the nose, and move up, coming together as they do.

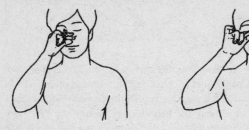

SNOWFLAKE (snō′ flāk), *n.* (Descending and settling.) The sign for SNOW is made: the fingers wriggle repeatedly as the downturned hands move slowly down. The right thumb and index, forming a circle, then settle gently on the back of the downturned left hand.

SO-CALLED (sō′ kôld′), *adj.* (The quotation marks are indicated.) The curved index and middle fingers of both hands, held palms out, move slightly to either side of the body, as if drawing quotation marks in the air. *Cf.* QUOTATION, QUOTE, SUBJECT, TITLE, TOPIC.

SOCIAL SECURITY *n.* (The "S" letters.) The signer finger-spells the letters "S-S."

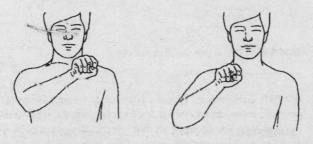

SOCIAL STUDIES *n.* The right hand makes the letter "S" twice, moving slightly to the right after the first time.

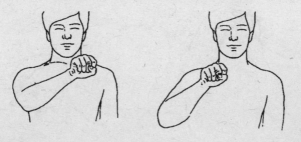

SODA POP *n.* (Corking a bottle.) The left "O" hand is held with thumb edge up, representing a bottle. The thumb and index finger of the right "5" hand represent a cork, and are inserted into the circle formed by the "O" hand. The palm of the open right hand then strikes down on the upturned edge of the "O" hand, as if forcing the cork into the bottle. *Cf.* POP, SODA WATER.

SODA WATER *n. phrase.* See SODA POP.

SO FAR *adv. phrase.* (From a point up and over.) In the "D" position, palms down, both index fingers touch the right shoulder and then are brought up and over, ending in a palm-up position, pointing straight ahead of the body. *Cf.* ALL ALONG, EVER SINCE, SINCE I, THUS FAR.

SOLAR SYSTEM *n.* (The movement of the planets.) The right "S" hand makes a clockwise circle around its left counterpart. Both "S" hands, palms forward, then separate and draw "Z"s in the air. This latter sign means SYSTEM.

SOME (sŭm; *unstressed* səm), *adj.* (Cutting off or designating a part.) The little finger edge of the open right hand moves straight down the middle of the upturned left palm. *Cf.* PART 1, PIECE, PORTION.

SOMERSAULT (sŭm′ ər sôlt), *n., v.* (The natural sign.) The signer mimes a somersault: the right bent "V" hand, palm facing forward, executes a somersault, twisting into a palm-up position.

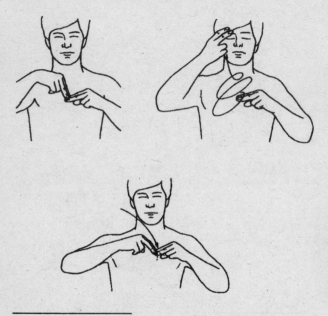

SOMETIME(S) (sŭm′ tīmz′), *adv.* (The "1" finger is brought up very slowly.) The right index finger, resting in the open left palm, which is facing right, swings up slowly from its position to one in which it is pointing straight up. The movement is repeated slowly, after a pause. *Cf.* OCCASIONAL, OCCASIONAL-LY, ONCE IN A WHILE.

SON (sŭn), *n.* (Male, baby.) The sign for MALE is made: The thumb and extended fingers of the right hand are brought up to grasp an imaginary cap brim. This is followed by the sign for BABY: The arms are held with one resting on the other, as if cradling a baby.

SONG (sông, sŏng), *n.* (A rhythmic, wavy movement of the hand, to indicate a melody; the movement of a conductors hand in directing a musical performance.) The right "5" hand, palm facing left, is waved back and forth next to the left hand, in a series of elongated figure-eights. *Cf.* MUSIC, SING.

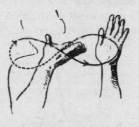

SOPHOMORE (sof′ ə môr), *n.* (College student.) The right index finger touches the middle finger of the left hand.

SORROW (sŏr' ō, sôr' ō), *n*. (The heart is circled, to indicate feeling, modified by the letter "S," for SORRY.) The right "S" hand, palm facing the body, is rotated several times over the area of the heart. *Cf.* APOLOGIZE 1, APOLOGY 1, REGRET, REGRETFUL, SORROWFUL 2, SORRY.

SORROWFUL 1 (sŏr' ə fəl, sôr'-), *adj*. (The facial features drop.) Both "5" hands, palms facing the eyes and fingers slightly curved, drop simultaneously to a level with the mouth. The head drops slightly as the hands move down, and an expression of sadness is assumed. *Cf.* GLOOM, GLOOMY, GRIEF, SAD.

SORROWFUL 2, *adj*. See SORROW.

SORRY (sŏr' ĭ, sôr' ĭ), *adj*. See SORROW.

SO-SO (sō sō), *phrase*. (Neither this way nor that.) The down-turned "5" hand flips over and back several times.

SPACE (spās), *n*. (The movement upward and outward.) Both "A" hands, palms facing forward and thumbs touching, open to the "5" position as they move upward and outward, with the signer looking up.

SPEAK (spēk), *v.*, SPOKE, SPOKEN, SPEAKING. (Words tumbling from the mouth.) The right index finger, pointing left, describes a continuous small circle in front of the mouth. *Cf.* HEARING, MENTION, SAID, SAY, SPEECH 1, TALK 1, TELL.

SPECIAL (spěsh′ əl), *adj.* (Selecting a particular item from among several.) The index finger and thumb of the right hand grasp and pull up the left index finger. *Cf.* EXCEPT, EXCEPTION.

SPECIALIZE (spěsh′ ə līz′), *v.*, -IZED, -IZING. (A straight, *i.e.*, special, path.) The hands are held in the "B" position, one above the other, with left palm facing right and right palm facing left. The little finger edge of the right hand moves straight forward along the index finger edge of the left. *Cf.* SPECIALTY.

SPECIALTY (spĕsh ′ əl tĭ), *n., pl.* -TIES. See SPECIALIZE.

SPECIFIC 1 (spĭ sĭf′ ĭk), *adj.* (The fingers come together precisely.) The thumb and index finger of each hand, palms facing, the right above the left, form circles. They are brought together with a deliberate movement, so that the fingers and thumbs now touch. Sometimes the right hand, before coming together with the left, executes a slow clockwise circle above the left. *Cf.* EXACT, EXACTLY, PRECISE.

SPECIFIC 2, *adj.* (Pointing.) The signer points to the index finger.

SPECULATE 1 (spěk′ yə lāt′), *v.*, -LATED, -LATING. (A thought is turned over in the mind.) The index finger makes a small circle on the forehead. *Cf.* CONSIDER 1, SPECULATION 1, THINK, THOUGHT, THOUGHTFUL.

SPECULATE 2, *v.* (Turning thoughts over in the mind.) Both index fingers, pointing to the forehead, describe continuous alternating circles. *Cf.* CONSIDER 2, SPECULATION 2, WONDER.

SPECULATION 1 (spěk′ yə lā′ shən), *n.* See SPECULATE 1.

SPECULATION 2, *n.* See SPECULATE 2.

SPEECH 1 (spēch), *n.* (Words tumbling from the mouth.) The right index finger, pointing left, describes a continuous small circle in front of the mouth. *Cf.* HEARING, MENTION, SAID, SAY,

SPEAK, TALK 1, TELL.

SPEECH 2, *n*. (A gesture of an orator.) The right open hand, palm facing left, is held above and to the right of the head. It pivots, forward and backward, on the wrist several times. *Cf.* LECTURE, TALK 2.

SPEECHLESS (spēch' lĭs), *(colloq.)*, *adj*. (The mouth drops open.) The fingertips of both "V" hands are held curved and touching before the body, one hand above the other. Then the hands are suddenly drawn apart, and at the same instant the mouth drops open and the eyes open wide.

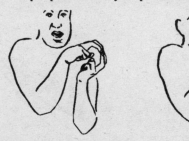

SPEED (spēd), *n., v.,* SPED, or SPEEDED, SPEEDING. (A quick movement.) The thumbtip of the upright right hand is flicked quickly off the tip of the curved right index finger, as if shooting marbles. *Cf.* FAST, IMMEDIATELY, QUICK, QUICKNESS, SPEEDY.

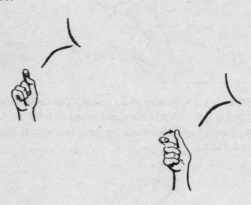

SPEEDY (spē' dĭ), *adj.* See SPEED.

SPEND (spĕnd), *v.,* SPENT, SPENDING. (Repeated giving forth.) The back of the upturned right hand, thumb touching fingertips, is placed in the upturned left palm. The right hand moves off and away from the left once or several times, each time opening into the "5" position, palm up. *Cf.* WASTE 1.

SPOON ON *phrase.* (The natural sign.) The signer, holding an imaginary spoon, tips it over slightly as if pouring off its contents.

SPORTS (spôrtz), *n.* (A challenge.) Both hands are held in the "A" position, knuckles facing and thumbs standing up. They come together forcefully.

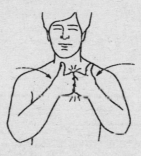

SPRING (spring), *n.* (Flowers or plants emerge from the ground.) The right fingers, pointing up, emerge from the closed left hand, and they spread open as they do. The action may be repeated. *Cf.* GROW, GROWN.

STAGE (stāj), *n.* The downturned right "S" hand sweeps forward along the downturned left arm.

STAMP (stămp), *n.* (Licking the stamp.) The tips of the right index and middle fingers are licked with the tongue, and then the fingers are pressed against the upturned left palm, as if affixing a stamp to an envelope.

STAND 1 (stănd), *v.*, STOOD, STANDING, *n.* (The feet planted on the ground.) The downturned right "V" fingers are thrust into the upturned left palm. *Cf.* STANDING.

STAND 2, *v.*, *n.* (Getting onto one's feet.) The upturned index and middle fingers of the right hand, representing the legs, are swung up and over in an arc, coming to rest in the upturned left palm. *Cf.* GET UP, STAND UP.

STANDARD (stan' dərd), *adj., n.* (The same all around.) Both downturned "Y" hands execute counterclockwise circles. *Cf.* COMMON.

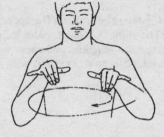

STANDING (stăn' dĭng), *n.* See STAND 1.

STAND UP *v. phrase.* See STAND 2.

STAPLER (stā' plər), *n.* (The natural sign.) The signer mimes hitting a stapler with the downturned hand.

START (stärt), *v.*, STARTED, STARTING. (Turning a key to open up a new venture.) The right index finger, resting between the left index and middle fingers, executes a half turn, once or twice. *Cf.* BEGIN, ORIGIN.

STARVATION (stär vā′ shən), *n.* (The upper alimentary tract is outlined.) The right "C" hand, palm facing the body, is placed with fingertips touching mid-chest. In this position it moves down a bit. *Cf.* STARVE, STARVED, WISH 2.

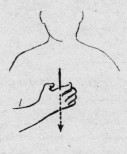

STARVE (stärv), *v.*, STARVED, STARVING. See STARVATION.

STARVED *v.* See STARVATION.

STATE (stāt), *n.* (The letter "S"; a collection of laws.) The right "S" hand moves down the open left palm, from fingertips to base.

STATISTICS (stə tis' tiks), *n.* (The letter "S"; the multiplication symbol.) Both "S" hands repeatedly cross each other as in the "X" symbol for multiplication.

STATUE (stăch' ōō), *n.* (Contours are indicated or outlined.) Both "A" hands, held about a foot apart before the face, with palms facing each other, move down simultaneously in a wavy, undulating motion. *Cf.* FIGURE 2, FORM 1, SHAPE.

STAY 1 (stā), *n., v.,* STAYED, STAYING. (Steady, uninterrupted movement.) The "A" hands are held with palms out, thumbs extended and touching, the right behind the left. In this position the hands move forward in a straight, steady line. *Cf.* CONTINUE, ENDURE 2, EVER 1, LAST 3, LASTING, PERMANENT, PERSEVERE, PERSIST, REMAIN, STAY STILL.

STAY 2, *v.* (Remaining in place.) One "Y" hand, held palm down, drops down a few inches.

STAY STILL *v. phrase.* See STAY 1.

STEAL 1 (stēl), *n., v.,* STOLE, STOLEN, STEALING. (The hand, partly concealed, takes something surreptitiously.) The index and middle fingers of the right hand, somewhat curved, are placed under the left elbow. As they move slowly along the left forearm toward the left wrist, they close a bit. *Cf.* ROB 1, THEFT 1, THIEF, THIEVERY.

STEAL 2, *(colloq.)*, *v.* (A sly, underhanded movement). The right open hand, palm down, is held under the left elbow. Beginning with the little finger, the hand closes finger by finger into the "A" position, as if wrapping itself around something, and moves to the right. *Cf.* ROB 2.

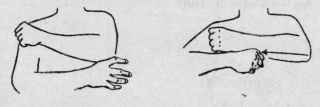

STEPBROTHER *n.* (Second brother.) The sign for SECOND is made: the right "L" hand, palm facing left and index straight up, moves forward so that the index now faces forward. This is followed by BROTHER: the thumb of the right "L" hand is placed at the right temple. The hand moves down to rest on top of the downturned left hand. The order of the two signs may be reversed.

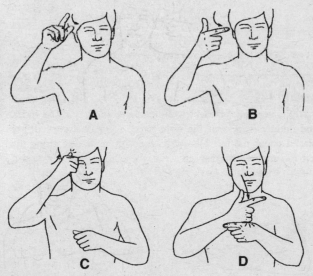

A   B

C   D

STEPFATHER *n.* (Second father.) The sign for SECOND is made: the right "L" hand, palm facing left and index straight up, moves forward so that the index now faces forward. This is followed by FATHER: the thumb of the right "5" hand is placed on the right temple. The FATHER sign may be made first, followed by SECOND.

STEPMOTHER *n.* (Second mother.) The sign for SECOND is made: the right "L" hand, palm facing left and index straight up, moves forward so that the index now faces forward. This is followed by MOTHER: the thumb of the right "5" hand is placed on the right jawline. The MOTHER sign may be made first, followed by SECOND.

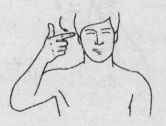

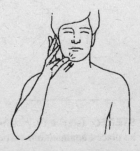

STEPSISTER *n.* (Second sister.) The sign for SECOND is made: the right "L" hand, palm facing left and index straight up, moves forward so that the index now faces forward. This is followed by SISTER: the thumb of the right "L" hand is placed on the right jawline. The hand moves down to rest on top of the downturned left hand. The order of the two signs may be reversed.

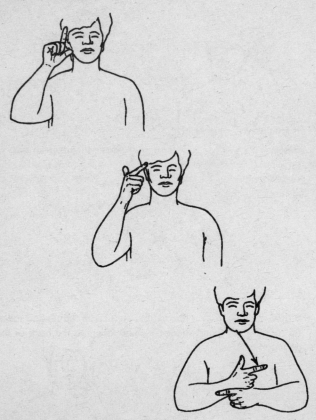

STEREO (ster' ē ō), *n.* (Sound waves.) One or both fists may be placed against their respective ears. The hand or hands then open and spread out in a wavy or wriggling movement.

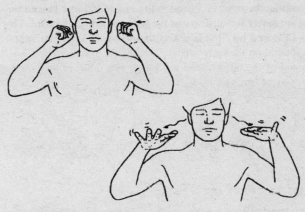

STILL (stĭl), *adv., conj.* (Duration of movement from past to present.) The right "Y" hand is held palm down in front of the right shoulder and is then moved slowly down and forward in a smooth curve.

STING (sting), *n., v.* (The natural sign.) The thumb and index of the right "F" hand suddenly come down on the back of the downturned left hand.

STINGY 1 (stĭn′ jĭ), *adj.* (Pulling things toward oneself.) Both prone open or "V" hands are held in front of the body with fingers bent. The hands are then drawn quickly and forcefully inward, as if raking things toward oneself. *Cf.* GREEDY 1, SELF-ISH 1.

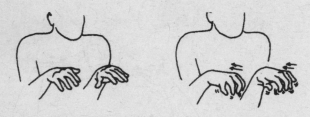

***

STINGY 2, *adj.* (Scratching the palm in greed.) The right fingers scratch the upturned left palm several times. A frowning expression is often used. *Cf.* GREEDY 2, SELFISH 2.

***

STOP (stŏp), *v.*, STOPPED, STOPPING, *n.* (A stopping or cutting short.) The little finger edge of the right hand is thrust abruptly into the upturned left palm, indicating a cutting short.

STORY (stôr' ĭ), *n.* (The unraveling or stretching out of words or sentences.) Both open hands are held close to each other, with fingers open and palms facing and almost touching. As the hands are drawn apart, the thumb and index finger of each hand come together to form circles. This is repeated several times. *Cf.* NARRATE, NARRATIVE, TALE.

STOVE (stōv), *n.* (Cooking and the shape.) The sign for COOK is made: The open right hand rests on the upturned left palm. The right hand flips over and comes to rest with its back on the left palm, as if it has turned over a pancake. The shape of the stove is then indicated: both downturned hands move apart and then, with palms facing each other, downwards.

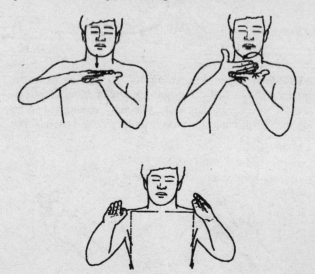

STRANGE (strănj), *adj.* (Something which distorts the vision.) The "C" hand describes a small arc in front of the face. *Cf.* CURIOUS 1, ODD, WEIRD.

STREET (strēt), *n.* (The path.) Both hands, palms facing and fingers together and extended straight out, move in unison away from the body, in a straight or winding manner. *Cf.* ROAD.

STRENGTH (strĕngkth, strĕngth), *n.* (Strength emanating from the body.) Both "5" hands are placed palms against the chest. They move out and away, forcefully, closing and assuming the "S" position. *Cf.* BRAVE, BRAVERY, HEALTH, HEALTHY, MIGHTY 2, WELL.

STRIKE (strīk), *v.*, STRUCK, STRIKING. (The natural sign.) The right "S" hand strikes its knuckles forcefully against the open left palm, which is held facing right. *Cf.* HIT 1, PUNCH 1.

STRONG (strông, strŏng), *adj.* (Flexing the muscles.) With fists clenched, palms facing down or back, the signer raises both arms and shakes them once, with force. *Cf.* MIGHT 1, MIGHTY 1, POWER 1, POWERFUL 1.

STUBBORN (stŭb' ərn), *adj.* (The donkey's broad ear; the animal is traditionally a stubborn one.) The open hand, or the "B" hand, is placed at the side of the head, with palm out and fingers pointing straight up. The hand moves forward and back, pivoting at the wrist, as in the case of a donkey's ears flapping. Both hands may also be used, at either side of the head.

STUCK (stŭk), *adj.* (Impaled on a stick, as a snake's head.) The "V" fingers are thrust into the throat.

STUDENT (stū' dənt, sto͞o'-), *n.* (One who learns.) The sign for LEARN is made: The downturned fingers of the right hand are placed on the upturned left palm. They close, and then the hand rises and the right fingertips are placed on the forehead. This is followed by the sign for INDIVIDUAL: Both open hands, palms facing each other, move down the sides of the body, tracing its outline to the hips.

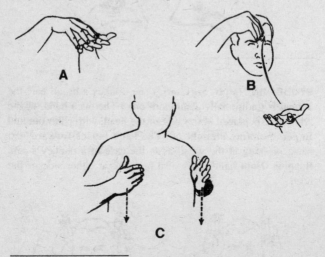

STUFFING (stuf' ing), *n.* The signer goes through the motions of pushing stuffing into the open cavity of a bird.

STUPID (stū′ pĭd, stoō′-), *adj.* (Knocking the head to indicate its empty state.) The "S" hand, palm facing the body, knocks against the forehead.

SUBJECT (sŭb′ jĭkt), *n.* (The quotation marks are indicated.) The curved index and middle fingers of both hands, held palms out, move slightly to either side of the body, as if drawing quotation marks in the air. *Cf.* QUOTATION, QUOTE, SO-CALLED, TITLE, TOPIC.

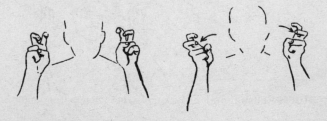

SUBMARINE (sub mə rēn′), *n*. (Cruising underwater.) The right "3" hand, palm facing left, moves forward under the shelter of the downturned left hand. The sign may be executed at eye level.

SUBMIT (səb mit′), *v*. (Throwing up the hands in a gesture of surrender.) The hands move palms up in an arc.

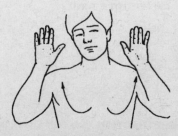

SUBSTITUTE (sŭb′ stə tūt′), *n., v.,* -TUTED, -TUTING. (Exchanging places.) The right "A" hand, positioned above the left "A" hand, swings down and under the left, coming up a bit in front of it. *Cf.* EXCHANGE, REPLACE, TRADE.

SUBTRACT (səb trăkt′), *v.,* TRACTED, -TRACTING. (Removing.) The right "A" hand, resting in the palm of the left "5" hand, moves slightly up and away, describing a small arc. It is then cast downward, opening into the "5" position, palm down, as if removing something from the left hand and casting it down. *Cf.* DEDUCT, ELIMINATE, REMOVE, SUBTRACTION.

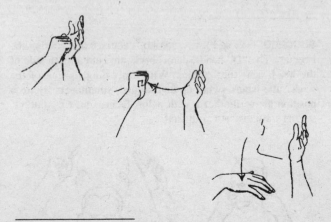

SUBTRACTION (səb trăk′ shən), *n.* See SUBTRACT.

SUBWAY (sub' wā), *n.* (An underground train.) The sign for TRAIN 1 is made: the downturned right "H" hand slides back and forth on its left counterpart. The right index finger then moves forward under the cupped left hand. The TRAIN 1 sign is often omitted.

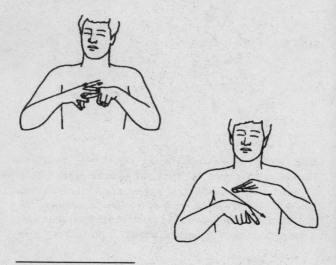

SUCCEED (sək sēd'), *v.*, -CEEDED, -CEEDING. (Penetrating the heights.) The "D" hands, palms back, are held at each side of the head, near the temples. With a pivoting motion of the wrists, the hands swing up and around, simultaneously, to a position above the head, with palms facing out. *Cf.* ACHIEVE, SUCCESS, SUCCESSFUL, TRIUMPH.

SUCCESS (sək sĕs'), *n.* See SUCCEED.

SUCCESSFUL (sək sĕs' fəl), *adj.* See SUCCEED.

SUFFER (sŭf' ər), *v.,* -FERED, -FERING. (A clenching of the fists; the rise and fall of pain.) Both "S" hands, tightly clenched, revolve about each other, slowly and deliberately, while a pained expression is worn. *Cf.* ENDURE 1.

SUGAR (shōōg' ər), *n.* (Titillating to the taste.) The fingertips of the right "U" hand, palm facing the body, brush against the chin a number of times beginning at the lips. *Cf.* CUTE 1, SWEET.

SUGGEST (səg jĕst′), *v.*, -GESTED, -GESTING. (An offering; a presenting.) Both hands, slightly cupped, palms up, are held close to the chest. They move up and out in unison, describing a very slight arc. *Cf.* OFFER, OFFERING, PRESENT 1, PROPOSE.

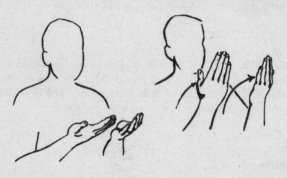

SUM (sŭm), *n.*, *v.*, SUMMED, SUMMING. (To bring up all together.) The two open hands, palms and fingers facing each other, with the left hand above the right, are brought together, with all fingers closing simultaneously. This sign is used mainly in the sense of adding up figures or items. *Cf.* ADD 1, ADDITION, SUMMARIZE 2, SUMMARY 2, SUM UP.

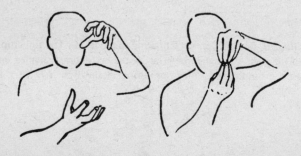

SUMMARIZE 1 (sŭm′ ə rīz′), *v.*, -RIZED, -RIZING. (To squeeze or condense into a small space.) The "C" hands face each other, with the right hand nearer to the body than the left. Both hands draw together and close deliberately, squeezing an imaginary object. *Cf.* MAKE BRIEF, SUMMARY 1.

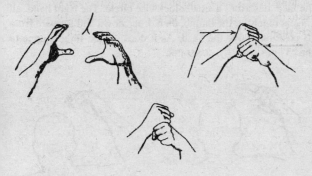

SUMMARIZE 2, *v.* See SUM.

SUMMARY 1 (sŭm′ ə rĭ), *n., adj.* Scc SUMMARIZE 1.

SUMMARY 2, *n.* See SUM.

SUMMER (sŭm′ ər), *n.* (Wiping the brow.) The downturned right index finger, slightly curved, is drawn across the forehead from left to right.

SUM UP *v. phrase.* See SUM.

SUN (sŭn), *n.*, *v.*, SUNNED, SUNNING. (The round shape and the rays.) The right index finger, pointing forward and held above the face, describes a small clockwise circle. The right hand, all fingers touching the thumb, then drops down and forward from its position above the head. As it does so, the fingers open to the "5" position. *Cf.* SUNSHINE.

SUNDAE (sŭn' də), *n.* (The whipped cream is spiraled on.) The right thumb is held pointing down over the left "S" hand, whose palm faces right. The thumb spirals up in a counter-clockwise manner.

SUNRISE (sŭn' rīz´), *n.* (The natural sign.) The downturned left arm, held horizontally, represents the horizon. The right thumb and index finger form a circle, and this circle is drawn up from a position in front of the downturned left hand.

SUNSET (sŭn′ sĕt′), *n.* (The natural sign.) The movement described in SUNRISE is reversed, with the right hand moving down below the downturned left hand.

SUNSHINE (sŭn′ shĭn′), *n.* See SUN.

SUPERFICIAL (soo pər fish′ əl), *adj.* (On the surface.) The right fingertips describe a small clockwise circle as they rub against the top of the downturned left hand.

SUPERVISE (sŏŏ′ pər vīz′), v., -VISED, -VISING. (The eyes sweep back and forth.) The "V" hands, held crossed, describe a counterclockwise circle before the chest.

SUPPORT (sə pôrt′), n., v. -PORTED, -PORTING. (Holding up.) The right "S" hand pushes up the left "S" hand. *Cf.* ENDORSE 1, SUSTAIN, SUSTENANCE.

SUPPOSE (sə pōz′), v., -POSED, -POSING. (To have an idea.) The little fingertip of the right "I" hand taps the right temple once or twice.

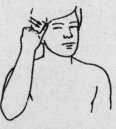

SURE (shŏŏr), *adj., adv.* (Coming forth directly from the lips; true.) The index finger of the right "D" hand, palm facing left, is placed against the lips. It moves up an inch or two and then

describes a small arc forward and away from the lips. *Cf.*
REAL, REALLY, SURELY, TRUE, TRULY, TRUTH.

SURELY (shŏŏr′ lĭ), *adv.* See SURE.

SURFING (sûrf′ ing), *n.* (The position and motion.) Both
hands face down. The right index and middle finger stand on
their left counterparts.

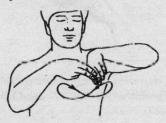

SURPRISE (sər prīz′), *v.*, -PRISED, -PRISING, *n.* (The eyes pop
open in amazement.) Both hands are held in modified "O"
positions with thumb and index fingers of each hand near the
eyes. These fingers suddenly flick open, and the eyes simultaneously pop open wide. *Cf.* AMAZE, AMAZEMENT.

SURRENDER (sə rĕn' dər), *v.*, -DERED, -DERING. (Throwing up the hands in a gesture of surrender.) Both "A" hands are held palms down before the chest and then thrown up in unison, ending in the "5" position. *Cf.* GIVE UP.

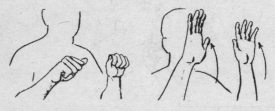

SUSPEND (sə spĕnd'), *v.*, -PENDED, -PENDING. (The natural sign.) The curved right index finger "hangs" on the extended left index finger.

SUSTAIN (sə stān'), *v.*, -TAINED, -TAINING. (Holding up.) The right "S" hand pushes up the left "S" hand. *Cf.* ENDORSE 1, SUPPORT, SUSTENANCE, UPHOLD.

SUSTENANCE (sŭs' tə nəns), *n.* See SUSTAIN.

SWEAR 1 (swâr), *v.* SWORE, SWORN, SWEARING. (The arm is raised.) The right index finger is placed at the lips. The right arm is then raised, palm out and elbow resting on the back of the left hand. *Cf.* PROMISE.

SWEAR 2, *v.* (Harsh words and a threatening hand.) The right hand appears to claw words out of the mouth. It ends in the "S" position, above the head, shaking back and forth in a threatening manner. *Cf.* CURSE 1.

SWEET (swēt), *adj., n.* (Titillating to the taste.) The fingertips of the right "U" hand, palm facing the body, brush against the chin a number of times beginning at the lips. *Cf.* CUTE 1, SUGAR.

SWEETHEART (swēt′ härt′), *(colloq.)*, *n.* (Heads nodding toward each other.) The "A" hands are placed together before the body with thumbs up. The thumbs wiggle up and down. *Cf.* LOVER.

SYMPATHY (sĭm′ pə thĭ), *n.* (Feelings from the heart, conferred on others.) The middle fingertip of the open right hand touches the chest over the heart. The same open hand then moves in a small, clockwise circle before the right shoulder, with palm facing forward and fingers pointing up. *Cf.* MERCY, PITY.

SYRUP (sir′ əp), *n.* (Wiping the mouth and pouring.) The upturned right index sweeps across the mouth, from right to left. The hand then forms the "A" shape, and pivots over so that the thumb represents a left arm.

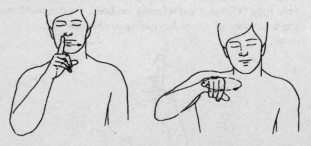

SYSTEM (sis′ təm), *n.* (An arrangement.) Both "S" hands, palms facing out, are positioned side by side. They separate, move down, and separate yet more, tracing a zigzag pattern.

TAKE (tāk), *v.* TOOK, TAKEN, TAKING, *n.* (Taking unto oneself.)
The right hand, palm out, is extended before the chest, index
finger and thumb in an open position, the other fingers separated and pointing up. The hand is drawn in toward the chest, and
the index and thumb close at the same time, indicating something taken to oneself. *Cf.* CHOOSE, SELECT 2.

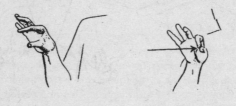

TAKE CARE OF *v. phrase.* (Slow, careful movement.) The
"K" hands are crossed, the right above the left, little finger
edges down. In this position the hands are moved up and down
a short distance. *Cf.* CARE 2, CAREFUL 2, KEEP, MAINTAIN, PRE-
SERVE.

TAKE UP *v. phrase.* (Responsibility.) Both hands, held palms
down in the "5" position, are at chest level. With a grasping

upward movement, both close into "S" positions before the face. *Cf.* ASSUME, PICK UP 1.

TALE (tāl), *n.* (The unraveling or stretching out of words or sentences.) Both open hands are held close to each other, with fingers open and palms facing and almost touching. As the hands are drawn apart, the thumb and index finger of each hand come together to form circles. This is repeated several times. *Cf.* NARRATE, NARRATIVE, STORY.

TALK 1 (tôk), *v.*, TALKED, TALKING. (Words tumbling from the mouth.) The right index finger, pointing left, describes a continuous small circle in front of the mouth. *Cf.* HEARING, MENTION, SAID, SAY, SPEAK, SPEECH 1, TELL.

TALK 2, *n., v.* (A gesture of an orator.) The right open hand, palm facing left, is held above and to the right of the head. It pivots on the wrist, forward and backward, several times. *Cf.* LECTURE, SPEECH 2.

TALK 3, *n., v.* (Movement forward from, and back to, the mouth.) The tips of both index fingers, held pointing up, move alternately forward from, and back to, the lips. *Cf.* CONVERSATION 1, CONVERSE.

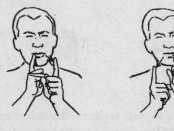

TALL 1 (tôl), *adj.* (The height is indicated.) The index finger of the right "D" hand moves straight up against the palm of the left "5" hand. *Cf.* HEIGHT 1.

TALL 2, *adj.* (The height is indicated.) The right right-angle hand, palm facing the left, is held at the height the signer wishes to indicate. *Cf.* BIG 2, HEIGHT 2, HIGH 2.

TAPE RECORDER *n.* (The movement of the spools.) Both hands are held downturned, with middle fingers hanging down. Both hands move in unison, in a clockwise direction.

TAX (tăks), *n., v.,* TAXED, TAXING. (Nicking into one.) The knuckle of the right "X" finger is nicked against the palm of the left hand, held in the "5" position, palm facing right. *Cf.* COST, EXPENSE, FINE 2, PENALTY, PRICE, TAXATION.

TAXATION (tăks ă' shən), *n.* See TAX.

TEA 1 (tē), *n.* (Dipping the teabag.) The right index finger and thumb raise and lower an imaginary teabag into a "cup" formed by the left "C" or "O" hand, held thumb side up.

TEA 2, *n.* (Stirring the teabag.) The hand positions in TEA 1 are assumed, but the right hand executes a circular, stirring motion instead.

TEACH (tēch), *v.*, TAUGHT, TEACHING. (Giving forth from the mind.) The fingertips of each hand are placed on the temples. They then swing out and open into the "5" position. *Cf.* EDUCATE, INSTRUCT.

TEEN (tēn), *n.* (The letter "T"; female and male.) The right "Thr" hand is placed first at the jaw and then at the temple.

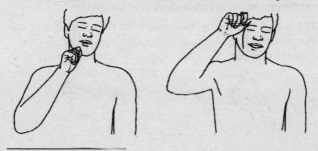

TELEPHONE (tĕl′ ə fōn′), *n., v.,* -PHONED, -PHONING. (The natural sign.) The right "Y" hand is placed at the right side of the head with the thumb touching the ear and the little finger touching the lips. This is the more modern telephone receiver. *Cf.* PHONE.

TELL (tĕl), *v.,* TOLD, TELLING. (Words tumbling from the mouth.) The right index finger, pointing left, describes a continuous small circle in front of the mouth. *Cf.* HEARING, MENTION, SAID, SAY, SPEAK, SPEECH 1, TALK 1.

TELL ME *phrase.* (The natural sign.) The tip of the index finger of the right "D" hand, palm facing the body, is first placed at the lips and then moves down to touch the chest.

TEMPERATURE (tĕm′ pər ə chər, -prə chər), *n.* (The rise and fall of the mercury in the thermometer.) The index finger of the right "D" hand, pointing left, moves slowly up and down the index finger of the left "D" hand, which is held pointing up. *Cf.* DEGREE 1.

TEMPT (tĕmpt), *v.*, TEMPTED, TEMPTING. (Tapping one surreptitiously at a concealed place.) With the left arm held palm down before the chest, the curved right index finger taps the left elbow a number of times. *Cf.* TEMPTATION.

TEMPTATION (tĕmp tā′ shən), *n.* See TEMPT.

TEND (tĕnd), *v.*, TENDED, TENDING. (The feelings of the heart move toward a specific object.) The tip of the right middle finger touches the heart. The open right hand, palm facing the body, then moves away from the heart toward the palm of the open left hand. *Cf.* TENDENCY.

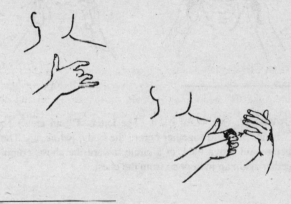

TENDENCY (tĕn′ dən sĭ), *n.* See TEND.

TENNIS (ten′ is), *n.* (Holding the racket.) The signer goes through the motions of manipulating a tennis racket. *Cf.* RACKET.

TERRIBLE (tĕr′ ə bəl), *adj.* (Throwing out the hands.) Both hands, their fingertips touching their respective thumbs, are held, palms facing each other, near the temples. They are thrown out before the face, assuming "5" positions, palms still facing. *Cf.* AWFUL.

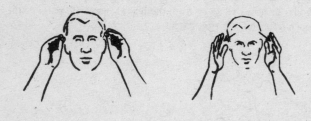

TERRITORY (ter′ ə tôr ē), *n.* (The letter "T"; an area.) The "T" hands are held together before the body, palms out. They separate and move back in a circle toward the chest, coming together again an inch or so from the chest.

TERROR 1 (tĕr′ ər), *n.* (The heart is suddenly covered with fear.) Both hands, fingers together, are placed side by side, palms facing the chest. They quickly open and come together over the heart, one on top of the other. *Cf.* AFRAID, FEAR 1,

FRIGHT, FRIGHTEN, SCARE(D).

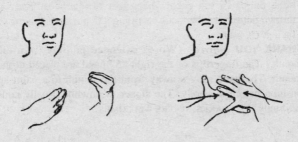

TERROR 2, *n* (The hands attempt to ward off something which causes fear.) The "5" hands, right behind left, move downward before the body, in a wavy motion. *Cf.* FEAR 2.

TEST (tĕst), *n.*, *v.*, TESTED, TESTING. (A series of questions, spread out on a page.) Both "D" hands, palms down, simultaneously execute a single circle, the right hand moving in a clockwise direction and the left in a counterclockwise direction. Upon completion of the circle, both hands open into the "5" position and move straight down a short distance. (The hands actually draw question marks in the air.) *Cf.* EXAMINATION 1.

THANKS (thăngks), *n. pl., interj.* See THANK YOU.

THANK YOU *phrase.* (Words extended politely from the mouth.) The fingertips of the right "5" hand are placed at the mouth. The hand moves away from the mouth to a palm-up position before the body. The signer meanwhile usually nods smilingly. *Cf.* THANKS, YOU'RE WELCOME 1.

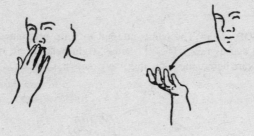

THAT (t͟hat, *unstressed* t͟hət), *pron.* (Something specific.) The downturned right "Y" hand is placed on the upturned left palm. *Cf.* THIS.

THAT ONE *(colloq.), phrase.* The downturned "Y" hand drops down abruptly, ending with a finger pointing at the one referred to. A knowing expression is assumed, or sometimes an exaggerated grimace, as if announcing a surprising fact.

THEFT 1 (thĕft), *n.* (The hand, partly concealed, takes something surreptitiously.) The index and middle fingers of the right hand, somewhat curved, are placed under the left elbow. As they move slowly along the left forearm toward the left wrist, they close a bit. *Cf.* ROB 1, STEAL 1, THIEF, THIEVERY.

THEFT 2, *n.* (A mustachioed thief.) The fingertips of both "H" hands, palms facing the body, are placed above the lips and are drawn slowly apart, describing a mustache. Sometimes one hand only is used. *Cf.* CROOK, ROB 3.

THEIR(S) (*ŧ͡hâr, unstressed ŧ͡hər*), *pron.* (Belonging to; pushed toward.) The open right hand, palm facing out and fingers together and pointing up, moves out a short distance from the body. This is repeated several times, with the hand moving an inch or two toward the right each time. The hand may also be swept in a short left-to-right arc in this position.

THEM (*ŧ͡hĕm, unstressed ŧ͡həm*), *pron.* (The natural sign.) The right index finger points in turn to a number of imaginary persons or objects. *Cf.* THEY.

THEMSELVES (*ŧ͡həm sĕlvz'*), *pron. pl.* (The thumb indicates an individual, *i.e., a self;* several are indicated.) The right hand, in the "A" position with thumb pointing up, makes a series of short forward movements as it sweeps either from right to left, or from left to right.

THEN 1 (t͟hĕn), *adv.* (Going from one specific point in time to another.) The left "L" hand is held palm facing right and thumb pointing left. The right index finger, positioned behind the left thumb, moves in an arc over the left thumb and comes to rest on the tip of the left index finger.

THEN 2, *adv.* (Same basic rationale as for THEN 1, but modified to incorporate the concept of nearness, *i.e.,* NEXT. The sign, then, is "one point [in time] to the next.") The left hand is held as in THEN 1. The extended right index finger rests on the ball of the thumb. The right hand then opens and arcs over, coming to rest on the back of the left hand, whose index finger has now closed.

THERAPY (ther' ə pē), *n.* (The letter "T"; helping.) The right "T" hand is placed palm down or palm left on the left palm. The left palm pushes up the right a short distance.

THERE 1 (ᵺâr), *adv.* (The natrual sing.) The right index finger points to an imaginary object, usually at or slightly above eye level, *i.e.,* "yonder."

THERE 2, *adv.* (Something brought to the attention.) The right hand is brought forward, simultaneously opening into the palm-up position.

THEREABOUTS (ᵺâr' ə boutz), *adv.* (In the general area.) The downturned open "5" hand moves in a counterclockwise direction in front of the body. *Cf.* ABOUT 3.

THEY (th̆ā), *pron.* (The natural sign.) The right index finger points in turn to a number of imaginary persons or objects. *Cf.* THEM.

THIEF (thĕf), *n.* (The hand, partly concealed, takes something surreptitiously.) The index and middle fingers of the right hand, somewhat curved, are placed under the left elbow. As they move slowly along the left forearm toward the left wrist, they close a bit. This is followed by INDIVIDUAL. *Cf.* ROB I, STEAL I, THEFT I, THIEVERY.

THIEVERY (thĕ'vɔ rĭ), *n.* See THIEF.

THIN I (thĭn), *adj.* (The drawn face.) The thumb and index finger run down the cheeks, which are drawn in.

THIN 2, *(sl.), adj.* (A thin, tapering object is described with the little fingers, the thinnest of all.) The tips of the little fingers, touching, one above the other, are drawn apart. The cheeks may also be drawn in for emphasis. *Cf.* SKINNY.

THING (thĭng), *n.* (Something shown in the hand.) The outstretched right hand, palm up and held before the chest, is dropped slightly and brought over a bit to the right.

THINK (thĭngk), *v.,* THOUGHT, THINKING. (A thought is turned over in the mind.) The index finger makes a small circle on the forehead. *Cf.* CONSIDER 1, SPECULATE 1, SPECULATION 1, THOUGHT, THOUGHTFUL.

THIRST (thûrst), *n*. (The parched throat.) The index finger moves down the throat a short distance. *Cf.* THIRSTY.

_____

THIRSTY (thûrs' tĭ), *adj*. See THIRST.

_____

THIS (t͡his), *pron., adj*. (Something specific.) The downturned right "Y" hand is placed on the upturned left palm. *Cf.* THAT.

_____

THIS MONTH *phrase*. (Now, month.) The sign for NOW is made: The upturned right-angle hands drop down rather sharply. The "Y" hands may also be used. This is followed by the sign for MONTH: The extended right index finger moves down along the upturned, extended left index finger. The two signs are sometimes given in reverse order.

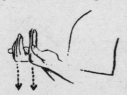

THOUGHT (thôt), *n.* (A thought is turned over in the mind.) The index finger makes a small circle on the forehead. *Cf.* CONSIDER 1, SPECULATE 1, SPECULATION 1, THINK, THOUGHTFUL.

THOUGHTFUL (thôt' fəl), *adj.* See THOUGHT.

THOUSAND (thou' zənd), *n.* ("M" for the Latin *mille,* thousand.) The tips of the right "M" hand are thrust into the upturned left plam.

THRILL (thrĭl), *(colloq.),* *n., v.,* THRILLED, THRILLING. (The feelings well up and come out.) The open hands are placed near the chest, with middle fingers resting on the chest. Both hands move up and out simultaneously. A happy expression is assumed. *Cf.* WHAT'S NEW?, WHAT'S UP?

THROUGH (thrōō), *adv., prep., adj.* (The natural movement.)
The open right hand is pushed between either the middle and
index or the middle and third fingers of the open left hand.

THUS FAR *adv. phrase.* (From a point up and over.) In the
"D" position, palms down, both index fingers touch the right
shoulder and then are brought up and over, ending in a palm-
up position, pointing straight ahead of the body. *Cf.* ALL,
ALONG, EVER SINCE, SINCE 1, SO FAR.

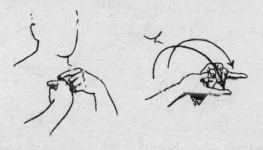

TICKET (tĭk′ ĭt), *n.* (A baggage check or ticket.) The sides of
the ticket are outlined with the thumb and index finger of each
hand. Then the middle knuckles of the second and third fingers
of the right hand squeeze the outer edge of the left palm, as a
conductor's ticket punch.

TIGER (tī′ gər), *n.* (The stripes on the face.) The claw hands trace the cat's stripes on the face.

TIGHTROPE (tīt′ rōp), *n.* (The natural activity.) The signer, arms outstretched, mimes walking a tightrope.

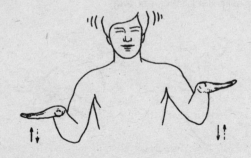

TILL (tĭl), *prep.* (From one point to the next.) The extended right index finger moves forward slowly and comes to rest on the tip of the extended, upturned left index finger. *Cf.* TO, TOWARD, UNTIL, UNTO, UP TO, UP TO NOW.

TIME 1 (tīm), *n.* (Time by the clock, indicated by the ticking of the clock or watch.) The curved right index finger taps the back of the left wrist several times.

TIME 2, *n.* (Time in the abstract, indicated by the rotating of the "T" hand on the face of a clock.) The right "T" hand is placed palm to palm in the open left hand. It describes a clockwise circle and comes to rest again in the left palm.

TINY (tī' ni), *adj.* (Indicating a small mass.) The extended right thumb and index finger are held slightly spread. They are then moved slowly toward each other until they almost touch. *Cf.* SMALL 1.

TIPTOE (tip′ tō), *n.*, *v.* (The feet touch lightly.) With both index fingers pointing down, the signer very lightly, slowly, and deliberately moves forward first one and then the other index finger. The shoulders are a little stooped, and with each successive forward movement of the index fingers, the signer moves forward very slightly.

TIRE (tīr), *v.*, TIRED, TIRING. (The hands collapse in exhaustion.) Both "C" hands are placed either on the lower chest or at the waist. The palms face the body. They fall away into a palms-up position. At the same time, the shoulders suddenly sag in a very pronounced fashion. An expression of weariness may be used for emphasis. *Cf.* TIRED.

TIRED (tīrd), *adj.* See TIRE.

TITLE (tī′ təl), *n.* (The quotation marks are indicated.) The curved index and middle fingers of both hands, held palms out, move slightly to either side of the body, as if drawing quota

tion marks in the air. *Cf.* QUOTATION, QUOTE, SO-CALLED, SUB-
JECT, TOPIC.

TO (too), *prep.* (From one point to the next.) The extended
right index finger moves forward slowly and comes to rest on
the tip of the extended, upturned left index finger. This sign
should never be used for an infinitive; it is simply omitted in
that case. *Cf.* TILL, TOWARD, UNTIL, UNTO, UP TO, UP TO NOW.

TODAY (tə dā′), *n.* (Now, day.) The sign for NOW is made:
The upturned right-angle hands drop down rather sharply. The
"Y" hands may also be used. This is followed by the sign for
DAY: The left arm, held horizontally, palm down, represents
the horizon. The right elbow rests on the back of the left hand,
with the right arm in a perpendicular position. The right "D"
hand, palm facing left, moves in an arc to the left until it is just
above the left elbow. The two signs may be reversed.

TOILET (toi′ lĭt), *n.* (The letter "T.") The right "T" hand is shaken slightly.

TOMORROW (tə môr′ ō, -mŏr′ ō), *n., adv.* (A single step ahead, *i.e.,* into the future.) The thumb of the right "A" hand, placed on the right cheek, moves straight out from the face, describing an arc.

TONIGHT (tə nīt′), *n.* (Now, night.) The sign for NOW is made: The upturned right-angle hands drop down rather sharply. The "Y" hands may also be used. This is followed by the sign for NIGHT: The left hand, palm down, is positioned at chest height. The downturned right hand, held an inch or so above the left, moves over the left hand in an arc, as the sun setting beneath the horizon. The two signs may be reversed.

TOOTHPASTE *n.* (Squeezing the tube.) The signer mimes squeezing toothpaste onto the outstretched left index finger.

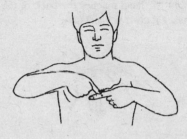

TOP DOG *n. (sl.)* (The senior year at school.) The downturned open right palm rests on the tip of the left thumb. *Cf.* SENIOR.

TOPIC (tŏp′ ĭk), *n.* (The quotation marks are indicated.) The curved index and middle fingers of both hands, held palms out, move slightly to either side of the body, as if drawing quotation marks in the air. *Cf.* QUOTATION, QUOTE, SO-CALLED, SUBJECT, TITLE.

TOUCH (tŭch), *n.*, *v.*, TOUCHED, TOUCHING. (The natural movement of touching.) The tip of the middle finger of the downturned right "5" hand touches the back of the left hand a number of times. *Cf.* CONTACT 1, FEEL 1.

TOUCHED (tŭcht), *adj.* (A piercing of the heart.) The tip of the middle finger of the right "5" hand is thrust against the heart. The head, at the same time, moves abruptly back a very slight distance. *Cf.* FEEL TOUCHED, TOUCHING.

TOUCHING (tŏuch' ĭng), *adj.* See TOUCHED.

TOURIST (tŏor' ist), *n.* (One who wanders around.) Using the downturned curved "V" fingers, the signer describes a series of small counterclockwise circles as the fingers move in ran

dom fashion from right to left. This is followed by the sign for
INDIVIDUAL.

TOWARD (tôrd, tə wôrd'), *prep.* (From one point to the
next.) The extended right index finger moves forward slowly
and comes to rest on the tip of the extended, upturned left
index finger. *Cf.* TILL, TO, UNTIL, UNTO, UP TO, UP TO NOW.

TRADE (trād), *n., v.,* TRADED, TRADING. (Exchanging places.)
The right "A" hand, positioned above the left "A" hand,
swings down and under the left, coming up a bit in front of it.
Cf. EXCHANGE, REPLACE, SUBSTITUTE.

TRAILER (trā′ lər), *n.* (The rig swings back and forth.) Both downturned hands are positioned with the left fingertips against the heel of the right hand, the cab. Both hands sway slightly back and forth as they move forward.

TRAIN 1 (trān), *n.* (Running along the tracks.) The "V" hands are held palms down. The right "V" moves back and forth over the left "V." *Cf.* TRANSPORTATION.

TRAIN 2, *v.,* TRAINED, TRAINING. (Polishing or sharpening up.) The knuckles of the downturned right "A" hand are rubbed briskly back and forth over the side of the hand and index finger of the left "D" hand. *Cf.* PRACTICE.

TRANSFER (trans' fər), *n., v.* (Shift position or travel.) The downturned curved right "V" fingers move forward in a horizontal arc.

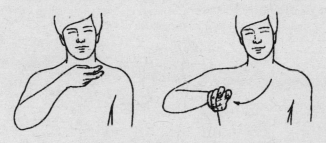

TRAP (trap), *n.* (The jaws of the trap snap together.) Both "X" hands, palms out, are held a few inches apart. They suddenly snap together.

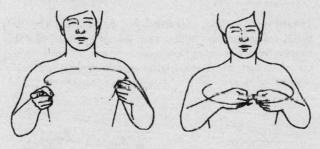

TRAVEL (trăv' əl), *n., v.,* -ELED, -ELING. (Moving around from place to place.) The downturned curved "V" fingers of the right hand describe a series of small counterclockwise circles as they move in random fashion from right to left.

TREE (trē), *n.* (The shape.) The elbow of the upright right arm rests on the palm of the upturned left hand. This is the trunk. The right "5" fingers wiggle to imitate the movement of the branches and leaves.

TRIUMPH (trī′ əmf), *n.* (Penetrating the heights.) The "D" hands, palms back, are held at each side of the head, near the temples. With a pivoting motion of the wrists, the hands swing up and around, simultaneously, to a position above the head, with palms facing out. *Cf.* ACHIEVE, SUCCEED, SUCCESS, SUCCESSFUL.

TROUBLE (trŭb′ əl), *n.*, *v.*, -BLED, -BLING. (A clouding over; a troubling.) Both "B" hands, palms facing each other, are rotat ed alternately before the forehead. *Cf.* PROBLEM 1, WORRIED, WORRY 1.

TRUE (trōō), *adj.* (Coming forth directly from the lips; true.) The index finger of the right "D" hand, palm facing left, is placed against the lips. It moves up an inch or two and then describes a small arc forward and away from the lips. *Cf.* REAL, REALLY, SURE, SURELY, TRULY, TRUTH.

TRULY (trōō′ lĭ), *adv.* See TRUE.

TRUTH (trōōth), *n.* See TRUE.

TRY 1 (trī), *n.*, *v.*, TRIED, TRYING. (Trying to push through.) The "A" hands, palms facing before the body, are swung around and a bit down, so that the palms now face out. The movement indicates an attempt to push through a barrier. *Cf.* ATTEMPT 1, EFFORT 1.

TRY 2, *v.*, *n.* (Trying to push through, using the "T" hands, for "try.") This is the same sign as TRY 1, except that the "T" hands are employed. *Cf.* ATTEMPT 2, EFFORT 2.

TUTOR (tōō′ tər), *n.*, *v.* (The letter "T"; taking knowledge from the mind and giving it to someone.) Both "T" hands, palms facing, are placed at the temples. They move forward and back again several times. Used as a noun, this sign is followed by the sign for INDIVIDUAL.

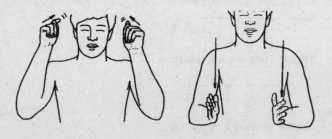

TWINS 1 (twinz), *n.* The right "T" hand moves from the left corner of the mouth to the right corner.

TWINS 2, *n.* The thumb edge of the right "T" hand is placed on the left corner of the mouth. It moves away and over to the right corner of the mouth.

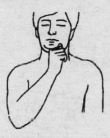

TWO MORE *(colloq.), phrase.* (Two fingers beckon.) The right hand is held palm up, with the index and middle fingers making very small and rapid beckoning movements.

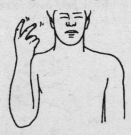

U

UNCERTAIN (un sûr′ tən), *adj.* (On a fence; unsure.) The downturned right "V" hand straddles the index finger edge of the left "B" hand, whose palm faces right. The right hand sways slightly, from left to right. *Cf.* ON THE FENCE, UNSURE, WAVER.

UNCLE (ŭng′ kəl), *n.* (The letter "U"; the "male" or upper portion of the head.) The right "U" hand is held near the right temple and is shaken slightly.

UNDER 1 (ŭn′ dər), *prep.* (Underneath something.) The right hand, in the "A" position, thumb pointing straight up, moves down under the left hand, held outstretched, fingers together, palm down. *Cf.* BELOW 2, UNDERNEATH.

UNDER 2, *prep.* (The area below.) The right "A" hand, thumb pointing up, moves in a counterclockwise fashion under the downturned left hand.

UNDERNEATH (ŭn´ dər nēth´, -nĕᵗh), *prep.* See UNDER 1.

UNDERSTAND (ŭn´ dər stănd´), *v* -STOOD, -STANDING. (An awakening of the mind.) The right "S" hand is placed on the forehead, palm facing the body. The index finger suddenly flicks up into the "D" position.

UNION (yōōn´ yən), *n.* (The "U" fingers, making a circle to indicate unity.) Both "U" hands, touching, with palms out, move in a circle until they touch again, with palms now facing in.

 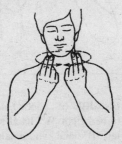

UNIVERSE (yōō′ nə vûrs), *n.* (The letter "U"; the planet.) The right "U" hand, palm out, makes a clockwise circle around the left "S" hand, representing a planet.

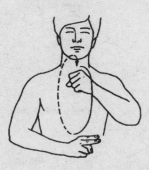

UNNECESSARY (un nes′ ə ser ə), *adj.* (Nothing there, in the area of necessity.) The sign for NECESSARY: the downturned curved index finger is thrust down and then the hand opens with a flourish to the palm-up position.

UNSURE (ŭn shŏŏr′), *adj.* (On a fence; uncertain.) The downturned right "V" hand straddles the index finger edge of the left "B" hand, whose palm faces right. The right hand sways slightly, from left to right. *Cf.* ON THE FENCE, UNCERTAIN, WAVER

UNTIL (ŭn tĭl'), *prep.* (From one point to the next.) The extended right index finger moves forward slowly and comes to rest on the tip of the extended, upturned left index finger. *Cf.* TILL, TO, TOWARD, UNTO, UP TO, UP TO NOW.

UNTO (ŭn' tōō), *prep.* See UNTIL.

UPSET (up set'), *adj.*, *v.* (The stomach is turned upside down.) The downturned open right hand is positioned horizontally across the stomach. It flips over so that it is now palm up.

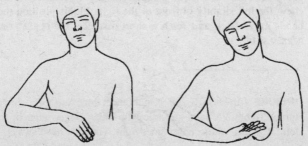

UP TO *prep. phrase.* (From one point to the next.) The extended right index finger moves forward slowly and comes to rest on the tip of the extended, upturned left index finger. *Cf.* TILL, TO, TOWARD, UNTIL, UNTO, UP TO NOW.

UP TO NOW *adv. phrase.* See UP TO.

URGE 1 (ûrj), *v.,* URGED, URGING, *n.* (Pushing forward.) Both "5" hands are held, palms out, the right fingers facing right and the left fingers left. The hands move straight forward in a series of short movements. *Cf.* ENCOURAGE, MOTIVATE, MOTIVATION.

URGE 2, *v.* (Shaking someone, to implant one's will into another.) Both "A" hands, palms facing, are held before the chest, the left slightly in front of the right. In this position the hands move back and forth a short distance. *Cf.* PERSUADE, PERSUASION.

US (ŭs), *pron.* (The letter "U"; an encompassing gesture.) The right "U" hand, palm facing the body, swings from right shoulder to left shoulder.

USE (*n.* ūs; *v.* ūz), *n.*, *v.*, USED, USING. (The letter "U.") The right "U" hand describes a small clockwise circle. *Cf.* USED, USEFUL, UTILIZE.

USED (ūzd), *v.* See USE.

USEFUL (ūs′ fəl), *adj.* See USE.

USE UP (ūz up), *v. phrase.* (Pull something off the hand.)
The right "C" hand, palm facing left, is placed on the upturned
left hand. The right hand, moving right, quickly leaves the left,
while closing into a fist.

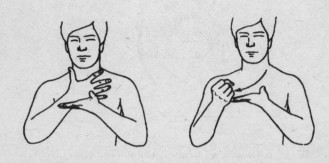

___

US TWO *phrase.* (Two persons interacting.) The right "V"
hand, palm up and fingers pointing left, is swung in and out to
and from the chest. *Cf.* BOTH OF US, WE TWO.

___

UTILIZE (ū′ tə līz′), *v.,* -LIZED, -LIZING. See USE.

V

VACATION (vā kā′ shən), *n*. (A position of idleness.) With thumbs tucked in the armpits, the remaining fingers of both hands wiggle. *Cf.* RETIRE.

VACUUM CLEANER (vak′ yoom klĕn′ ər), *n*. (Sucking up the dirt.) The extended right fingers are positioned above the upturned left palm. The right fingers move back and forth across the palm, while the fingers open and close very rapidly.

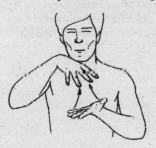

VALUABLE (văl′ yॡॡ ə bəl, văl′ yə bəl), *adj*. Both "F" hands, palms facing each other, move apart, up, and together in a smooth elliptical fashion, coming together at the tips of the thumbs and index fingers of both hands. *Cf.* IMPORTANT, SIGNIFICANCE 1, SIGNIFICANT, VALUE, WORTH, WORTHWHILE, WORTHY.

VALUE (văl′ ū), *n*. See VALUABLE.

VARIED (vâr′ ĭd), *adj*. (Separated many times; different.) The "D" hands, palms down, are crossed at the index fingers or are held side by side. They separate and return to their initial position a number of times. *Cf.* DIFFERENCE, DIFFERENT, DIVERSE 1, DIVERSITY 1.

VARIOUS (vâr′ ĭ əs), *adj*. (The fingertips indicate many things.) Both hands, in the "D" position, palms out and index fingertips touching, are drawn apart. As they move apart, the index fingers wiggle up and down. *Cf.* DIVERSE 2, DIVERSITY 2, VARY.

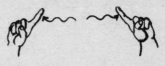

VARY (vâr´ ĭ), *v.*, VARIED, VARYING. See VARIOUS.

VCR *n.* (A fingerspelled loan sign.) The signer fingerspells "V-C-R."

VENETIAN BLINDS *n.* (The slats.) Both hands, palms down at chest level, are positioned with the right above the left, left fingers pointing right and right fingers pointing left. They both move down, while each wrist swivels back and forth, imitating the opening and closing of the blinds.

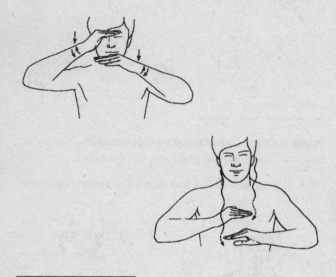

VERB (vûrb), *n.* (The letter "V.") The right "V" hand, palm facing the body and fingers pointing left, moves across the mouth from left to right.

VERY (vĕr′ ĭ), *adv.* (The "V" hands, with the sign for MUCH.) The fingertips of the "V" hands are placed together, and then moved apart.

VETERINARIAN (vet ər ə når′ ē ən), *n.* (A fingerspelled loan sign.) The signer spells out "V-E-T" with the fingers.

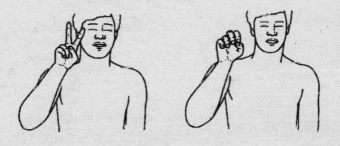

VICTORY 1 (vǐk′ tə rǐ), *n.* (Waving of flags.) Both upright hands, grasping imaginary flags, wave them in small circles. *Cf.* CELEBRATE, CELEBRATION, CHEER, REJOICE, WIN 1.

VICTORY 2, *n.* (Waving a flag.) The right "A" hand goes through the natural movement of waving a flag in circular fashion. Preceding this, the right hand may go through the motion of grabbing the flagstaff out of the left hand. *Cf.* WIN 2.

VIDEOTAPE (vĭd′ ē ō tāp), *n., v.* (The turning of the tape.) The left hand is held open, palm facing right. The right "V" hand makes a circle around the left palm, ending in the letter "T," and resting on the palm.

VIEW (vū), *n., v.,* VIEWED, VIEWING. (Look around.) The sign for LOOK is made: The right "V" hand, palm facing the body, is placed so that the fingertips are just under the eyes. Then both "V" hands are held with palms down and fingers pointing forward in front of the body. In this position the hands move simultaneously from side to side several times. *Cf.* VISION 1.

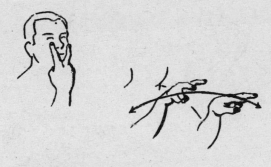

***

VISION 1 (vĭzh′ ən), *n.* (Look around.) The sign for LOOK is made: The right "V" hand, palm facing the body, is placed so that the fingertips are just under the eyes. Then both "V" hands are held with palms down and fingers pointing forward in front of the body. In this position the hands move simultaneously from side to side several times. *Cf.* VIEW.

VISION 2, *n.* (A sudden opening of the mind.) The sign for DREAM is made: the tip of the right index is placed on the forehead. Then both "S" hands are held in front of the forehead, the left in front of the right. They open into the "C" position, as the hands separate. The sign for DREAM may be omitted.

VISIT (vĭz'ĭt), *n., v.*, -ITED, -ITING. (The letter "V"; random movement, *i.e.*, moving around as in visiting.) The "V" hands, palms facing, move alternately in clockwise circles out from the chest.

VOLCANO (vol kă′ nō), *n*. (The shape and the eruption.) Both "V" hands move up, coming together to form a peak. The hands are then closed and opened explosively, describing the eruption.

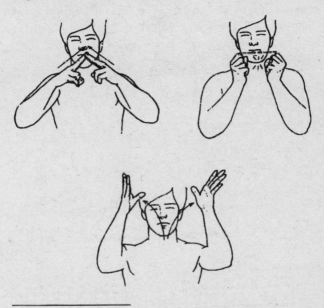

VOTE 1 (vōt), *n., v.,* VOTED, VOTING. (Placing a ballot in a box.) The right hand, holding an imaginary ballot between the thumb and index finger, places it into an imaginary box formed by the left "O" hand, palm facing right. *Cf.* ELECT, ELECTION.

VOTE 2, *n.*, *v.* (Placing the ballot in the box.) The thumb and index finger drop an imaginary ballot into a slot.

W

WAFFLE (wŏf′ əl), *n*. (The grid pattern.) Both hands face each other, fingertips forward and interlocked, right above left. The right hand moves down and back up a number of times, representing the cover of the waffle grill.

WAIT (wāt), *n., v.*, WAITED, WAITING. (The fingers wiggle with impatience.) The upturned "5" hands are positioned with the right behind the left. The fingers of both hands wiggle.

WAIVE (wāv), *v*. (A wiped off and clean slate.) The right hand wipes off the left palm several times.

WAKE UP (wăk), *v. phrase.* (Opening the eyes.) Both hands are closed, with thumb and index finger of each hand held together, extended, and placed at the corners of the closed eyes. Slowly they separate, and the eyes open. *Cf.* AWAKE, AWAKEN.

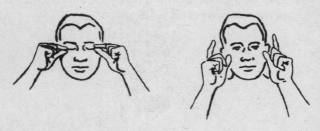

WALK (wôk), *n., v.,* WALKED, WALKING. (The movement of the feet.) The downturned "5" hands move alternately toward and away from the chest.

WALKIE-TALKIE (wô′ kē tô kē), *n.* (The shape at the ear.) The "Y" hand is held thumb against mouth, and then it moves up so that the thumb is against the ear. The movement is repeated.

WALLET 1 (wol' it), *n*. (Folding the wallet.) The two hands held with fingertips touching are brought together palm to palm and move flat against each other as if closing a wallet. This is a generic sign.

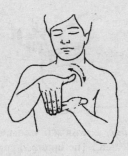

WALLET 2, *n*. (Placing the bills in.) The little finger edge of the open right hand, palm facing the body, is slipped into the space created by the thumb and other fingers of the left hand. The signer then mimes placing the wallet into a back pocket.

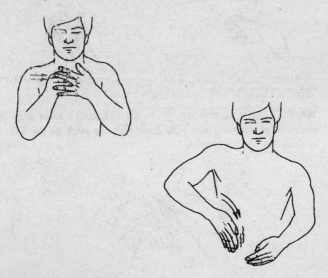

WANT (wŏnt, wônt), *v.*, WANTED, WANTING. (Grasping something and pulling it in.) The upturned "5" hands, held side by side before the chest, close slightly into a grasping position as they move in toward the body. *Cf.* DESIRE, NEED 2, WISH 1.

WARM (wôrm), *adj., v.*, WARMED, WARMING. (The warmth of the breath is indicated.) The upturned cupped right hand is placed at the slightly open mouth. It moves up and away from the mouth, opening into the upturned "5" position, with fingers somewhat curved.

WARN (wôrn), *v.*, WARNED, WARNING. (Tapping one to draw attention to danger.) The right hand taps the back of the left several times. *Cf.* CAUTION.

WAS (wŏz, wŭz; *unstressed* wəz), *v.* (Something past, behind.) The upraised right hand, in the "5" position with palm facing the body, is held just above the right shoulder and is thrown back over it. *Cf.* PAST, PREVIOUS, PREVIOUSLY, WERE.

WASH 1 (wŏsh, wôsh), *n., v.,* WASHED, WASHING. (Rubbing the clothes.) The knuckles of the "A" hands rub against one another, in circles.

WASH 2, *v.* (The natural sign.) The closed hands move up and down against the chest as if scrubbing it. *Cf.* BATH, BATHE.

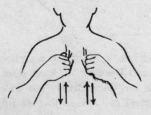

WASH DISHES *v. phrase.* (The natural sign.) The downturned right "5" hand describes a clockwise circle as it moves over the upturned left "5" hand.

WASTE 1 (wăst), *n., v.,* WASTED, WASTING. (Repeated giving forth.) The back of the upturned right hand, thumb touching fingertips, is placed in the upturned left palm. The right hand moves off and away from the left once or several times, each time opening into the "5" position, palm up. *Cf.* SPEND.

WASTE 2, *n., v.,* (The "W" is indicated.) The same movement as in WASTE 1 is used, except that the right hand assumes the "W" position and keeps it.

WATCH 1 (wŏch), *n., v.,* WATCHED, WATCHING. (The eyesight is directed forward.) The right "V" hand, palm facing the body, is placed so that the fingertips are just under the eyes. The hand swings around and out, so that the fingertips are now pointing forward. *Cf.* LOOK 1, PERCEIVE, PERCEPTION, SEE, SIGHT.

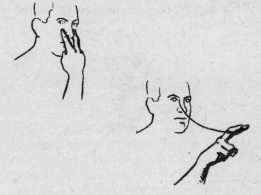

WATCH 2, *n.* (The shape of the wristwatch.) The thumb and index finger of the right hand, forming a circle, are placed on the back of the left wrist.*Cf.* WRISTWATCH.

WATER (wô′ tər, wŏt′ ər), *n.* (The letter "W" at the mouth, as in drinking water.) The right "W" hand, palm facing left, touches the lips a number of times.

WAVER (wā′ vər); *v.*, -VERED, -VERING. (On a fence; uncertain.) The downturned right "V" palm faces right. The right hand sways slightly, from left to right. *Cf.* ON THE FENCE, UNCERTAIN, UNSURE.\

WE 1 (wē; *unstressed* wĭ), *pron.* (An encompassing movement.) The right index finger points down as it swings over from the right shoulder to the left shoulder.

WE 2, *pron.* (The letter "W.") The right "W" hand, fingers pointing up, goes through the same motion as in WE 1.

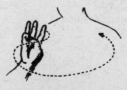

WEAK (wēk), *adj.* (The knees buckle.) The right "V" hand is placed with fingertips resting in the upturned left palm. The knuckles of the "V" fingers buckle a bit. This motion may be repeated. *Cf.* WEAKNESS.

WEAKNESS (wĕk′ nĭs), *n.* See WEAK.

WEALTH (wĕlth), *n.* (A pile of money.) The sign for MONEY is made: The back of the upturned right hand, whose thumb and fingertips are all touching, is placed in the upturned left palm. The right hand then moves straight up, as it opens into the "5" position, palm facing down and fingers somewhat curved. *Cf.* RICH, WEALTHY.

WEALTHY (wĕl′ thĭ), *adj.* See WEALTH.

WEAR (wâr), *n. v.*, WORE, WORN, WEARING. (Draping the clothes on the body.) With fingertips resting on the chest, both hands move down simultaneously. The action is repeated. *Cf.* CLOTHES, CLOTHING, DRESS, SHIRT.

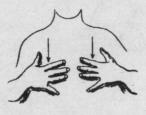

WEATHER (weŧh′ ər), *n.* (The letter "W.") The right "W" hand, palm out, moves straight down before the body, trembling slightly as it does.

WEDDING (wĕd′ ĭng), *n.* (A joining of hands.) The down-turned "B" hands are joined together with a flourish.

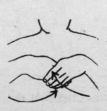

WEEK (wĕk), *n.* The upright, right "D" hand is placed palm-to-palm against the left "5" hand, whose palm faces right. The right "D" hand moves along the left palm from base to finger-tips.

WEIGH (wā), *v.,* WEIGHED, WEIGHING. (The balancing of the scale is described.) The fingers of the right "H" hand are centered on the left index finger and rocked back and forth. *Cf.* POUND 1, WEIGHT.

WEIGHT (wāt), *n.* See WEIGH.

WEIRD (wĭrd), *adj.* (Something which distorts the vision.) The "C" hand describes a small arc in front of the face. *Cf.* CURIOUS 1, ODD, STRANGE.

WELCOME (wĕl′ kəm), *n., v.,* -COMED, -COMING. (Opening or leading the way toward something.) The open right hand, held up before the body, sweeps down in an arc and over toward the left side of the chest, ending in the palm-up position. Reversing the movement gives the passive form of the verb, except that the hand does not arc upward but rather simply moves outward in a small arc from the body. *Cf.* INVITE.

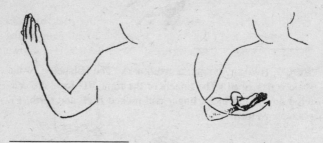

WELL (wĕl), *adj.* (Strength emanating from the body.) Both "5" hands are placed palms against the chest. They move out and away, forcefully, closing and assuming the "S" position. *Cf.* BRAVE, BRAVERY, HEALTH, HEALTHY, MIGHTY 2, STRENGTH.

WE'LL SEE *phrase.* (Modified from the sign for SEE.) The index finger of the right "V" hand, palm facing left, is placed at the corner of the right eye. The hand makes several very small back and forth movements. This is often accompanied by a very slight nodding.

WERE (wûr, *unstressed* wər), *v.* (Something past, behind.) The upraised right hand, in the "5" position with palm facing the body, is held just above the right shoulder and is thrown back over it. *Cf.* PAST, PREVIOUS, PREVIOUSLY, WAS.

WET (wĕt), *adj., n., v.,* WET or WETTED, WETTING. (The wetness.) The right fingertips touch the lips, and then the fingers of both hands open and close against the thumbs a number of times.

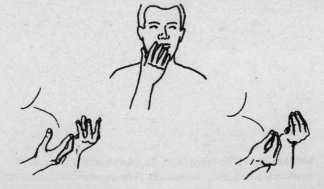

WE TWO *phrase*. (Two people interacting.) The right "V" hand, palm up and fingers pointing left, is swung in and out to and from the chest. *Cf.* BOTH OF US, US TWO.

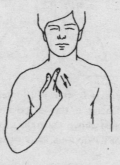

WHALE 1 (hwāl), *n*. (The blowhole.) The right hand, in the AND position, fingers pointing up, is placed on top of the head. It moves up off the head and opens into the "5" position, representing the whale blowing out through the blowhole.

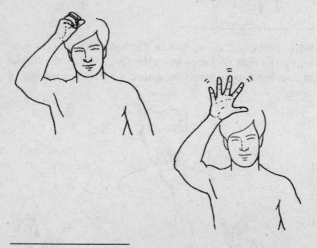

WHALE 2, *n*. (The letter "W"; the movement.) The right "W" hand makes a series of undulating dive movements in front of the downturned left arm, which represents the surface of the water.

W-H-A-T? *(colloq.), interj.* (A fingerspelled loan sign.) The letters "W-H-A-T" are spelled out rather slowly, but with force and deliberation, while the signer assumes a look of incredulity. This is the equivalent of a shouted interjection.

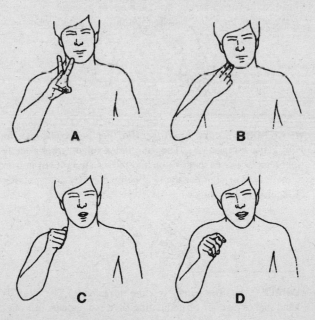

WHAT 1 (hwŏt, hwŭt; *unstressed* hwət), *pron., adj., adv., interj., conj.* (The finger passes over several specifics to bring out the concept of "which one?") The right index finger passes over the fingers of the upturned left "5" hand, from index to little finger.

WHAT 2, *pron., adj., adv., interj., conj.* (Throwing out the hands as a gesture of inquiry.) Both upturned open hands move slightly back and forth in front of the chest. The signer assumes a look of wonderment, emphasized by slightly upturned shoulders, raised eyebrows, or furrowed brow.

WHAT FOR? *(colloq.), phrase.* (For-For-For?) The sign for FOR is made repeatedly: The right index finger, resting on the right temple, leaves its position and moves straight out in front of the face. The sign is usually accompanied by an expression of inquiry, or annoyance.

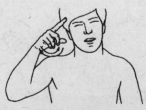

WHAT IS THE PRICE? (Amount of money is indicated.) The sign for MONEY is made: The upturned right hand, grasping some imaginary bills, is brought down into the upturned left palm a number of times. The right hand then moves straight up, opening into the "5" position, palm up.

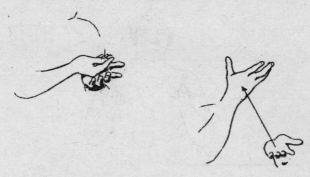

WHAT'S NEW? (The feelings well up and come out.) The open hands are placed near the chest, with middle fingers resting on the chest. Both hands move up and out simultaneously. A happy expression is assumed. *Cf.* HOW ARE YOU, THRILL, WHAT'S UP?

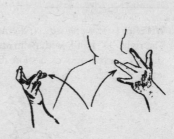

WHAT'S UP? See WHAT'S NEW?

WHAT TO DO? *(colloq.), phrase.* (Do-Do-Do?) This is a modified fingerspelled loan sign. The signer makes palm-up "D"s with both hands. These quickly assume the "O" position, with the palms remaining up. This is repeated several times, quickly, with an expression of despair or inquiry.

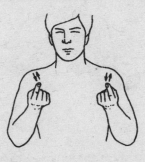

WHEN (hwĕn), *adv., conj., n.* (Fixing a point in time.) The left "D" hand is held upright, palm facing the body. The right index finger describes a clockwise circle around the left, coming to rest on the left index fingertip.

WHERE 1 (hwâr), *adv.* (Alternate directions are indicated.) The right "D" hand, with palm out and index finger straight or slightly curved, moves a short distance back and forth, from left to right.

WHERE 2, *adv.* The open "5" hands, palms up and fingers slightly curved, move back and forth in front of the body, the right hand to the right and the left hand to the left. *Cf.* HERE.

WHETHER (hwĕth' ər), *conj.* (Considering one thing against another.) The "A" hands, palms facing and thumbs pointing straight up, move alternately up and down before the chest. *Cf.* EITHER 3, OR, WHICH.

WHICH (hwĭch), *pron. (esp. interrog. pron.)*, *adj.* See WHETHER.

WHILE (hwīl), *conj. only.* (Parallel time.) Both "D" hands, palms down, move forward in unison, away from the body. They may move straight forward or may follow a slight upward arc. *Cf.* DURING, MEANTIME.

WHILE AGO, A 1, *phrase*. (The slight movement represents a slight amount of time.) With the closed right hand held with knuckles against the right cheek, the thumbtip flicks off the tip of the curved index finger a number of times. The eyes squint a bit and the lips are drawn out in a slight smile. The hand remains against the cheek during the flicking movement. Sometimes, instead of the flicking movement, the tip of the curved index finger scratches slightly up and down against the cheek. In this case, the palm faces back toward the shoulder. The same expression is used as in the flicking movement. *Cf.* RECENT, RECENTLY.

WHILE AGO, A 2, *phrase*. (Time moved backward a bit.) The right "D" hand, palm facing the body, is placed in the palm of the left hand, which is facing right. The right hand swings back a bit toward the body, with the index finger describing an arc. *Cf.* FEW SECONDS AGO, JUST A MOMENT AGO.

WHISPER (hwis' pər), *n., v.* (Two people talk back and forth.) The right index and middle fingers rest on the lips.

They individually go back and forth repeatedly striking the lips.

WHO (hōō), *pron.* (The pursed lips are indicated.) The right index finger traces a small counterclockwise circle in front of the lips, which are pursed in the enunciation of the word. *Cf.* WHOM.

WHOM (hōōm), *pron.* See WHO.

WHOSE (hōōz), *pron.* (Who; outstretched open hand signifies possession, as if pressing an item against the chest of the person spoken to.) The sign for WHO is made: The right index finger traces a small counterclockwise circle in front of the lips, which are pursed in the enunciation of the word. Then the right "5" hand, palm facing out, moves straight out toward the person spoken to or about.

WHY (hwī), *adv., n., interj.* (Reason--coming from the mind -- modified by the letter "Y," the phonetic equivalent of WHY.) The fingertips of the right hand, palm facing the body, are placed against the forehead. The right hand then moves down and away from the forehead, assuming the "Y" position, palm still facing the body. Expression is an important indicator of the context in which this sign is used. Thus, as an interjection, a severe expression is assumed; while as an adverb or a noun, the expression is blank or inquisitive.

WIDE (wīd), *adj.* (The width is indicated.) The open hands, fingers pointing out and palms facing each other, separate from their initial position an inch or two apart. *Cf.* WIDTH.

WIDTH (wĭdth), *n.* See WIDE.

WIFE (wīf), *n.* (A female whose hand is clasped in marriage.) The FEMALE root sign is made: The thumb of the right "A" hand moves down along the right jawbone, almost to the chin.

The hands are then clasped together, right above left.

WILD (wĭld), *adj.* (The "W"s; the mind is in a state of disarray.) Both "W" hands, palms facing, describe alternate clockwise circles at the temples. This sign should be accompanied by an appropriate look of agitation, or a threatening look.

WILL (wĭl), *v.* (Something ahead or in the future.) The upright, open right hand, palm facing left, moves straight out and slightly up from a position beside the right temple. *Cf.* FUTURE, IN THE FUTURE, LATER 2, LATER ON, WOULD.

WIN 1 (wĭn), *v.*, WON, WINNING, *n.* (Waving of flags.) Both upright hands, grasping imaginary flags, wave them in small circles. *Cf.* CELEBRATE, CELEBRATION, CHEER, REJOICE, VICTORY 1.

WIN 2, *v.*, *n.* (Waving a flag.) The right "A" hand goes through the natural movement of waving a flag in circular fashion. Preceding this, the right hand may go through the motion of grabbing the flagstaff out of the left hand. *Cf.* VICTORY 2.

WIND (wĭnd), *n.* (The blowing back and forth of the wind.) The "5" hands, palms facing and held up before the body, sway gracefully back and forth, in unison. The cheeks meanwhile are puffed up and the breath is being expelled. The nature of the swaying movement--graceful and slow, fast and violent, etc.--determines the type of wind. The strength of exhalation is also a qualifying device.

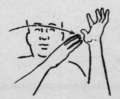

WINDOW (wĭn' dō), *n.* (The opening of the window.) With both palms facing the body, the little finger edge of the right hand rests atop the index finger edge of the left hand. The right hand then moves straight up and down. *Cf.* OPEN THE WINDOW.

WINDSURFING *n.* (The natural movement.) The signer, standing on an imaginary windsurfer and grasping the boom, executes a series of swaying maneuvers, as if guiding a surfboard.

WINE (wīn), *n*. (The "W" hand indicates a flushed cheek.) The right "W" hand, palm facing the face, rotates at the right cheek, in either a clockwise or a counterclockwise direction.

_____

WINTER 1 (wĭn′ tər), *n*. (The trembling from cold.) Both "S" hands, palms facing, are placed at the sides of the body. In this position the arms and hands shiver. *Cf.* COLD 1, SHIVER.

_____

WINTER 2, *n*. (The letter "W.") The upright "W" hands, palms facing or forward, are brought together forcefully before the body one or two times.

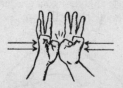

_____

WIPE (wīp), *v*. (Wiping with a cloth or towel.) The flattened right hand makes a series of clockwise wiping movements against the open left palm.

WISDOM (wĭz′ dəm), *n*. (Measuring the depth of the mind.) The downturned "X" finger moves up and down a short distance as it rests on mid-forehead. *Cf.* WISE.

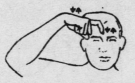

WISE (wīz), *adj*. See WISDOM.

WISH 1 (wĭsh), *v*., WISHED, WISHING. (Grasping something and pulling it in.) The upturned "5" hands, held side by side before the chest, close slightly into a grasping position as they move in toward the body. *Cf.* DESIRE, NEED 2, WANT.

WISH 2, *v., n.* (The upper alimentary tract is outlined.) The right "C" hand, palm facing the body, is placed with fingertips touching mid-chest. In this position it moves down a bit. *Cf.* STARVATION, STARVE, STARVED.

WITH (wĭth), *prep.* (The two hands are together, *i.e.,* WITH each other.) Both "A" hands, knuckles together and thumbs up, are moved forward in unison, away from the chest. They may also remain stationary.

WITHDRAW 1 (wĭth drô′, wĭth-), *v.,* -DREW, -DRAWN, -DRAW-ING. (Pulling away.) The downturned open hands are held in a line, with fingers pointing to the left, the right hand behind the left. Both hands move in unison toward the right. As they do so, they assume the "A" position. *Cf.* DEPART, LEAVE.

WITHDRAW 2, *v.* (Pulling out.) The index and middle fingers of the right "H" hand are grasped by the left hand. The right hand pulls out of the left. *Cf.* QUIT, RESIGN.

WITHIN (wĭth ĭn′, wĭth-), *adv.*, *prep.* (The natural sign.) The fingers of the right hand are thrust into the left. *Cf.* IN, INSIDE, INTO.

WITHOUT (wĭth out′, wĭth-), *prep.*, *adv.* (The hands fall away from the WITH position.) The sign for WITH is formed The hands then drop down, open, and part, ending in the palms-down position.

WOMAN (wŏŏm′ ən), *n*. (A big female.) The FEMALE prefix sign is made: The thumb of the right "A" hand moves down along the line of the right jaw, from ear almost to chin. This outlines the string used to tie ladies' bonnets in olden days. This is a root sign to modify many others. The downturned right hand then moves up to a point above the head, to indicate the relative height.

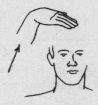

WONDER (wŭn′ dər), *v*., -DERED, -DERING. (Turning thoughts over in the mind.) Both index fingers, pointing to the forehead, describe continuous alternating circles. *Cf.* CONSIDER 2, SPECULATE 2, SPECULATION 2.

WONDERFUL (wŭn′ dər fəl), *adj., interj*. (The feelings are titillated.) With the thumb resting on the upper part of the chest, the fingers are wiggled back and forth. *Cf.* ELEGANT, FINE 1.

WON'T (wōnt, wŭnt), *v.* Contraction of *will not.* (Holding back.) The right "A" hand, palm facing left, moves up sharply to a position above the right shoulder. *Cf.* REFUSE.

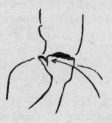

WORD (wûrd), *n.* (A small part of a sentence, *i.e.,* a word.) The tips of the right index finger and thumb, about an inch apart, are placed on the side of the outstretched left index finger, which represents the length of a sentence.

WORD PROCESSING *n.* (A fingerspelled loan sign.) The signer fingerspells "W-P."

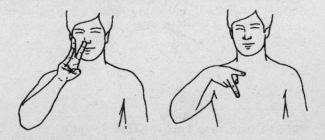

WORK (wûrk), *n.*, *v.*, WORKED, WORKING. (Striking an anvil.) Both "S" hands are held palms down. The right hand strikes against the back of the left a number of times. *Cf.* JOB.

WORLD (wûrld), *n.* (The letter "W" in orbit.) The right "W" hand makes a complete circle around the left "W" hand and comes to rest on the thumb edge of the left "W" hand. The left hand frequently assumes the "S" position instead of the "W," to represent the stationary sun.

WORRIED (wûr′ ĭd), *v.* (A clouding over; a troubling.) Both "B" hands, palms facing each other, are rotated alternately before the forehead. *Cf.* PROBLEM 1, TROUBLE, WORRY 1.

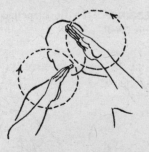

WORRY 1 (wûr′ ĭ), *v.*, -RIED, -RYING. See WORRIED.

WORRY 2, *v., n.* (Drumming at the forehead, to represent many worries making inroads on the thinking process.) The right fingertips drum against the forehead. The signer frowns somewhat, or looks very concerned.

WORSE 1 (wûrs), *adj.* The "V" hands, palms facing the body, cross quickly. The comparative degree suffix sign -ER is often used after this sign: The upright thumb of the right "A" hand is brought sharply up to a level opposite the right ear.

WORSE 2, *adj.* The same movements as in WORSE 1 are used, except that the "W" hands are employed. The comparative degree suffix sign may likewise follow.

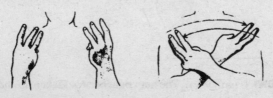

WORTH (wûrth), *adj., n.* Both "F" hands, palms facing each other, move apart, up, and together in a smooth elliptical fashion, coming together at the tips of the thumbs and index fingers of both hands. *Cf.* IMPORTANT, SIGNIFICANCE 1, SIGNIFICANT, VALUABLE, VALUE, WORTHWHILE, WORTHY.

WORTHWHILE (wûrth′ hwīl′), *adj.* See WORTH.

WORTHY (wûr′ tʰ̌i), *adj.* See WORTH.

WOULD (wŏŏd, *unstressed* wəd), *v.* (Something ahead or in the future.) The upright, open right hand, palm facing left, moves straight out and slightly up from a position beside the right temple. *Cf.* FUTURE, IN THE FUTURE, LATER 2, LATER ON, WILL.

WOW! (wou), *interj.* The limp right hand is shaken up and down repeatedly, while the signer assumes a look of open mouthed surprise.

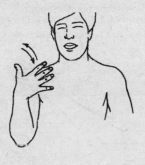

WRAP (rap), *v., n.* (Wrapping up a package.) Both down-turned hands, fingers pointing to each other, make a series of alternate clockwise circles, as if spreading wrapping paper around an object.

WRISTWATCH *n.* (The shape of the wristwatch.) The thumb and index finger of the right hand, forming a circle, are placed on the back of the left wrist. *Cf.* WATCH 2.

WRITE (rīt), *v.*, WROTE, WRITTEN, WRITING. (The natural movement.) The right index finger and thumb, grasping an imaginary pen, write across the open left palm.

WRONG (rông, rŏng), *adj., n.* (Rationale obscure; the thumb and little finger are said to represent, respectively, right and wrong, with the head poised between the two.) The right "Y" hand, palm facing the body, is brought up to the chin. *Cf.* ERROR, MISTAKE.

XEROX (zĭr′ ŏks), *n.* (The letter "X"; the movement of the light as it moves under the item to be copied.) The "X" finger moves back and forth rather rapidly under the downturned hand.

XMAS, *n.* See CHRISTMAS.

Y

YARD (yärd), *n.* (The letter "Y"; arm's length.) The down-turned right "Y" hand is placed on the shoulder of the down-turned left arm. The right hand moves down the arm to the left fingertips.

YEAR (yĭr), *n.* (A circumference around the sun.) The right "S" hand, palm facing left, represents the earth. It is positioned atop the left "S" hand, whose palm faces right, and represents the sun. The right "S" hand describes a clockwise circle around the left, coming to rest in its original position.

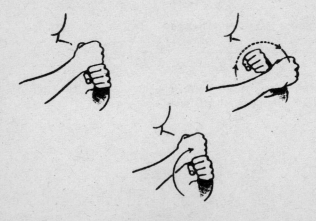

YEAR-ROUND *adj.* (Making a revolution around the sun.) The right index finger, resting on the left index, goes forward around the left once, coming back to where it began.

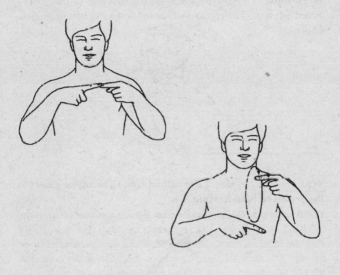

YEARS (yĭrs), *n. pl.* The sign for YEAR is made twice.

YES (yĕs), *(colloq.), adv., n.* (The nodding.) The right "S" hand, imitating the head, "nods" up and down.

YESTERDAY (yĕs′ tər dĭ, -dā′), *adv., n.* (A short distance into the past.) The thumbtip of the right "A" or "Y" hand, palm facing left, rests on the right cheek. It then moves back a short distance.

YOU 1 (ū), *pron. sing.* (The natural sig*n*.) The signer points to the person he is addressing.

YOU 2, *pron. pl.* (The natural sign.) The signer points to several persons before him, or swings his index finger in an arc from left to right.

YOUNG (yŭng), *adj.* (The spirits bubbling up.) The fingertips of both open hands, placed on either side of the chest just below the shoulders, move up and off the chest, in unison, to a point just above the shoulders. This is repeated several times. *Cf.* YOUTH, YOUTHFUL.

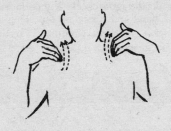

YOUR (yŏŏr), *pron., adj.* (The outstretched open hand indicates possession, as if pressing an item against the chest of the person spoken to.) The right "5" hand, palm facing out, moves straight out toward the person spoken to. *Cf.* YOURS.

YOU'RE WELCOME 1, *phrase.* (Words extended politely from the mouth.) The fingertips of the right "5" hand are placed at the mouth. The hand moves away from the mouth to a palm-up position before the body. The signer meanwhile usually nods smilingly. *Cf.* THANKS, THANK YOU.

YOU'RE WELCOME 2, *phrase.* (A straightening out.) The right hand, fingers together and palm facing left, is placed in the upturned left palm, whose fingers point away from the body. The right hand slides straight out along the left palm, over the left fingers, and stops with its heel resting on the left fingertips. *Cf.* ALL RIGHT, O.K. 1, RIGHT 1.

YOURS (yŏŏrz, yôrz), *pron.* See YOUR.

YOURSELF (yŏŏr sĕlf′), *pron.* The signer moves his upright thumb in the direction of the person spoken to. *Cf.* -SELF.

YOURSELVES (yŏŏr sĕlvz′), *pron. pl.* The signer moves his upright thumb toward several people before him, in a series of small forward movements from left to right.

YOUTH (ūth), *n.* See YOUNG.

YOUTHFUL (ūth′ fəl), *adj.* See YOUNG.

Z

ZERO 1 (zĭr´ ō), *(colloq.)*, *n.* (An emphatic movement of the "O," *i.e.*, ZERO, hand.) The little finger edge of the right "O" hand is brought sharply into the upturned left palm.

ZERO 2, *n.* (The natural sign.) The right "O" hand, palm facing left, is held in front of the face. It then moves an inch or two toward the right.

ZIPPER (zĭp´ ər), *n.* (The movement of the zipper.) The signer mimes opening and closing a zipper on the chest or the side of the body.

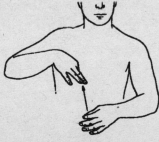

A concise edition of "the most comprehensive and clearly written dictionary of sign language ever published." —*Los Angeles Times*

AMERICAN SIGN LANGUAGE CONCISE DICTIONARY

· REVISED EDITION ·

More than 2,500 signs and 3,750 illustrations

········ **FEATURING** ········

500 NEW SIGNS AND 750 NEW ILLUSTRATIONS MANY NEVER BEFORE PUBLISHED

MARTIN L. A. STERNBERG